CALLUM MORTON

VALHALLA
2007 VENICE BIENNALE

Valhalla, 2007
Digital imaging Callum Morton and Nick Hubicki

—

185 Flinders Lane Melbourne 3000
T +613 9654 6131
mail@annaschwartzgallery.com
www.annaschwartzgallery.com

ANNA SCHWARTZ GALLERY

contents

492

498

614

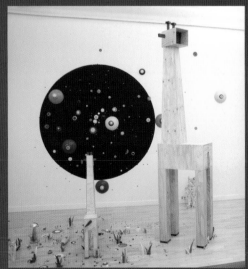

Books

Review

RIPE:
ANZ Private Bank / Art & Australia
Contemporary Art Award

570

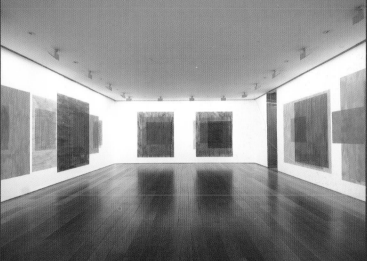

576

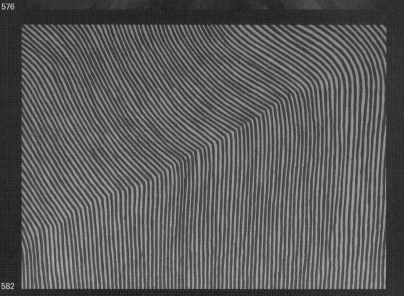

cover, detail
Rosemary Laing, burning Ayer #6, 2003,
type-C photograph, 110 x 224 cm, courtesy
the artist and Tolarno Galleries, Melbourne.

582

Art & Australia Vol. 44/4

Winter 2007 June/July/August
Art Quarterly ISSN 0004-301 X
Published by Art & Australia Pty Ltd
11 Cecil Street, Paddington
NSW 2021 Australia
Tel 61 2 9331 4455 Fax 61 2 9331 4577

Publisher & Editor-in-Chief
Eleonora Triguboff
publisher@artandaustralia.com.au

Editor
Katrina Schwarz
katrina.schwarz@artandaustralia.com.au

Publication Manager
Marni Williams
marni.williams@artandaustralia.com.au

Editorial Assistant
Jesse Stein
jesse.stein@artandaustralia.com.au

Editorial Advisory Board
Claire Armstrong, Greg Burke, Rex Butler,
Joanna Capon, Max Delany, Brian Ladd,
Victoria Lynn and Nick Waterlow

Consultant to Art & Australia
Claire Armstrong

Contributing Editor, Books
Andrea Stretton

Design
Clinton Duncan

Advertising & Trade Manager
Karen Brown
karen.brown@artandaustralia.com.au

Marketing & Development Manager
Fiona David
fiona.david@artandaustralia.com.au

Subscriptions
info@artandaustralia.com.au
Tollfree (Australia only) 1800 224 018

Subscribe online
www.artandaustralia.com.au

Newsagent distribution
Australia Network Distribution Co.

editorial

Like the airborne, turbulence-tossed women in her photographs, Rosemary Laing is flying fast. George Tjungurrayi journeys on foot out of the Gibson Desert; his conceptual abstractions chronicle Tingari stories of continuous travel from place to place. In Madrid, Narelle Jubelin maps a geography of displacement. What, if anything, holds these artists together within the nebulous concept of 'Australian-ness'?

As artists cross borders and artistic trends become more globalised, ideas of nationhood and of fixed identity begin to unravel. In this climate, the question of what it means to be an Australian artist and, moreover, of what it means to represent Australia internationally, is contested ground.

As Art & Australia turns its gaze towards Australian artists who live beyond our borders, those who exhibit overseas and in 'globefests'[1] such as the Venice Biennale and documenta, we do so with an awareness that an artist's country of origin, or the fact of their expatriation, should never be the most important or privileged aspect of their identity. Writing her inaugural column for the magazine, curator Juliana Engberg notes: 'Artists prefer to think that their own work is distinctive and free from nationalism; that their artistic vision is a unique, individual insight.'

And yet the urge remains to think about art as a product of its cultural context, as does the need to honour and observe local histories and genealogies – from George Tjungurrayi's deep connection with the land, to what Rex Butler identifies as Rosemary Laing's well-earned place within the long tradition of Australian landscape depiction.

While Australia's tourism industry has no reservation about pushing the notion of a discrete national identity, one personified, in its latest beguiling incarnation, as a pneumatic bikini-clad blonde, the art world is decidedly more tentative. With its insistence on the collapsing of national distinctions, of borders and essentialist tropes, contemporary art posits a new context – one not located within a particular country, but rather in a state of transit, a liminal space – a geography of displacement, a journey from place to place, flying fast.

Katrina Schwarz
Editor

1 Juliana Engberg, 'Dig it!', Art & Australia, vol. 44, no. 4, 2007, p. 488.

The images on page 428 of Art & Australia, vol. 44, no. 3, were incorrectly attributed to Gertrude Contemporary Art Spaces, Melbourne.

ROSEMARY LAING
2007 VENICE BIENNALE

www.tolarnogalleries.com

5.10am, 15 December 2004 (detail), C Type photograph, 85 x 169.5 cm

contributors

Daniel Baumann lives in Basel and is an art historian, freelance curator and writer for *Pacemaker, Parabol, Parkett,* and *Spike Art Quarterly,* among others. He is Director of the Adolf Wölfli-Foundation, Museum of Fine Arts in Bern, curator of Nordtangente-Kunsttangente, a project for art in public spaces in Basel, and founder of an ongoing exhibition series in Tbilisi, Georgia.

Lily Brett is an Australian author living in New York. Her books of essays, *In Full View* (1997), *New York* (2001) and *Between Mexico and Poland* (2002), were critical successes, and her novel *Too Many Men* (1999) was a bestseller in Australia, Germany and the United States.

Rex Butler is Senior Lecturer in art history in the Department of English, Media Studies and Art History at the University of Queensland. His research interests include contemporary Australian art and art criticism, postwar American art and postmodernism. He has written several books, including *Slavoj Zizek: Live Theory* (2005) and *A Secret History of Australian Art* (2002) and was editor of *Radical Revisionism* (2005), among other titles.

Judith Ryan is Senior Curator of Indigenous Art at the National Gallery of Victoria, Melbourne. She has published extensively, including *Mythscapes: Aboriginal Art of the Desert* (1989), *Images of Power: Aboriginal Art of the Kimberley* (1993), *Ginger Riley* (1997) and *Colour Power: Aboriginal Art Post 1984* (2004).

Rachel Spence is a freelance journalist living in Venice. She writes on art for the *Financial Times,* the *Jewish Quarterly* and www.artinfo.com.

Ann Stephen is an art historian and curator at the Powerhouse Museum, Sydney. Her latest books are *On Looking at Looking: The Art and Politics of Ian Burn* (2006) and, reviewed in this issue, *Modernism and Australia: Documents on Art, Design and Architecture 1917–1967* (2006).

Daniele Balit is a freelance curator and art critic based in Paris. He is a PhD candidate at Université La Sorbonne, and is a founding member of 1:1projects, a platform for cultural production based in Rome and London.

Edmund Capon AM, OBE, has been Director of the Art Gallery of New South Wales, Sydney, since 1978.

Andrew Clifford is a freelance writer and sound artist. He works as curatorial assistant at the University of Auckland's Centre for New Zealand Art Research and Discovery.

Michael Condon is a freelance writer based in Tokyo.

Ashley Crawford is the author of *Wimmera: The Work of Philip Hunter* (2002) and co-author of *Spray: The Work of Howard Arkley* (1997).

Juliana Engberg is Artistic Director of the Australian Centre for Contemporary Art (ACCA), Melbourne, and was visual arts curator for the Melbourne International Arts Festival in 2005.

Zane Fischer is an arts writer and columnist for Santa Fe's alternative weekly publication *The Santa Fe Reporter.*

Andrew Frost is a writer and arts journalist who lives on the Central Coast of New South Wales.

Anthony Gardner is completing his PhD at the Centre for Contemporary Art and Politics, University of New South Wales, Sydney, and teaches contemporary art and theory at the University of Melbourne.

Paddy Johnson, author of the blog *Art Fag City,* is a writer who lives and works in Brooklyn, New York. Her writing has been featured in the *New York Observer, Flavorpill, FlashArt, NYFA Current* and *ArtKrush.* She has lectured at Yale University and the Whitney Independent Study Program.

John Kaldor AM was Commissioner for the Australian pavilion at the 2005 and 2007 Venice biennales. He is on the International Council of the Museum of Modern Art (MoMA) in New York, and Tate Modern in London and the Board of the Biennale of Sydney. He is the founder of John Kaldor Fabricmaker.

Rachel Kent is Senior Curator at the Museum of Contemporary Art, Sydney. She has written for a range of local and international journals including, most recently, *Parkett.*

Geoffrey Legge is a director of Watters Gallery, Sydney.

Joanna Mendelssohn is an Associate Professor at the College of Fine Arts, University of New South Wales. She has written extensively on Australian art and is currently researching the work of Richard and Pat Larter, and is one of the instigators of the *Dictionary of Australian Artists Online.*

Nina Miall is a London-based curator with the gallery Haunch of Venison. She recently curated Philippe Parreno's first solo exhibition in the United Kingdom, and has written art criticism for a variety of international art publications.

Louis Nowra is a playwright, novelist and screenwriter. His latest book is *Chihuahuas, Women and Me* (2005), a collection of essays.

Ingrid Periz has written for *Art & Text, World Art* and *ARTnews* and has taught at the University of Melbourne and New York University. Her book on Adam Cullen was published in 2004. A Harkness Fellowship took her to New York in 1987, and she now lives outside New York City.

Valeria Schulte-Fischedick is an art historian and curator based in Berlin. She has supervised the international studio program in Künstlerhaus Bethanien since 2005 and writes for various art magazines and catalogues.

Barry Schwabsky is an American art critic and poet living in London. His books include *The Widening Circle: Consequences of Modernism in Contemporary Art* (1997) and *Vitamin P: New Perspectives in Painting* (2002).

David Teh is a writer, curator and lecturer based in Bangkok, where he recently curated a multi-exhibition project called 'Platform'. He is a director of Sydney's Half Dozen artist-run initiative.

Veronica Tello is a freelance writer and curator based in Melbourne. She is currently undertaking postgraduate research at the University of Melbourne. In 2005 she was part of the Gertrude Contemporary Art Spaces Emerging Writers' Program.

Anna Waldmann is Director of Visual Arts at the Australia Council. Before joining the Australia Council, she worked as a curator at the Art Gallery of New South Wales and as program manager (Visual Arts and Crafts and Museums and Galleries) at the NSW Ministry for the Arts. She is a member of numerous art and cultural committees and has published books, catalogues and articles on Australian and European art.

SHAUN GLADWELL

MUSEUM OF CONTEMPORARY ART, SANTIAGO CHILE 26.4–1.7
52ND INTERNATIONAL ART EXHIBITION VENICE BIENNALE 10.6–21.11
ARTSPACE, SYDNEY 20.9–20.10
SHERMAN GALLERIES 30.11–22.12

Planet and Star Sequence, Pioneer Studios, Sydney, 2006, Photograph Josh Raymond

Dig it

Juliana Engberg

At this year's Venice Biennale that mysterious femme, Sophie Calle, will inhabit the neoclassical rotunda of the French pavilion with works that speak of pain and self-examination. Across the way, Tracey Emin will no doubt do her utmost to dishevel and disobey the authoritarianism of Britain's imperial edifice. In the idealist and weirdly miniaturised Jefferson-styled pavilion of the United States of America, works by the late Felix Gonzales Torres, offering a utopian fantasy, will presumably twinkle and illuminate the terrazzo and stone. In the Netherlands' strictly modernist pavilion, Aernout Mik will derange the principles of clarity with surreally scatological works that are prone to collapse into bodily decadence.

Each of these artists will 'represent' their country, but in the scheme of things, does it matter to anyone other than their funding bodies if they are 'French', 'English', 'American' or 'Dutch'? Most artists picked to exhibit at a 'globe fest' like the Venice Biennale would like to think not. Generally artists prefer to believe that their work is distinctive and free from 'nationalism'; that their artistic vision is a unique, individual insight. Most artists do not want to be associated with the governmental inference attached to being a national 'representative'. You can see their point. After all, who wants to be associated with bad policies, colonial misdemeanours and global terrorism? Artists are wary of being seen to be cultural ambassadors for ideals that they do not share.

While that is true, it is nevertheless interesting to think about the kind of cultural context that produces contemporary work. That context is not necessarily attached to 'nationalism', but it can rarely be dislodged from the aesthetics and philosophies that circulate around the creation of art in a certain place.

For instance, it is hard to imagine Sophie Calle's art coming from a culture other than that of France. Her focus on vignette images and texts which question the construction of the self and of others seem so located within the philosophical musing of writers such as Roland Barthes, whose wistful introspections of love and pain, joy and loss characterise a whole tradition of ennui from Proust to filmmaker Catherine Breillat.

There is something so wonderfully *fatigué* about Calle's whole enterprise. Beds of course dominate: beds to be shared, beds to be alone in, beds to be left unmade, beds to wallow in, beds to be queen in for a day, and beds to spy upon. It's unlikely that an American artist, say, would have enough tolerance for the languidness of such endless introspection, or the philosophical existentialism to care. *Viva la France* I say. Hoorah for madeleines and for time lost and remembrance of things past. Yes, Sophie Calle is indeed French, from the tip of her petite stilettos to her Anouk Aimée bob.

Tracy Emin's beds are different. These are dissolute, dishevelled, despised beds. Not froufrou like Calle's princess-diva ones. Emin's beds reek of squats and coin-operated gas meters, and 'where the hell am I's?', and 'can I crash at yours's?'. This is not so much introspection as exhibitionism of a squalid, self-effacing, self-loathing, yet determinedly survivalist kind. Post-Blitz make do, and post-punk fuck-off. Emin's works join a long line of British destitution; they are the latter-day *Rake's progress* of William Hogarth and William Holman Hunt's 'fallen woman' translated to modern, post-Thatcher London.

Emin is absolutely British. As well as fulfilling the above conditions of urban squalor and modern disenfranchisement, Emin's works acknowledge the British version of 1970s feminist practice. Emin's quilts and blankets with their sewn testimonials relate to works like the abject nappy-liners of Mary Kelly's *Post partum document*, 1973–79, as well as to suffragettes' banners and union pendants. Emin has taken a traditional folk form – used by dissenters through millennia to convey a message, and as a symbol of belonging to a clan, cult or club – and resurrected it with sincerity and punch.

Emin's blankets have resonance and significant pathos. One is struck by the use of felt and candy colours, the desperate rose bouquets and floral designs, the manual labour of their making and emblemised narratives of racism, sexism, abuse and inequality. These works fit into the British living room of pattern upon pattern, cheery bucolic and class distinction. And like the stiff-upper-lip-dom that underpins a certain British ethos they strangely contain hope and sorrow

In equal parts – victim and survivor in mutual need.

So Calle is French and Emin is a Brit, but what about Felix Gonzales Torres? Is he American? Well, not perhaps in the ways one might expect. Not in a James Rosenquist, US of A, big spaghetti way, or in Richard Prince cowboy fashion, or in a Warholian production-line system, or in a Kosuthian cool, minimal, conceptual manner. At any rate, which way is American? There is no pure American art; it is all continentally drifted, huddle massed, attracted to the lifted light like tired moths.

This is the 'Americanesque' of Felix Gonzales Torres: the luminous light bulb memorials to so many souls, the gentle pillows of lovers departed, the corner of fortune cookies with their messages of inspiration, the sheets of printed clouds offered as a gift. His is an art that exemplifies the finest, loftiest aims of a country whose forefathers sought a more humane society, even if the current incumbents cannot. It takes an immigrant to point this out. It requires the humility of a person who fled Cuba for a welcoming shore in order to escape persecution and to seek a home, bringing with him a lingering aesthetic of mysticism, ritual and reliquary.

Felix Gonzales Torres turned on lights to try and shed enlightenment on a society which had lost its way and had lost some of its most creative spirits. What a wonderful choice he is to 'represent' the United States. An outsider of sorts, yet still one embraced. Not cynical, not bombastic, not straight. Not here in body, but certainly in spirit as a kind of lingering hope for better times.

Aernout Mik is almost the opposite. His work is apt to slump, implode and enact a scatological disturbance. At first this seems paradoxical in view of what we understand about modern Holland. Neat, industrious, sane, measured Holland, where the cleanliness of Dutch baroque and protestant restraint sends a pearly cream, Vermeer-like glow over a winter day. And where, in its architectural genre paintings, lofty cathedrals with unadorned interiors dwarf the occupants while they contemplate God's greatness.

But what about the dog pissing in the corner, the drunk collapsed on a column, the amorous groping going on near the pulpit, or the merchant huddle making deals? Ah yes. Holland has always had its grubby side as exemplified by its still-life works with rotting apples, infested fruit and spilt wine. Where there is pious righteousness, there exists, almost of necessity, debauchery and dissolution as a counterpoint to didacticism.

Mik's works are particularly Dutch in this respect. His shattered stock exchange types – men dressed in the uniform of modernity: shirt, tie, sensible trousers found palpitating and levitating amidst the debris of commerce – are the contemporary equivalents of the destitute and wicked non-converts in the genre scenes of the seventeenth century. The mess of Mik's works relate strongly to Dutch still lifes and to that artform's message of morality. In Mik's works there is as much compelling veracity and realism, combined with surreal fantasy, as there is in Dutch baroque paintings.

To dislodge Mik from his aesthetic ancestors would be wrong. The power of his work resides as much in the history he attaches to and fights against as it does in being encountered as a singular, monumentally individual event. In this sense it's good to be Dutch. The same applies to Calle, Emin and Gonzales Torres. Representing your country is, in my view, often taken too literally and too much at face value, and too aligned with a governmental position of the day. Generally I think curators and artists are well aware of this, and they play the game with a brilliantly informed strategy of meta-comment. After all, art is much more sedimentary than mere collateral surface … and Venice is a great dig.

Image Problem?

Australian art and international perception

Edmund Capon and John Kaldor, 2007,
courtesy Art Gallery of New South Wales, Sydney.
Photograph Mim Stirling.

Edmund Capon: Let's kick off with some thoughts on the image of Australian art. The image of Australian art at the moment is so conditioned by Aboriginal art that I think it is actually slightly distorting. I think it is a pity that while that is a very distinctive language and a unique one, it tends to be the sole representation of the Australian artistic image abroad. The Art Gallery of New South Wales is always trying to promote Australian art abroad and yet it is really hard to get major overseas institutions interested in Australian art, other than, every now and then, Aboriginal art.

John Kaldor: So how can we change that?

EC: The first thing, and this is what you have helped so much with, is the Venice Biennale, which is a great showcase. The other thing is that individual artists and individual dealers are now making their own inroads into the world. There are artists – Bill Henson, Tracey Moffat, Mike Parr ...

JK: Ricky Swallow

EC: who have now made terrific images, but what we need is a consolidated presence, rather than a series of individual images.

JK: But can you do that? There are very few countries that have a solid image. Isn't it that individual artists from every country make their mark?

EC: Yes, it is – but it is a cumulative effect, and one of the problems is that Australia has not accumulated enough mass, if you like, to create that cumulative image. Today a centre of contemporary art no longer exists, whereas forty or fifty years ago it was Paris and then New York. But, nonetheless, there is a certain coherent image to the art of contemporary Germany, of contemporary Italy, of contemporary Britain, China, Japan. And I don't think there is the same sort of consolidated image in Australia.

JK: I am not sure I agree with you totally there, because we have, almost, a school of model-makers. If you take people like Ricky Swallow, James Angus, Patricia Piccinini and even young ones like Tim Silver, they are all modelling in some way. I am also surprised how many good, young Australian video artists there are. I think [they are] better than painters or sculptors.

EC: It is an interesting choice for Venice this year. I am a great admirer of Callum Morton, I think he is wonderful.

JK: I saw his work before it got packed up to go to Venice. It is mind-blowing. It will be fantastic. It is a building, like a public sculpture. It is monumental.

EC: In the rather diffused world of contemporary art it is difficult to consolidate an image.

JK: Is it more a question of marketing? Look at how China exploded onto the international market over the period of a few years. How does that happen?

EC: I don't know if it is purely marketing. I think it is about intrigue and opportunity. If you look at major international collections of contemporary art, whether private or public, the Australian component is small or non-existent. Because of the perception of Australia as a country 'over there', the western world, and maybe even the eastern world, expects to see something different, which is why Aboriginal art fits the bill so conveniently. And when Australia

John Kaldor, commissioner for the Australian pavilion at the 2005 and 2007 Venice biennales, in conversation with **Edmund Capon**, Director of the Art Gallery of New South Wales

produces artists that fit comfortably into the global image of contemporary art it doesn't fulfil that certain expectation.

Tell me what happens if someone goes to the Venice Biennale this year and sees Callum Morton, Daniel von Sturmer and Susan Norrie; do we often manage to sell works?

JK: Yes, if the works are good they will sell. One phenomenon today is the absolute blurring between biennales and art fairs, because biennales are getting very commercial and art fairs are becoming curated shows. Basel, which is the best art fair in the world, now has a curated section, and at the 2005 Venice Biennale every Gilbert and George work sold before the opening.

EC: John, when it comes to selecting three artists for Venice, to me, Norrie, von Sturmer and Morton seem like completely different artists.

JK: That is what we wanted. What I learned from the 2005 biennale is that no matter how successful or good an artist is, they can never really represent a country's art. When I took on the biennale the second time I said I wanted to have more than one artist. I also wanted to have something outside the Giardini because it has become very classical; it hasn't got the excitement of the Arsenale or of the outside pavilions. Art now overtakes the whole of Venice – in every church, in every palazzo and warehouse. My mantra is: we want to show the *best* of contemporary Australian art, as represented by these *three* artists. If there is a theme, the theme is diversity.

EC: I am always mistrustful of themes. It is a bit like titles. The art world is full of contrived titles.

JK: Hopefully with three artists and three different sites it will create an impact. Plus we are very fortunate that Robert Storr has selected a further three artists, Shaun Gladwell, Christian Capurro and Rosemary Laing [for the curated show at the 2007 Venice Biennale], so there is a total of six Australian artists. But long range, it is hard to get a foothold on the international circuit.

EC: To get firmly implanted in people's imaginations and psyches you need something that coalesces all the strengths. I suppose one of the things we say is that travel is a great educator – people [in Australia] travel relentlessly.

JK: Part of our biennale effort is sending curators, including Indigenous curators, to Venice. And this year we are also sending four educators, because good art schools create good artists.

I think our aim should be to have a handful of 'international artists who are of Australian origin' rather than 'Australian artists'. Take Switzerland, it is well known for chocolates, beautiful scenery …

EC: cuckoo clocks, tax evasion.

JK: Switzerland is not known for great creative art, but now you have a handful of great contemporary artists – if you take Pipilloti Rist, Ugo Rondinone, Urs Fischer – they are not regarded as 'Swiss artists', but as 'international artists who happen to have been born in Switzerland'.

EC: That is exactly right, and let's face it, there *are* artists like that – great artists who happen to be Australian. One of the other things that has been a constraining factor is the financial independence of artists and their capacity to sell their work. Australian artists find it easier, naturally, to sell their works in Australia and therefore that reliance on the home market has often dimmed their aspiration to be seen more widely.

JK: I think that was more with the previous generation of artists, not so much with the younger generation, who have a much more international horizon.

EC: You are right, there is a more open spirit and greater aspiration.

JK: So the art has to grow up and the artist has to grow up. But if we take William Kentridge, his art is very much based on South Africa: he takes that as the base of his inspiration but makes it into a very global and international art. The roots of his art are in South Africa but the result is universal and that is what our artists have to do.

EC: If you look at the history of twentieth-century Australian art, it has retained a very strong sense of place – to the exclusion, almost, of being recognised and appreciated beyond Australia. Certainly, the universal language of contemporary art is such that the place of origin is irrelevant, pretty much. I feel sometimes frustrated when I go and see what is happening in other cities around the world. I feel, if only I could pluck out those works here and put them over there. It is quite frustrating.

JK: We do make an effort to show Australian art in institutions internationally. I think we equally need to make an effort to get artists into good commercial galleries internationally.

EC: I agree with that, but the point is the institutions are the difficult ones – that is the public window which brings public recognition. Commercial galleries are very active but the imprimatur of the institutions is crucial and where we have not yet succeeded. It is a constant quest. What you do is you get the people who come here, like Storr, and get them sufficiently enthused to do what he has done with Venice – to say: 'A larger world should be able to see some of this.'

JK: Our sportsmen wouldn't be happy breaking just Australian records, they would want to break world records. Our artists should be the same.

3 artists,
3 projects

Newly commissioned projects by three Australian artists – Daniel von Sturmer, Callum Morton and Susan Norrie – will be unveiled at the 2007 Venice Biennale. The artists tell us about their works and their hopes for Venice.

Susan
Norrie

Susan Norrie, courtesy the Australia Council for the Arts. Photograph Gary Herry.

'The title of my new project for the Venice Biennale 2007 is *HAVOC*. I have been working with video artist David Mackenzie (camera/sound/editing) and Justin Hale (journalist/interpreter) in Indonesia.

I decided to focus on the 'ring of fire', the volcanic/geographic region of the South Pacific. I travelled to Porong in East Java where a catastrophic oil/gas drilling accident has caused an unstoppable flow of hot mud. This environmental disaster has left thousands homeless and will also affect generations to come.

The model and the process behind making this work has been confrontational and challenging. There was an enormous amount of risk in making a new work for the Venice Biennale in the Third World, as one needs to be respectful and not harm people. Through this uncertainty a margin of manoeuvrability emerged, so rather than focusing on success or failure there was an opening to experiment .

HAVOC continues my interests in man-made and natural disasters. This is also a time of thermodynamics, suggesting an historical progression towards disorder. I also wanted to deal with the disparities between Third World and First World countries – to close the gap.

I decided to deal with this issue of nationality through situating Australia within the Asia-Pacific region. I also felt that Indonesia is a kind of micro-version of the world, and I think it is dealing with enormous and complex issues in an extraordinary way.'

Daniel
von Sturmer

Daniel von Sturmer, courtesy the Australia Council
for the Arts. Photograph Eamon Gallagher.

'I started by looking at the exhibition space, and the work I have created
is a response to the Australian pavilion and an attempt to work with the internal
logic of its architecture. I hadn't been to Venice before, so I had no real idea
about the pavilion space, except for what people had told me – so I was
pleasantly surprised. It was bigger than I first imagined and while I could see
there were some difficult aspects to the architecture – the pavilion has two
levels – it was also an interesting challenge. I wanted to find a way to unify the
two levels of the pavilion and to give some added reason for how you might
interact with the height shift as you move through the space.

The central structure I have created is a two-dimensional plane that changes
height and shifts direction, and which is itself a platform for video events, video
projections and objects. The structure wraps around the space – it unfolds
around corners or folds into corners – and sometimes it is above head height.
The point for me is to activate the viewers' awareness of how they view the
space and walk through the gallery, how they interact with the work and find
meaning through the different correlations between, say, a video and an object,
a video and the structure, and the architecture framing all these things. It is
a question of interplay, negotiation and intervention.

Some of the objects used in the installation are found objects or have been
bought "off the shelf". Another category of objects is based on an existing form
that I have modified slightly, such as shredded paper, which I compress into
another shape. There will be a number of videos dispersed through the space,
atop or beneath the structure. The videos will be projected onto small screens

and are another "space" for the viewer to engage with. It is interesting to
look at the space of the gallery as one container, within which there is another
container for other kinds of spaces, and the video again is another kind of space
on another scale. There is also a sense of the viewers' own scale shifting as they
move through the space – at times they will be much smaller than the structure
and at times they will tower above it.

The other aspect of the work is that the pavilion has been closed off for
many years. It was originally built to be quite a light space and when you reveal
those windows again it makes sense of the building's volume. By opening the
windows the pavilion is reconnected to its surroundings and a sense of light and
view are reintroduced to the space.

I don't specifically think about the work going to an international audience
and what that might mean but it is always a great opportunity when that does
happen. The difficulty with any national survey is that it is never going to be a
true representation of everything that happens in a place. National surveys are
interesting for looking at nationalistic boundaries, but personally I don't see
the value in ascribing "this is Australian art", "that is American art". The actual
situation is that there is a kind of pluralism, a great interchange of information
and ideas. Because we are on a shared platform – we are shopping in very
similar places, we are experiencing very similar things – to a large degree we
can share experience in real time, although there will always be those local
influences and local ways of doing things. Artists move, boundaries shift and,
at the end of it, it is the ideas and interchange that define the whole event.'

Callum Morton

Callum Morton, courtesy the Australia Council for the Arts. Photograph Richard Crompton.

'For the Venice Biennale I am rebuilding in three-quarter scale the facade of a house I used to live in, and which my father designed, when I was a child. It was a significant house in many ways, and in searching for a subject for Venice, I came to realise its influence on my practice. It was a modernist house from the 1970s – concrete block on formed slab – a standard building technology used across the globe, only it was left unrendered on purpose.

The Venice commission, like all my work, began with an image, in this instance an image of a ruin, something fairly anonymous. When I drove up the street my family used to live in and saw that the house was no longer there, the experience collided with my thinking about images of violence, of holes and the aftermath of destruction – all that residual stuff that is part of the media landscape. I started thinking about this house as an erased thing, as an absence. It was nice to have a personal connection to the building and although it is not my way to be intensely biographical, I am interested in taking a biography, or a form that is biographical, and making it fictive. I have collided two things – a media image with a personal memory – to rebuild the house. But it is a house brought back from the dead and sutured together.

It is a massive piece. Like all my work, it is some dysfunctional form of architecture but this time it is actually architectonic, it needed to be engineered. It is essentially a public sculpture and has to sit outside for six months. As with my earlier installation *Babylonia* [2005], the viewer enters the work. They go inside to find a corporate office foyer that is completely white and which has three lifts that go down – they only go down. In many senses, it is a kind of purgatory, like all waiting rooms are. The house has risen up (from the grave) and the lifts swallow you up and take you back down with it – to hell. Connecting with another early work, *Cellar* [1998], the [Venice] installation is illuminated at night. Light will pour, poltergeist-like, through the holes. I am interested in how everyday life has been inflected by this narrative of foreboding and how it has become almost cinematic.

I've never been to the Venice Biennale and that has been a good thing for me. It is sometimes referred to as the 'World Cup of contemporary art', but I am not so sure about that analogy, even though I understand its relevance to an event so dealer and collector driven. To describe the biennale as a 'World Cup' implies that all artists are competing against each other under the national rubric, that they are simply the 'talent' within the superstructure of the art world and that the economies of scale, money and audience are the same. The funny thing is I am on an Armenian soccer pitch, one of the smallest and the most pathetic little soccer pitches you are likely to encounter. It is perfect for my work.

I have done a number of international shows that collect together Australian artists and although it is a great way to get overseas and get a project up, my preference is reserved for exhibitions like the 'Istanbul Pedestrians Exhibitions' [for which Morton created the installation *Stonewash* in 2005]. I was invited to Turkey as an artist alongside other artists, not, specifically, as an Australian. Because there was little focus on national representation the show and the work was liberated from a host of expectations and assumptions. It was an enlightening and exciting experience.'

Australian arts:
Gained in translation?

Anna Waldmann

I think 'home' is as much geography as ideal. I often wonder if in fact we are all on the periphery, trying to cross a purely notional gap of knowledge and experience. The sense of dislocation and of personal and cultural repositioning that characterises the twenty-first century can be negotiated through art and by artists who have the ability to redefine our parameters by subtly shifting the conventions of national and intellectual traditions.

Australian artists have a shared affinity for exile. Trying to cross the gap of knowledge and experience through forums, exhibitions, residencies and exchanges, the Australia Council's Visual Arts Board supports artists, writers and curators, helping them to create and develop professional opportunities nationally and internationally. It funds a national network of contemporary art spaces, craft/design councils, new media organisations, art magazines, exhibition touring agencies and museums such as Sydney's Museum of Contemporary Art. The Australia Council supports major exhibitions, including the Asia-Pacific Triennial, the Biennale of Sydney, the Biennial of Electronic Art in Perth, and the Adelaide Biennial.

Although it funds an Australian presence at many biennales, the council collaborate closely with a small number of international exhibitions: documenta, and the biennales and triennales in Istanbul, Gwangju, Liverpool, São Paulo and Berlin. It invites the curators associated with these events to Australia so that they can visit with and choose Australian artists for their exhibitions. In recent years the Australia Council has hosted Dan Cameron, Sukwon Chang, Klaus Biesenbach, Saskia Bos, Okwui Enwezor, Yuko Hasegawa, Ruth Noack, Lisette Lagnado, Robert Storr and Roger Buergel. This year Simryn Gill and Juan Davila will be included in documenta 12, selected by Ruth Noack, and Robert Storr has chosen Shaun Gladwell, Rosemary Laing and Christian Capurro for the curated exhibition at the 2007 Venice Biennale.

The other side of the international coin is the Australia Council's overseas studio residency program. Over the past twenty years it has hosted approximately 700 artists in residencies in Berlin, Barcelona, London, Los Angeles, Tokyo, Rome, Paris, Milan and New York. It would be a failure of the imagination not to realise the impact of three months in one of these locations, and how much the experience liberates and nourishes artists.

The council is regularly offered new studios around the world and called upon to support international exhibitions and collaborations. Australian art has a freshness and sophisticated energy and it gains in translation in the world of 'soft globalisation'. Australia's love affair with the rest of the world shows how essential art is in negotiating the complexities of modern society and in defining the parameters of 'us' so that we can know the 'other'.

In conversation:
Rachel Kent speaks
with Curator Ruth Noack
about documenta 12

documenta is a major international exhibition – the largest of its kind – that takes place in Kassel, Germany, every five years. Established in 1955 by Arnold Bode as an adjunct to the city's National Garden Festival, it was originally conceived as a singular event to showcase modernist art practices formerly shunned by the Nazis under the banner of 'degenerate art'. Exhibited at the neo-classical Fridericianum Museum, which, like much of Kassel, had been badly damaged by allied bombing a decade earlier, its physical presentation acknowledged the provisional nature of the space itself, which was then only partially restored. The exhibition also made active use of everyday construction materials and modes of presentation that placed artworks, viewers and their physical surrounds in a dialogue unusual for its time. Originally entitled 'European Art of the Twentieth Century', Bode's documenta took as its focus the origins or 'roots' of contemporary artistic production, guided by the question: 'Where does art stand today, where do we stand today?'[1]

Now in its twelfth incarnation, the current documenta is co-curated by Roger Buergel and Ruth Noack who have been researching and developing the exhibition since 2003. On display between June and September 2007 at selected venues throughout Kassel, including the Fridericianum, it is built around three conceptual parameters or 'guiding questions' devised by the curators in response to their research.

Rachel Kent: Ruth, in your recent visit to Sydney as part of your research for documenta, you spoke in depth about the three leitmotifs of documenta 12 and I'd like to explore them here. Can you outline your three guiding questions and how they intersect with one another in regards to the exhibition?

Ruth Noack: Our three guiding questions are about modernity, life and education. Contemporary artists all around the world are dealing with one or another of these subjects, though they might mean different things in different places. Yes, they intersect, but you'll have to come to Kassel to see how. To us, an exhibition is a medium which helps us to find answers to questions that are, and need to be, asked around the world today.

RK: I'm very interested in your ideas regarding education and audience in relation to documenta as so often – as you note – education is outsourced or simply 'added on' to the experience of the exhibition itself. In your recent Sydney address you spoke of a purpose-built 'pavilion', to be constructed in Kassel, for a range of contextual purposes parallel to the exhibition display. Could you expand on this concept?

RN: We found that the existing buildings in Kassel did not allow us to think of the public as an integral part of the exhibition proper. Architecture always transports with it a society's attitudes and exclusions, and the eighteenth, nineteenth and twentieth centuries had different ideas of a public than we do. We think of the public as a body which constitutes itself at the instance of perception and discourse. So we need spaces in which both contemplation and discussion can take place.

RK: Unlike the previous documenta and others before it, documenta 12 is not accompanied by a large, singular catalogue publication that frames works in the exhibition. Instead, it is introduced by a three-issue magazine developed by an independent team, based in Vienna and led by Editor-in-Chief Georg Schöllhammer, that comes out in the lead-up to the exhibition itself. Can you speak a little about this concept and its relationship to the exhibition?

RN: *documenta magazine* is based on a network of around ninety-five journals, online platforms and radio stations around the world, all of which have three things in common: they are read and respected by artists, they are interested in discussing our leitmotifs from their own local perspectives, and they want to establish a dialogue, which functions trans-locally and independent of Kassel.

Ruth Noack, 2006,
courtesy documenta, Kassel.
Photograph © Marianne Menke.

The exhibition has profited enormously from the wisdom, insight and enthusiasm of these local experts – they have helped us make sense of local scenes and cultural contexts. Visitors to documenta can use the three issues of the magazine to read up on our leitmotifs in preparation for the exhibition. On the other hand, the magazine allows people to access the exhibition even if they cannot physically come to Kassel.

RK: A word about the art and artists in documenta 12. In your recent address you spoke in detail about the issue of context. This is a complex issue facing all curators and exhibitions when presenting a range of artworks from locations beyond the local. Could you speak a little about the issue of context – global and local – and how this informs the exhibition, at both the micro and macro level?

RN: Loss of context always raises problems, as works of art are imbued with meanings that depend on specific fields of knowledge, be they historical, cultural, geographical, or simply due to the fact that artists are experts in their fields. How to make up for this loss is one of the big curatorial questions. The answer is simple: you cannot. But what one can do is to create new contexts for works of art, by placing them into dialogue with each other, enabling them to speak a more complex text, or to shine in a larger tonal range than if they were isolated, solely dependent on, say, a white cube reading.

Roger M. Buergel, 'Der ursprung (The origins)', *50 Jahre / Years documenta, Archive in Motion*, Steidl, Germany, 2005, pp. 174–75.

documenta 12, Kassel, 16 June – 23 September 2007.

Howard Arkley, **Floriated residence, 1994**, acrylic on canvas, 203 x 153 cm, collection Vizard Foundation Art Collection of the 1990s, Melbourne, acquired 1994, courtesy National Gallery of Victoria, Melbourne. © The artist's estate.

Howard Arkley:
Myths and
Misconceptions

Anthony Gardner

I have a confession to make: I am part of a generation that got hooked on contemporary art at the end of the 1990s. For us, the Melbourne art scene was entrenched firmly in Fitzroy and decidedly not in Prahran and Richmond. The artist-run space Store 5 was consigned to art history, while 'Popism', Paul Taylor's 1982 exhibition of postmodern Australian art, seemed an archaeological relic. And what we knew about Melbourne's 'painter of the moment', Howard Arkley, came to us mainly as myths: his legendary enthusiastic and influential teaching, his high-profile drug overdose, even his celebrity as the scion of suburban dreaming. In the years since Arkley's death in 1999, it proved surprisingly difficult to rectify that situation of second-hand knowledge and to actually encounter an Arkley work. Solo shows, let alone an institution-based retrospective, were thin on the ground; our best bet was to visit a contemporary art auction and witness the rapid turnover of Arkley's paintings in the early years of his posthumous renown.

The National Gallery of Victoria's (NGV) touring retrospective of Arkley's career is therefore highly anticipated and long overdue. But this superbly presented exhibition, spearheaded by NGV curator Jason Smith, shows that our nearly decade-long wait provides unexpected benefits. It has given the NGV team the benefit of time to thoroughly research and collate the 130 or so works that comprise the exhibition and which span the breadth of Arkley's career from his first solo show in 1975 at Tolarno Galleries, Melbourne, to 1999's 'The Home Show' in the Australian pavilion at the Venice Biennale. This collation alone is an impressive feat, and one made more difficult by the numerous transfers of Arkley's works from one collection to another. Thankfully, this problem is largely redressed by both this exhibition and a new book published in conjunction with it, *Carnival in Suburbia* (2006), by Arkley's brother-in-law and Monash University academic, John Gregory. Through much painstaking labour, both the monograph and exhibition allow viewers to easily relocate and revisit works that risked being lost in the recent storm of sales.

The second benefit relates to interpretation. The moment has passed when we could view Arkley's works through a prism of pathos or, worse, premonition. By presenting *Suicide*, 1983, alongside some of its source material from (among other things) weekly tabloid magazines, Smith succeeds in drawing the painting away from ghoulishly biographical connotations and back to Arkley's process of building content. Arkley's signature 'psychedelic' blur, created through the skilled use of a spray-gun, reveals a consistent attempt to merge 'low' and 'high' art manufacture, tagging or tattooing and op art. (The inclusion of a painting of

a person shooting up, *The ritual*, 1986, is arguably a less successful locking of Arkley to drug subcultures.)

What emerges throughout this exhibition is not a facile narrative based on the artist's biography. Instead, Smith provides a sustained focus on Arkley's most important aesthetic trait: his cannibalism of (Western) art's histories and his attempt to question art's vanguardism when filtered through new, contemporary contexts. Does synthetic cubism maintain its significance when transposed through wallpaper patterning, as when chintz stands in for shrubbery in Arkley's many images of suburban houses? Can the rationalist utopias of de stijl survive their translation into visual forms of muzak, as in *Muzak mural*, 1980–81, where day-glo dots on canvas leach onto the three dimensions of the chairs that stand before them? Pieter Saenredam's multi-perspective views within baroque Dutch churches, abstraction from before and after 'The Field', even contemporaries such as Alun Leach-Jones and Brian Dunlop, get tangled in Arkley's web of allusions and illusions.

But as this exhibition makes clear, Arkley's postmodernism was not the usual cliché of allusion for its own sake. At its heart lay an important conceptual tension, as Chris McAuliffe notes in an online podcast accompanying the exhibition (and which is itself an important innovation that demands to be followed by other galleries across the country). That was the tension between the avant-garde ambitions of art past and the question of where painting could go once it had been reduced to décor and design in the 1980s. In a sense, then, Arkley's aesthetic was neo-modernist rather than postmodern – a replay of Clement Greenberg's dialectic of avant-garde and kitsch in the context of (yet another) 'death of painting'. But we can be more specific again, particularly in relation to the heyday of Arkley's suburban home series in the 1990s. What was really at stake was the delicate balance between the painting of domestication and the domestication of painting. The exhibition's greatest success is its focus on these conceptual tensions, rather than limiting the Arkley show to stereo-typical content or his mythologised biography. It provides an important and timely reminder of why Arkley was such an influential painter – for both his postmodern peers and the generations emerging in his wake who, like me, may never before have had the opportunity to witness Arkley's talent firsthand.

Howard Arkley, The Ian Potter Centre: National Gallery of Victoria Australia, Melbourne, 17 November – 25 February 2007; Art Gallery of New South Wales, Sydney, 10 March – 6 May 2007; Queensland Art Gallery, Brisbane, 6 July – 16 September 2007.

MICHAEL LANDY
19 JULY – 12 AUGUST

SHERMAN GALLERIES

16–20 GOODHOPE STREET PADDINGTON NSW 2021 AUSTRALIA TEL +61 2 9331 1112 FAX +61 2 9331 1051 TUE TO FRI 10–6 SAT 11–6
www.shermangalleries.com.au info@shermangalleries.com.au

SHANE COTTON
28 JUNE – 14 JULY

Red Shift (detail), 2007

John Mawurndjul 2006, type C photograph, 120 x 120 cm

SONIA PAYES
31 JULY – 25 AUGUST 2007

CHARLES NODRUM GALLERY
267 CHURCH STREET RICHMOND MELBOURNE VICTORIA 3121 AUSTRALIA
www.charlesnodrumgallery.com.au gallery@charlesnodrumgallery.com.au
TEL: +61 3 9427 0140 FAX: +61 3 9428 7350 HOURS: TUES - SAT 11

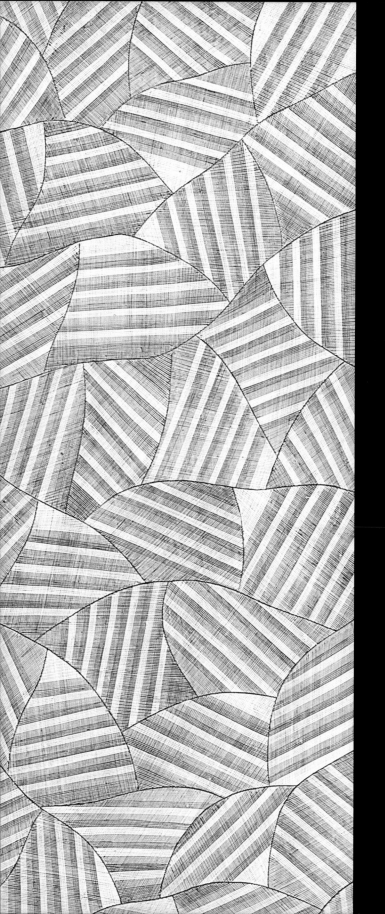

GUNTER CHRISTMANN

SAMUEL NAMUNJDJA

3 – 28 July 2007

NIAGARA
GALLERIES

245 Punt Road Richmond Victoria 3121 Australia
Tel: +61 3 9429 3666   Fax: +61 3 9428 3571
mail@niagara-galleries.com.au
www.niagara-galleries.com.au
Hours: Tue 11.00–8.00pm Wed–Sat 11.00 6.00pm ACGA

Samuel Namunjdja *Gungura (Wind dreaming)*. 2006 ochre pigments with PVC fixative on stringybark 150.5 x 48cm

Opening:
By invitation
Wednesday 04 July, 6.30pm
For more information call
us or visit our website.

Johnnie Dady 2007
Drawing/sculpture
04 July – 12 August 2007

Untitled 2006
120 x 40 x 120cm
Cardboard

Über Gallery

52 Fitzroy Street
St Kilda 3182 Australi.
Tel +613 8598 9915
info@ubergallery.com
www.ubergallery.com

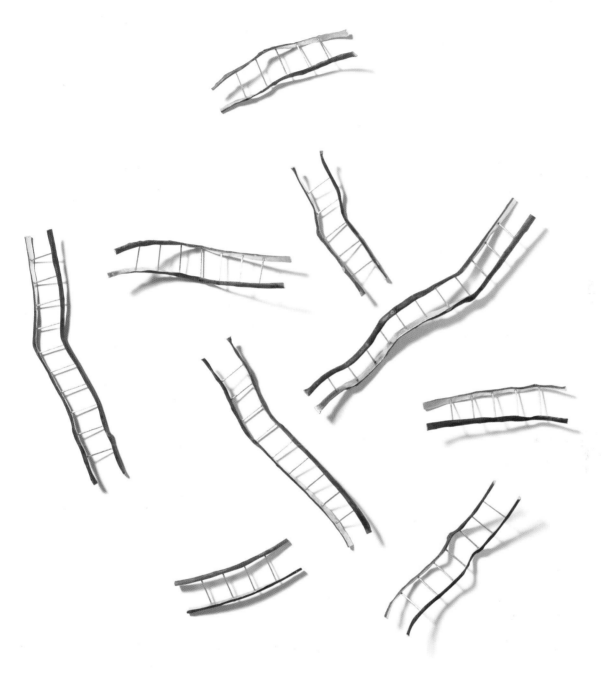

geag

GREENAWAY ART GALLERY : ADELAIDE   39 Rundle Street, Kent Town SA 5067   T +61 8 8362 6354   E gag@greenaway.com.au   W www.greenaway.com.au

1 – 26 August, 2007
A SALA Festival exhibition

HOSSEIN VALAMANESH & ANGELA VALAMANESH

ROSEMARY LA
ROBERT ROO
TIM MAG
PETER GRA
BROOK AND
ANDREW BRO
LOUISE HEAR
TIM JOH

TOLARNO GALLERIES

LEVEL 4, 289 FLINDERS LANE, MELBOURNE

VICTORIA 3000, AUSTRALIA

TEL 61 3 9654 6000 EMAIL mail@tolarnogalleries.com

www.tolarnogalleries.com DIRECTOR JAN MINCHIN

DANIEL CROOKS
1–23 JUNE

S H E R M A N   G A L L E R I E S

16–20 GOODHOPE STREET PADDINGTON NSW 2021 AUSTRALIA TEL +61 2 9331 1112 FAX +61 2 9331 1051 TUE TO FRI 10–6 SAT 11–6
www.shermangalleries.com.au info@shermangalleries.com.au

Letter from London

Barry
Schwabsky

right, detail
Tomma Abts, Eppe, 2006, acrylic and oil on canvas,
48 cm x 38 cm, courtesy greengrassi, London,
Galerie Daniel Buchholz, Cologne, and Galerie Giti
Nourbakhsch, Berlin.

Maybe the watershed year was 2000. That's not only the year London got a proper contemporary art museum in the Tate Modern, but also when it became strikingly clear that the most interesting thing about the British art scene was precisely that it's not very British. In 2000 only one of the four artists shortlisted for the country's most highly publicised annual art event, the Turner Prize, was actually born in the United Kingdom. Glenn Brown, the English painter, was joined by Michael Raedecker, who is Dutch; Tomoko Takahashi from Japan; and German-born Wolfgang Tillmans, who won the prize.

London in the 1990s became famous (or notorious) for the yBas – the young British artists – such as Tracey Emin, Damien Hirst, Sarah Lucas, Gavin Turk, and so on. In retrospect, it might be more apt to dub them the lBas: the last British artists. Not because significant art is no longer coming out of Britain – far from it; rather, because London's significance has been reinforced as it has become a magnet for non-British artists. The yBas deserved their name insofar as they did not merely happen to be British, but were artists whose work was profoundly, sometimes outrageously, British in content and attitude. British art critic Matthew Collings had a great time making fun of the notion that these artists were 'cheeky cockneys and punk rockers oppressed by the Thatcher junta, dodging IRA bombs, living in squats, and making rough and ready art that screams with rage', but the very fact that they could generate such a description was the essence of their work. Even now, if a London taxi driver finds out you're an art critic, watch out: you'll have to hear his opinion of Hirst or Emin. Art became a pop-cultural phenomenon in Britain like nowhere else – in great part because the yBas's recognisably British personae struck a chord with the general public, evoking an English working class that is fast disappearing as the working class has itself become, through immigration, highly multicultural.

Fast-forward a decade and how different everything looks. This year, Tomma Abts is the second German-born winner of the Turner Prize, and the British scene is notably short on cheeky cockneys. The London art world has become cosmopolitan in a way that could never have been imagined at the time of the original 'Freeze' exhibition staged by Hirst in 1988. And yet, strangely enough, the seeds for the change were sown precisely then and there. For one thing, that is when Charles Saatchi – Baghdad-born, don't forget! – began collecting contemporary British art in earnest, and in quantity, thereby kick-starting what had previously been an almost dormant market. And 'Freeze' was the show that identified the new British scene as essentially the work of Goldsmiths College graduates – something that was never quite true, but an important part of the myth.

There are a number of reasons for the unexpected rise of London as an international art mecca, and some of them have nothing to do with art. The opening of European borders has been vital, but that doesn't explain why it is London rather than Paris or Brussels (or even Europe's number two city for

artists, Berlin) that has benefited. The most important reason for London's ascent is its concentration of highly regarded art schools, led at first by Goldsmiths, and more recently by the Royal College of Art. But there are many more: Chelsea College of Art and Design, Central St Martins College of Art and Design, the Royal Academy of Arts, and so on. Many foreign students come here to study; a lot of them decide to stay on. And the schools have a strong incentive to take overseas students whom they can charge vastly higher fees than British students pay. Looking back to that 2000 Turner Prize, Raedecker undertook a Masters at Goldsmiths, Takahashi attended Goldsmiths and the Slade School of Fine Art (intriguingly, she also studied ethnomusicology at SOAS, the School for Oriental and African Studies); Tillmans studied, not in London but close enough, at the Bournemouth and Poole College of Art and Design.

Of course, especially in a city as horrifyingly expensive to live in as London, artists need something to live on once they've finished their studies. They need a market – something that the gratifyingly inexpensive Berlin sorely lacks. London has an art market in great part thanks to Charles Saatchi – not only thanks to his money but to his massive public support of contemporary art, which has made collecting contemporary art fashionable among those who can afford to do so, as it had not previously been in Britain. Of course, the other element in the popularisation of contemporary art in Britain has been the Turner Prize itself.

But even Saatchi, an Iraqi-born Jew, could never have been so influential in old London. There was one further change necessary for all the pieces of London's internationalism to fall into place. That change has to do with a transformation of the rules governing the City of London – Britain's financial heart. I'm too much of a layman to explain it in any detail, but a deregulation of the financial markets in 1986, which resulted in a so-called 'big bang', led to London becoming the financial capital for all of Europe, and possibly the world, even eclipsing New York. As the *Independent* recently put it: 'Out went parochialism and long lunches at the club; in came American banks, electronic trading and the cut-throat competitive ethos that has put London at the heart of international finance.'

As a result, just as there are now a vast number of internationals working as artists here, there is an even bigger number earning vast amounts of money in banking and finance. These foreigners constitute the real collecting base for London. London's collectors are Italians, Germans, Americans, Russians, Iranians – almost anything but English. If London has become one of the world's great cities for art, it's because London is no longer English – it's something more like the world.

Coco Pops

Louis Nowra

opposite, clockwise from top left
**Philip Taaffe, Chi-Chi meets the death
of painting, 1985**, acrylic over linoprint on
paper, 284.5 x 114.3 cm, courtesy Gagosian
Gallery, New York.

Robert Ryan, Lenny, 2005, oil on canvas,
134 x 123 cm, courtesy Arthouse Gallery,
Sydney.

Coco, courtesy the author.
Photograph Roslyn Sharp.

For many people, the chihuahua is not so much a dog but a rat-like creature used as a fashion accessory by bubble-headed blonde celebrities such as Jayne Mansfield, Britney Spears and Paris Hilton. Yet they are thought to have been bred by the Toltecs, Mayans and Aztecs, who either ate them, or ritually killed them, in order to guide dead priests and other important men through the hideous underworlds of hell.

My obsession with chihuahuas has been as long-running as my fascination with art. Not only are they the smallest canines, but their appearance is also plain weird. They have bug eyes, apple-shaped skulls and ears like triangular leaves. When afraid or cold they shake uncontrollably as if they have Parkinson's disease. But they love human company and are ferociously loyal. They appear as comic characters in films, logos for restaurants, and crop up in a surprisingly large range of art.

I have written about chihuahuas at length in articles and essays and an art gallery owner recently approached me to curate a show featuring the chihuahua. I was on holidays with my wife, Mandy, and our chihuahua, Coco, near Byron Bay, and I was mentally drawing up a list for the perfect exhibition. It would begin with Toltec pottery, which featured deliberately fattened chihuahua-like dogs, and an Aztec child's toy in the shape of a chihuahua. All such ancient representations are very stylised, as if the artists distilled the dog to its pure form.

Of modern artists and photographers there would be Philip Taaffe's *Chi-Chi meets the death of painting*, 1985, a haunting work where, on a red background, six white living chihuahuas arranged in a vertical line stare at six white chihuahua corpses. It's like a disturbing canine version of the Mexican Day of the Dead. In opposition to this I would also include the one-off lithograph Davida Allen created for me of a couple having sex on a bed, underneath which four chihuahuas linger patiently, as if having created the erotic moment. Then there would be Elliott Erwitt's many photographs of chihuahuas, in which he manages to make all of them resemble the alien out of the movie *E.T.* (1982).

Over the Byron Bay holiday week I began to draw up a list – one that was more wish-fulfilment than practical. As luck would have it, Mandy, Coco and I were in a beer garden when a middle-aged man came up to us and asked for a cigarette light. His eyes landed on Coco and he said he also had a chihuahua. Of course, chihuahua owners always find fellow owners fascinating and we got to talking. He said his chihuahua was called Lenny Pascoe. Anyone who names his chihuahua after the test cricketer and fiery fast bowler obviously has a quirky slant on life, and it turned out he was a painter who lived nearby. The only art I had seen by local artists was either kitsch (dolphins, rainbows) or brightly coloured abstract patterns, obviously painted under the influence of drugs.

Lenny Pascoe's owner was called Robert Ryan. We had all had a few drinks and Robert talked of how annoyed he got when people would ask, after he told them he was a painter, 'What sort of stuff do you paint – abstract or figurative?'. I have met many painters over the years and always found some of the best were defensively combative, as if trying to avoid putting into words that which they can only communicate artistically. At the end of the evening Robert asked if I wanted to come and see his work in the morning. At first I was reluctant. What if I didn't like it? But even if I didn't, I could at least meet Lenny Pascoe.

I arrived slightly hung-over the next morning and knocked on his door. Robert was surprised that I had come and escorted me into his studio. The first thing that struck me was how narrow the studio was.

I sat down and before me was a huge canvas, maybe 2.5 metres by 2 metres. It was unfinished and Robert was racing against time to get it ready for his next exhibition at Art Galleries Schubert in Queensland. At first it was hard to get a fix on it because there was little room to step back and examine it as a whole. The work was intricate and powerful, like a colourful tapestry of hieroglyphic marks, small figures and objects. Its complexity was almost overwhelming. It was decorative yet exquisite in its graphics and storytelling texture. It would be easy to say that the animal and childlike figures were primitive but, with a sophisticated elegance, he had refined them to their essence.

Clutching a can of bourbon and coke, and enjoying myself thoroughly, I studied the other painting behind me. It, too, had the same initial complexity that made one look closely at it to unlock its subtle interweaving of colour and figures. Then, out of the corner of my eye, Lenny Pascoe drifted into the studio. He was larger than Coco and with spikier hair, but he was indeed a chihuahua. Then something occurred to me. I turned around and gazed closely at the first painting and saw that Robert had incorporated Lenny a couple of times into the work, not in a naturalistic way but as if he had distilled Lenny to his essential being. I had seen this depiction of chihuahuas before. The dog in the painting was startlingly similar to the way the Mayan and Aztec artists had represented it. I was thrilled. It was as if the essence of the chihuahua had been passed, over a span of more than 1000 years, to this modern artist from Byron Bay.

I returned to my holiday shack. Coco ran out to greet me. Sure, she isn't immortalised in a painting, but, it's a consolation to know, as any objective judge will confirm, that she's much more attractive than Lenny. Besides, Lenny can't beg, do Hi-Fives, and pirouette on cue like Coco can.

RICHARD McMILLAN
1944–2006

Richard McMillan. Photograh courtesy Ross Plapp.

Andrew Frost

When Artspace first opened in the early 1980s it shared a floor of a run-down rag trade building in Randall Street in Sydney's Surry Hills with the offices of the pioneering art magazine *Art Network*. I was working as a volunteer gallery assistant at Artspace and it was there that I first met Richard McMillan, then editor of the magazine. McMillan had no real reason to speak to me, a student without a clue to how the world worked, let alone be such a nice bloke, yet he happily engaged in art-world banter and responded to the nonsense I spouted with a respectful seriousness. It was a mark of the man that, although he didn't need to do either of these things, he did so with charm and wit.

McMillan, who died last year after an eighteen-month battle with a brain tumour, was a well-known and much-liked personality on the Sydney art scene. He was a writer, photographer, sculptor, art scholar and curator. But perhaps more than any of those things he was also a true bon viveur, someone who knew how to live well.

Although a raconteur, he was also a private person whose background was, even to many of his closest friends, something of a mystery. He was born in Syracuse, New York in 1944, and grew up in the small Rockwell-esque town of Geneseo, New York. He attended Syracuse University, majoring in English, but before he completed his bachelor's degree he was drafted into the United States Army. He served as an artillery officer in Vietnam, eventually returning to finish his studies in 1969. His experiences in Vietnam deeply affected him and he rarely spoke of them.

With a rich American accent untroubled by his nearly thirty years in Australia, his response to the question 'Where are you from?' was: 'I left home at eighteen and have been on the road ever since.' A traveller with a passion for the arts, he first worked at the Library of Congress in Washington D.C. and then at the Fine Arts Museum in Boston. He also proudly carried the counter-culture badge of credibility of having attended the 'original' Woodstock in 1969. He went to the concert with Jon Plapp, the man with whom he would spend the rest of his life. Later in 1969 he and Plapp moved to Toronto where McMillan worked at the David Mirvish Gallery.

McMillan emigrated to Australia in 1977, a year after Plapp had returned to Sydney. Reunited, they converted an engineering shop into a warehouse apartment and studio while McMillan set about making Sydney his new home town. Around 1979 McMillan became involved with the fledgling *Art Network*, then under the stewardship of editor Ross Wolfe and publisher Peter Thorn. McMillan helped out on early issues, eventually becoming its editor from issue 8

in 1983, following Wolfe's departure. Among McMillan's achievements with the magazine was an issue dedicated entirely to contemporary photography, one of the first ever by an Australian art magazine.

In 1977 McMillan and Plapp met Margaret Tuckson, the widow of the painter Tony Tuckson, at an opening at Watters Gallery. McMillan became a close friend of Tuckson and helped with the cataloguing of her late husband's vast trove of paintings and drawings. Weekly visits eventually turned into ongoing employment as McMillan became an expert on Tony Tuckson's work. Renowned as someone who undertook meticulous research, McMillan received a Master of Fine Art from the University of New South Wales in 1997, writing his thesis on Tuckson's drawings. He later joined the Oceanic Art Society in which he was active, and in 2004 he became a dual Australian-American citizen.

McMillan is fondly remembered not only for his many achievements, which he played down with considerable self-effacement, but also for his mischievous sense of humour. He always seemed to be in touch with all the goings-on of the art world and revealed information to you in a tone of conspiratorial fun. He often used his insider knowledge of the art world to help young artists make their way and, with Plapp, collected work by artists from around the world. A number of these works were donated to the National Gallery of Australia, Canberra. Like many charming people, McMillan could also be mercurial and had a propensity for alarming jokes – Ross Wolfe recalls a road trip to Brewarrina with McMillan behind the wheel. When Wolfe attempted to play a Willie Nelson tape, McMillan drove the car into the gravel at high speed until the music was ejected. Although he had officially given up smoking, McMillan always happily accepted my cigarettes on the occasions I met him for coffee. In public he had the demeanour of a kid who had just been caught pulling a prank and it was always great to see him at an opening.

McMillan is survived by his mother, his brother Thomas and his sister Dorothy. In an email to this writer Dorothy recalled that: 'Richard was a wonderful brother. At his memorial service my mother told a story of how he had – when he was about four and I was two and we lived out in the country – taken me outside at night to see the cabbages growing in the moonlight. He was always pointing out the beauty.'

JON PLAPP
1938–2006

Jon Plapp. Photograh courtesy Ross Plapp.

Geoffrey Legge

Whenever I think of Jon Plapp I recall the unswerving integrity of the man and his art. His many friendships involved no compromise on his part; he was he same gentle, thoughtful, responsive Jon Plapp to everyone. His paintings oo were uncompromising. Critical comment, the earliest being that of Elwyn Lynn, perceived the humanity in Plapp's paintings despite a fairly strict formal aesthetic.

For all my best endeavours, expressions of feelings about Jon Plapp seem o ring hollowly against my recollections of his quiet steadfastness. It is wise, herefore, to retreat from feelings and embrace facts. Plapp, having acquired a Bachelor of Arts degree from the University of Melbourne, left in 1966 for he United States and Canada. When, eleven years later, he returned to settle n Sydney, he possessed the three co-ordinates of his future life. He had earned a PhD from Washington University, St Louis, which would qualify him to practise as a psychologist. More important and contrary to what he had earlier conceived as possible, he had become an artist. And, most importantly, he had met his life partner, Richard McMillan.

Jon's professions as psychologist and artist did not have much social overlap. His colleagues at Rivendell Child and Adolescent Unit held him in high regard as a psychologist for whom painting was a spare-time activity. In the art world he was thought of as an artist with a day job. His important contribution to his day job' is attested to by his friend and colleague at Rivendell, Professor Marie Bashir, Governor of New South Wales. Her excellency said:

Jon first came into the life of myself and friends and colleagues … when he joined the team at Rivendell in the late 1970s. I had waited for several years to fill a very important position on the team, hoping that someone special enough – wise and knowledgeable and sensitive – would some day appear. A person with all those qualities, and countless more, arrived! We could not believe our good fortune … And across those years at Rivendell, every professional colleague, every young person in need and their families, every member of the household staff, every school counsellor and countless others, had the benefit of his qualities and skills.

As artists, Jon and Richard became obsessed with the work of Tony Tuckson. This led to a close friendship with Tuckson's widow, Margaret, over a thirty-year period. For all his tireless commitment to the Art Gallery of New South Wales, Tuckson was, in his self-image, an artist. Jon Plapp mirrored Tuckson in this, for despite his effective involvement at Rivendell, Plapp thought of himself as an artist. His early work was well received and, over the years, it has lost nothing

of its freshness and interest. Any overt influences from the artists he admired in the United States and Canada disappeared as his work developed, so much so that someone familiar with his paintings from 1985 onwards might have difficulty identifying Plapp's earlier work.

Hanging over his work and life for some years was the stalking spectre of Parkinson's disease. In his most recent paintings Plapp turned the affliction to his advantage: the variations in density of line, which was the touchstone for the pulse of humanity in his work, acquired an even greater vitality as he devised strategies to discipline his shaking hand. But not for very much longer would his failing body be able to make manifest the insights of his enquiring mind.

A sculptor, Richard McMillan constructed wall reliefs in which vertical and horizontal elements were animated by diagonals. Is it a coincidence that Plapp, who was for many years preoccupied with the vertical/horizontal grid, should introduce diagonals in his work at the end of his life? We can never know what will emerge from the furnace of our infatuations – and Jon was infatuated with Richard, and Richard with Jon. The early symptoms of Plapp's disease triggered the thought, 'Thank God he's got Richard'. But Richard became the victim of a brain tumour and Jon became his carer. When he knew his time was short, Richard's concern was for Jon, not for himself. 'It's Jon I'm sorry for', he said. Richard's death in July 2006 was a sorrow Plapp could not share. He gave little evidence of his grief. Long months after Richard's death he'd find himself cooking a meal for them both. Then the realisation would flood in that no-one was going to clatter down the wooden stairs to join him. 'Isn't it silly of me?' Jon said. No, it was not silly, it was heartbreaking, for it was touching evidence of such deep devotion.

Jon died on 26 November 2006, a little over four months after Richard's passing. He left many friends, including his brother and sister-in-law, Ross and Liz Plapp.

TRENT PARKE 2006

MAGNUM PHOTOS
60TH ANNIVERSARY EXHIBITION
22.08.07 - 22.09.07

TRENT PARKE//MARK POWER//
ANTOINE D'AGATA//JONAS BENDIKSEN//
ALEC SOTH

36 GOSBELL STREET, PADDINGTON NSW AUSTRALIA
+61 2 9331 7775   WWW.STILLSGALLERY.COM.AU

sullivan+strumpf
FINE ART

44 Gurner St Paddington Sydney 2021 Australia
T. +61 2 9331 8344 F. +61 2 9331 8588
art@ssfa.com.au www.ssfa.com.au
Tuesday–Friday 10am–6pm, Saturday 11am–5pm
Sunday 2–5pm, or by appointment

Sydney Ball *Traxus* 2007 acrylic on canvas, 118 x 137 cm (detail)

SYDNEY BALL
STRUCTURES II

31 JULY – 19 AUGUST 2007

GEORGE LAMBERT
RETROSPECTIVE
heroes & Icons

29 JUNE – 16 SEPTEMBER 2007
National Gallery of Australia, Canberra

George Lambert *Self-portrait with gladioli* 1922 (detail) oil on canvas National Portrait Gallery, Canberra Gift of John Schaeffer AO in 2003

domenico de clario
that time

tuesday 7 august – 1 september, 2007

'not a sound only the old breath and the leaves turning and then suddenly
this dust whole place suddenly full of dust when you opened your eyes from
floor to ceiling nothing only dust and not a sound only what was it said
come and gone was it something like that come and gone come and gone
in no time gone in no time'

From Samuel Beckett's 'That Time' (Collected Shorter Plays,1967)

45 Flinders Lane   T 613 9650 0589   mail@arc1gallery.com
Melbourne VIC 3000   F 613 9650 0591   www.arc1gallery.com

LORETTA QUINN:
A DECADE OF SCULPTURE
20 June - 28 July

Dream-Memory (2001) Mild steel, wire mesh, fibreglass, resin, copper (handcut leaves) 185.0 x 115.0 x 115.0cm
Collection of the Artist

Stonington Stables Museum of Art
Deakin University, Melbourne Campus at Toorak
336 Glenferrie Road Malvern 3144 t 03 9244 5344 f 03 9244 5254
e stoningtonstables@deakin.edu.au www.deakin.edu.au/artmuseum
Tuesday to Friday 12 - 5 Saturday 1 - 5
Melways reference 59 c6 free entry

STONINGTON STABLES
museum of art

DEAKIN
UNIVERSITY

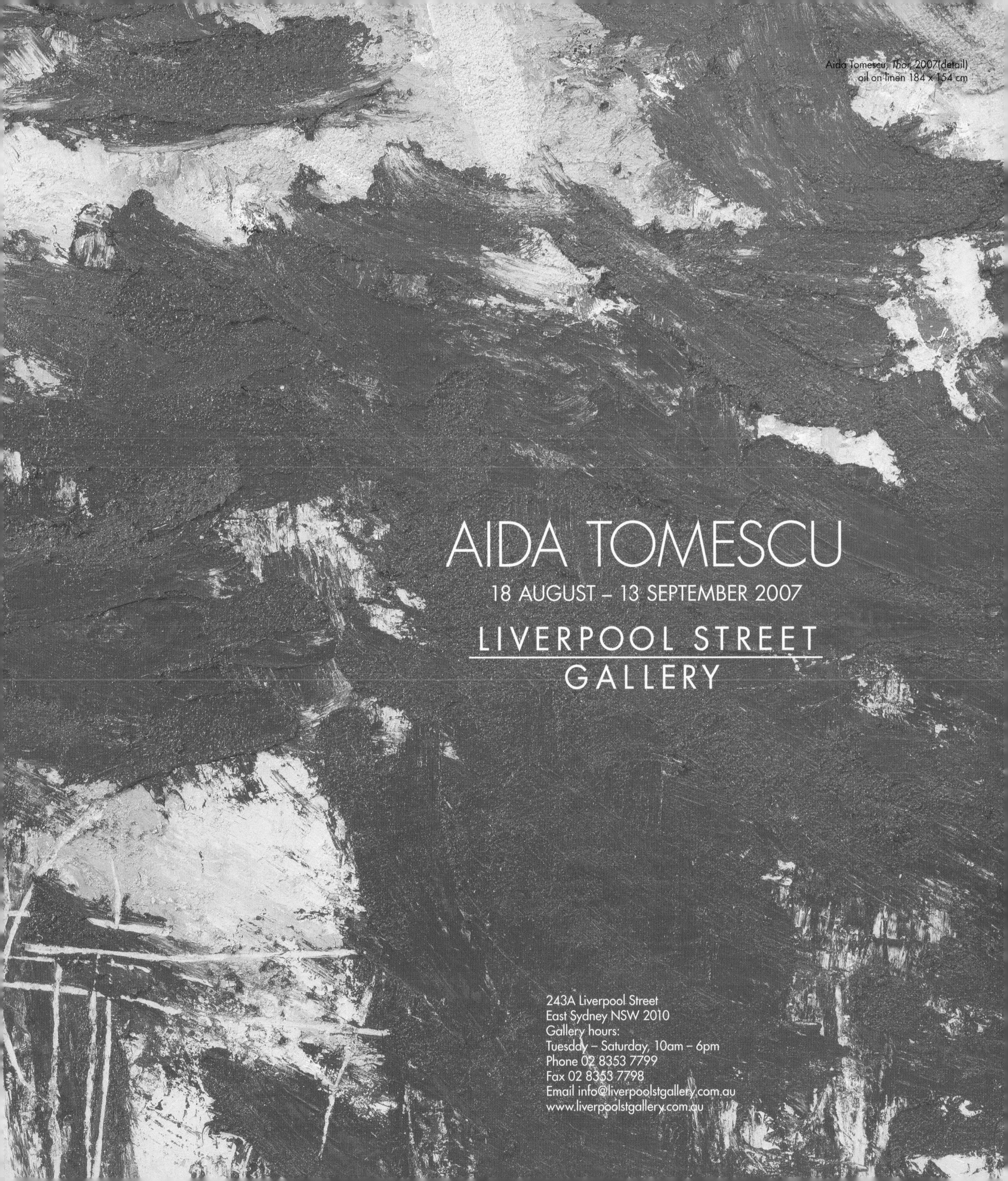

Aida Tomescu, *Thor*, 2007(detail)
oil on linen 184 x 154 cm
AIDA TOMESCU
18 AUGUST – 13 SEPTEMBER 2007
LIVERPOOL STREET
GALLERY
243A Liverpool Street
East Sydney NSW 2010
Gallery hours:
Tuesday – Saturday, 10am – 6pm
Phone 02 8353 7799
Fax 02 8353 7798
Email info@liverpoolstgallery.com.au
www.liverpoolstgallery.com.au

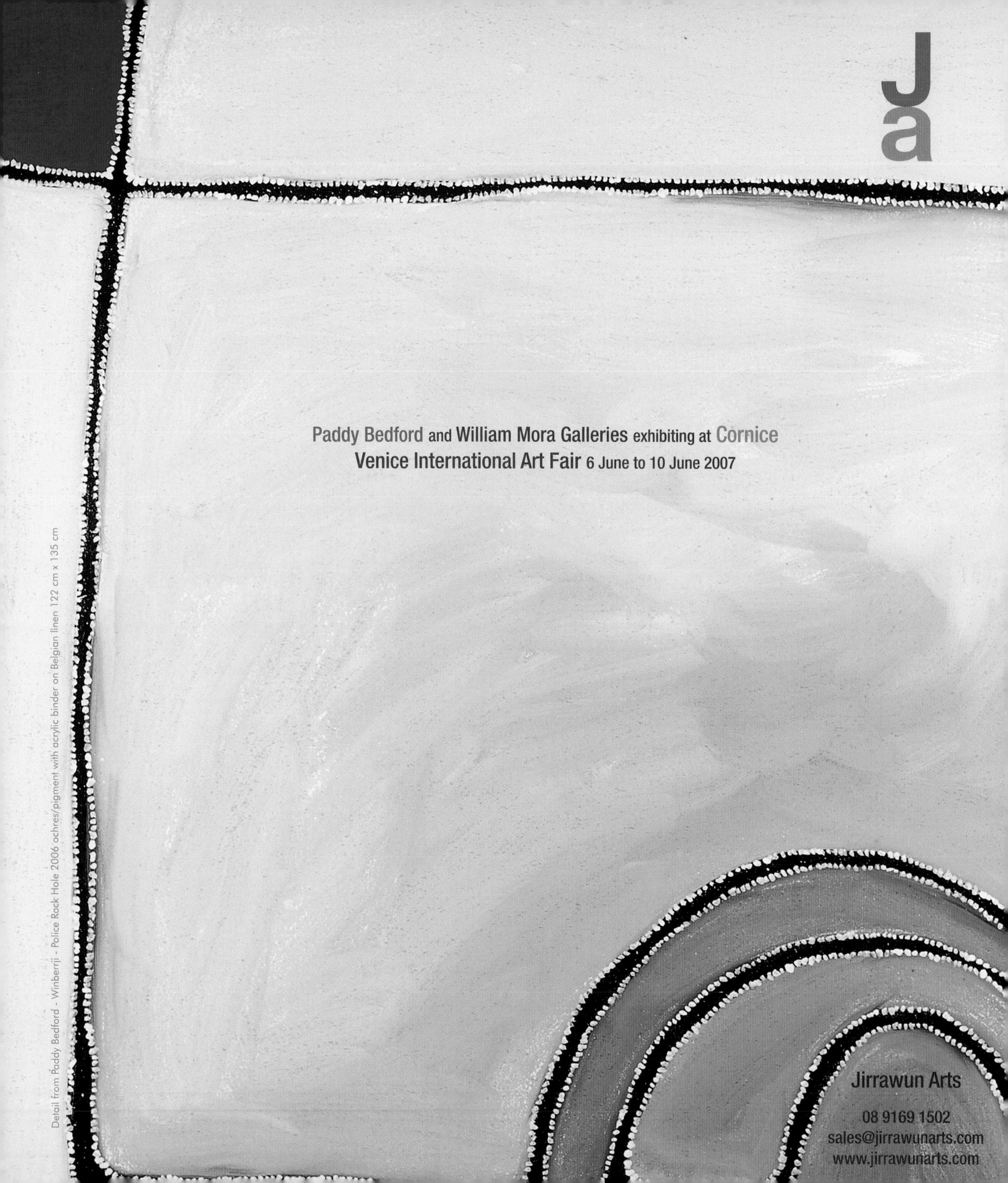

J
a

Paddy Bedford and William Mora Galleries exhibiting at Cornice
Venice International Art Fair 6 June to 10 June 2007

Detail from Paddy Bedford - Winberriji - Police Rock Hole 2006 ochres/pigment with acrylic binder on Belgian linen 122 cm x 135 cm

Jirrawun Arts

08 9169 1502
sales@jirrawunarts.com
www.jirrawunarts.com

LV/L'Ennui 2006 charcoal on paper 120 x 85 cm

Michael Zavros

July

Marina Mirage Seaworld Drive
Main Beach Qld 4217 T +61 7 55710077
E: info@schubertcontemporary.com.au
www.schubertcontemporary.com.au

SCHUBERT CONTEMPORARY

ARTHUR GUY MEMORIAL PAINTING PRIZE

AQUISITIVE PRIZE OF $50,000
EXHIBITION DATES
30 JUNE – 5 AUGUST 2007

**Bendigo
Art Gallery**

42 VIEW ST
BENDIGO
VICTORIA 3550
T 03 5434 6088
F 03 5443 6586

BENDIGOART
GALLERY.COM.AU

TIM OLSEN GALLERY

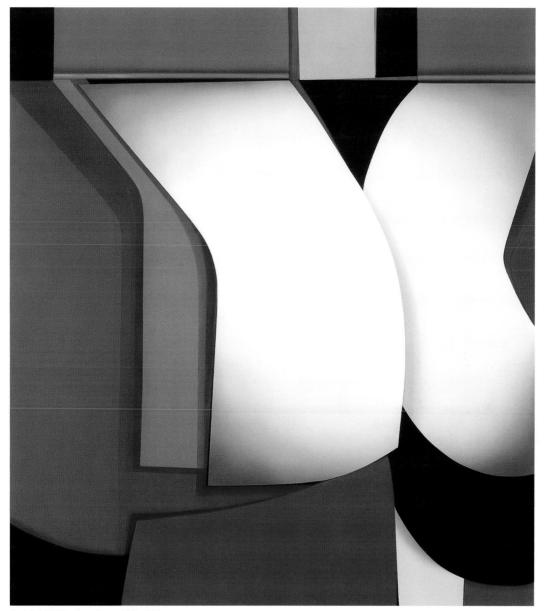

Untitled, 2007, oil on linen, 200 x 180cm

TIM OLSEN

QUEEN STREET

GALLERY

MARIE HAGERTY
31 July - 18 August 2007

80a QUEEN STREET, WOOLLAHRA NSW 2025 TEL 61 2 9362 4300 FAX 61 2 9360 9672
EMAIL info@timolsengallery.com www.timolsengallery.com GALLERY HOURS Tuesday - Friday 10am - 6pm, Saturday 11am - 5pm

Grace Crowley
BEING MODERN

27 July – 28 October 2007
North Terrace   Adelaide
www.artgallery.sa.gov.au

■ national gallery of **australia**
travelling exhibitions

ART GALLERY
of South Australia

Grace Crowley, Australia, 1890–1979, *Mirmande*, 1928, oil on canvas; Bequest of the artist 1981. Art Gallery of South Australia, Adelaide

david jolly

new works 2007

suttongallery

254 brunswick street | t:+61 3 9416 0727 | art@suttongallery.com.au
fitzroy 3065 | f:+61 3 9416 0731 | www.suttongallery.com.au
victoria australia |

GARETH SANSOM

NEW PAINTINGS

13 - 30 JUNE 2007

JOHN BUCKLEY GALLERY

8 Albert St, Richmond VIC 3121, Australia   Gallery hours: 12 – 6pm Wed–Sat   Tel: +61 3 9428 8554 Fax: +61 3 9428 8939 www.johnbuckley.com.au

Gareth Sansom, *Fish story (La Chinoise)*, 2006, 124 x 124 cm, Oil and enamel on linen

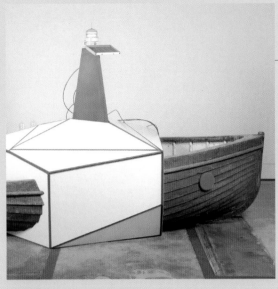

AUGUST
**CHRIS FOX
HITESH NATALWALA**

JULY
**HAYDEN FOWLER
SOUTH AFRICA ON PAPER**

gbk

gallery barry keldoulis

JUNE
**On tour...
Sydney gallery closed**

**2 Danks Street
Waterloo Sydney**

Tue - Sat, 11-6
barry@gbk.com.au
www.gbk.com.au
02 8399 1240
0414 864 445

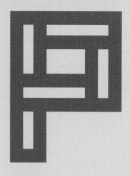

Discovering Egypt

The Ian Potter Museum of Art
The University of Melbourne

31 March –
26 August 2007

Shabti figurine (faience)
Egypt, Late Period,
664–332 BCE
The University of
Melbourne Art Collection
Flinders Petrie Collection

Funded by
2006 Donor Program

Acknowledgement
Queen's College,
University of Melbourne

Potter event supporter

Tuesday to Friday 10am – 5pm
Saturday and Sunday 12 – 5pm

Enquiries 03 8344 5148
potter-info@unimelb.edu.au

Listings of all events
www.art-museum.unimelb.edu.au

Arachne, Kalorama 2006 oil on linen 60 × 76 cm

MELBOURNE WORKS ON PAPER
31 MAY UNTIL 24 JUNE 2007

50 SMITH STREET • COLLINGWOOD • VIC • 3066

T 03 9417 0800 **F** 03 9417 0699
E enquiries@australiangalleries.com.au
W www.australiangalleries.com.au

MEMBER OF AUSTRALIAN COMMERCIAL GALLERIES ASSOCIATION INCORPORATED

MARY TONKIN

NEAR THE TOP DAM

AUSTRALIAN **G**ALLERIES
ESTABLISHED 1956

OUR WAY
CONTEMPORARY
ABORIGINAL ART
FROM
LOCKHART RIVER

5 May – 1 July 2007

A major survey exhibition by

The University of Queensland Art Museum

The James and Mary Emelia Mayne Centre
A cultural initiative of The University of Queensland
St. Lucia, Brisbane

Open: 10am – 4 pm Tuesday to Sunday
Telephone 07 3365 3046   www.maynecentre.uq.edu.au

Samantha Hobson *Bust 'Im Up Again 2001* – detail Synthetic polymer paint and glaze on canvas 125 x 171cm

THE UNIVERSITY OF QUEENSLAND
AUSTRALIA

Queensland Government

Australian Government | Queensland Government
THE VISUAL ARTS AND CRAFT STRATEGY

Our Way, Contemporary Aboriginal Art from Lockhart River has been supported by the Australian Government and the Queensland Government through Arts Queensland, Department of Education, Training and the Arts, as part of the Visual Arts and Craft Strategy and the Queensland Indigenous Arts Marketing and Export Agency (QIAMEA), Department of the Premier and Cabinet. QIAMEA promotes Queensland's Indigenous arts industry through marketing and export activity throughout Australia and internationally.

gallery

gabrielle
pizzi

Balgo Group
Exhibition

In association with Warlayirti Artists
26 June – 21 July 2007

Boxer Milner *Purkitji* 2006 120 x 80 cm acrylic on linen

**Representing Contemporary
Australian Aboriginal Artists since 1983**

Level 3 75-77 Flinders Lane Melbourne 3000 Australia
T 61 3 9654 2944 F 61 3 9650 7087
gallery@gabriellepizzi.com.au www.gabriellepizzi.com.au
Member ACGA

turner galleries

TURNER GALLERIES NOW OPEN.

From 1999 to 2006, TURNER GALLERIES was known as The Church Gallery and located in Claremont, Western Australia.

In March 2007 the gallery relocated to a refurbished 1920's workshop in Northbridge, near the city centre.

It continues to show culturally significant artworks by outstanding Australian artists and sponsors an innovative artist in residence programme. Turner Galleries is directed by Helen Morgan and managed by Allison Archer.

2007 EXHIBITIONS

23 MARCH - 21 APRIL
MARION BORGELT

27 APRIL - 26 MAY
PETER DAILEY
HOLLY STORY

1 JUNE - 30 JUNE
MATTHEW HUNT

6 JULY - 4 AUGUST
JILLIAN GREEN
GRAHAM MILLER

10 AUGUST - 8 SEPTEMBER
JULIE GOUGH
LORRAINE BIGGS

14 SEPTEMBER - 13 OCTOBER
STUART ELLIOTT

19 OCTOBER - 17 NOVEMBER
LISA WOLFGRAMM

23 NOVEMBER - 19 DECEMBER
ANNETTE BEZOR

TURNER GALLERIES
470 WILLIAM STREET
NORTHBRIDGE WA 6003
tel 08 9227 1077
fax 08 9227 1011

www.turnergalleries.com.au
info@turnergalleries.com.au

OPEN
tuesday - saturday
11am - 5pm

dianne tanzer gallery

11.8.07
Unitl 8.9.07

108 - 110 Gertrude St
Fitzroy VIC 3065
Australia

t 03 9416 3956
dtanzer@ozemail.com.au
www.diannetanzergallery.net.au

ACGA

NEIL HADDON
STRANDED

Wendy Teakel
Drylands
7 – 25 August 2007

Wendy Teakel will also be represented
by Catherine Asquith Gallery during
Kunstherbst 15 Sept – 15 Oct 2007 &
Art Forum Berlin 29 Sept – 3 Oct 2007,
in Berlin.

Also representing:

Andrew Kaminski

Ann-Heather White

Anthony Curtis

Christine Maudy

Dianne Fogwell

Geoff Todd

Helen Geier

Helen Lehmann

Hu Ming

Iris Fischer

Jarek Wojcik

Karina Wisniewska *(Switzerland)*

Katherine Boland

Lisa Gipton

Liz Caffin

Melitta Perry

Meg Buchanan

Michelle Day

Ragnhild Lundén *(Sweden)*

Rina Franz

Wendy Stokes

William Ferguson

Xue Mo *(China)*

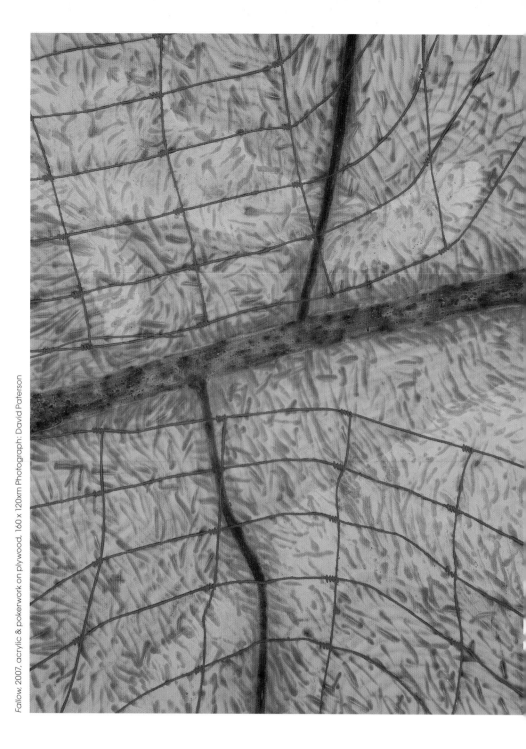

Fallow, 2007, acrylic & pokerwork on plywood, 160 x 120㎝ Photograph: David Paterson

catherine asquith gallery
melbourne/berlin
ground floor, 130 flinders street, melbourne vic 3000
telephone +613 9654 7257 mobile 0438 001 482
enquiries@catherineasquithgallery.com
www.catherineasquithgallery.com

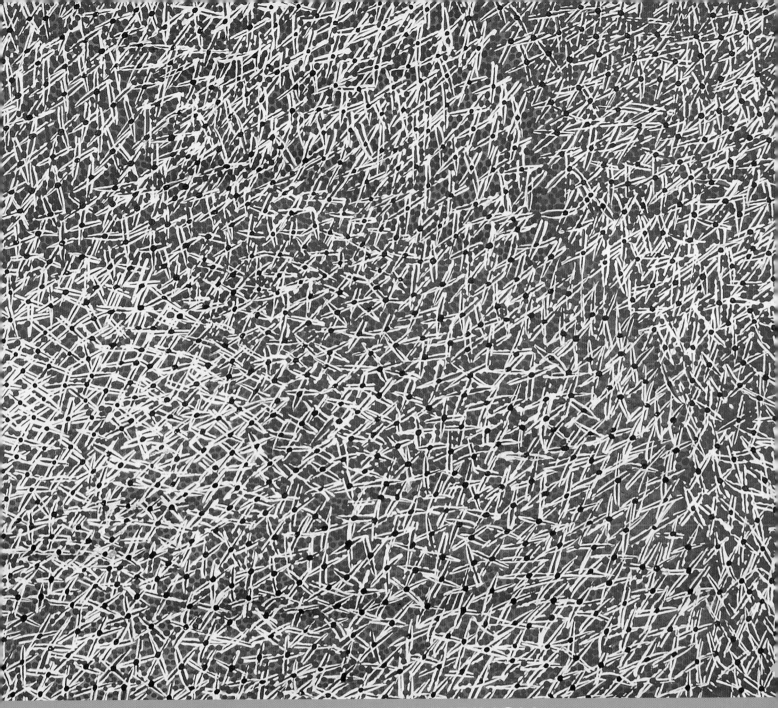

GULUMBU YUNUPINGU

Bark paintings and Larrakitj (Memorial Poles)

17 – 28 July, 2007

Alcaston Gallery @ Depot Gallery, 2 Danks Street, Waterloo, Sydney, NSW

Preview in Melbourne June 2007. View online from 12 July, 2007 at www.alcastongallery.com.au

ALCASTON GALLERY

11 Brunswick Street, Fitzroy Vic 3065 • T 61 3 9418 6444 • F 61 3 9418 6499
E art@alcastongallery.com.au W www.alcastongallery.com.au
Tuesday – Friday 10am – 6pm • Saturday 11am – 5pm

Credit details: Gulumbu Yunupingu *Ganyu-Stars* (detail) 2007 natural ochres on bark, 150 x 72cm

CRITERIONGALLERY

12 CRITERION STREET HOBART O3 6231 3151
CRITERIONGALLERY.COM.AU

SCOTT REDFORD

REPRESENTED BY CRITERION GALLERY

JASPER KNIGHT

14 Nov – 2 Dec 2007

1214 High Street Armadale VIC 3143

T: 03 9500 8511
F: 03 9500 8599

www.metro5gallery.com.au

METRO 5 GALLERY

Black and Yellow Jetty (detail)

Anne Judell - *Waltz*, 2006/07, charcoal/graphite on Hahnemuhle paper, 107x78cm

THIS WINTER AT MARS

Anne Judell
William Eicholtz
Giuseppe Romeo
Beverley Veasey
Domenico De Clario
Amanda Robins
Saffron Newey

[MARS] MELBOURNE
ART ROOMS

418 Bay Street Port Melbourne VIC 3207
Phone: 03 9681 8425

WWW.HATWINES.COM

www.marsgallery.com.au

Specialists in Important Art

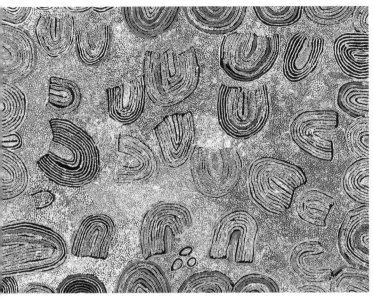

Clockwise from top: Naata Nungarrayi, *The Rockhole and Soakage Water Site of Marrapinti* 2001 (detail), sold for $153,250 (a record price for the artist); Gilt Bronze Figure of Bhodisatva, early 18th century (detail), sold for $96,000; John Peter Russell, *Gros Temps a Belle-Ile* (Stormy Weather at Belle-Ile), sold for $810,000; Diamond Pendant/Brooch (detail), Tiffany & Co, sold for $40,800

JANET DAWSON SURVEY

a Bathurst Regional Art Gallery travelling exhibition

This exhibition examines Janet Dawson's remarkable career from 1953 to 2006 and confirms her place as one of Australia's most accomplished living artists.

Curated by art historian Christine France, the exhibition will tour nationally in 2007:

Drill Hall Gallery ANU
15 February – 25 March

S.H. Ervin Gallery
30 April – 10 June

Queensland University Art Museum
7 July – 19 August

Tasmanian Museum & Art Gallery
6 September – 21 October

Mornington Peninsula Regional Gallery
30 October – 2 December

Publication sponsor

Image: Janet Dawson, *Moon at dawn through a telescope* January 2000, oil on canvas, 122.0 diameter, collection: National Gallery of Australia, Canberra © Janet Dawson. Licensed by VISCOPY, Australia 2006.

marina
strocchi
painting

sam
leach
painting

richard
stringer
sculpture

darren
siwes
photography

robert
doble
painting

• nellie castan gallery | www.nelliecastangallery.com

ACGA

ADAM CHANG

Brian, the dog and the doorway. Oil on canvas, 210cm x 137cm. 2007 Archibald Prize finalist. Collection Brian and Gene Sherman

Pengosekan still life 2007 (detail)
watercolour, 49x42.5cm

Thornton Walker
Works on Paper

17 July – 11 August 2007

HEISERGALLERY

90b Arthur Street
Fortitude Valley Qld 4006
Telephone 07 3254 2849
Facsimile 07 3254 2859
Email bh@heisergallery.com.au

Peter Cameron

Guthega #52, 2006, oil on linen, 84 x 76cm

'Guthega' part 3
19/07/07 – 11/08/07

rex-livingston art dealer

156 commonwealth street surry hills nsw 2010
Tues to Sat 11am to 5pm
tel : (02) 9280 4156   art@rex-livingston.com   www.rex-livingston.com

Urban view 2006 oil on canvas 46 × 61 cm

MELBOURNE PAINTING AND SCULPTURE
26 JUNE UNTIL 15 JULY 2007

35 DERBY STREET • COLLINGWOOD • VIC • 3066

T 03 9417 4303 F 03 9419 7769
E enquiries@australiangalleries.com.au
W www.australiangalleries.com.au

MEMBER OF AUSTRALIAN COMMERCIAL GALLERIES ASSOCIATION INCORPORATED

TERRY MATASSONI

MULTITUDE AND SOLITUDE

AUSTRALIAN GALLERIES

ESTABLISHED 1956

JAMES COCHRAN

8 June - 30 June 2007

Tokyo Neon Street Scene, 2006, aerosol enamel on canvas, 180 x 240cm [2 panels]

MAHONEYS GALLERIES

68 Hardware Lane Melbourne Vic 3000

t 3 9642 1095 Mon-Fri 9-5.30 Sat 10-4

mahoneysgalleries.com.au

James Makin Gallery
WINTER 2007

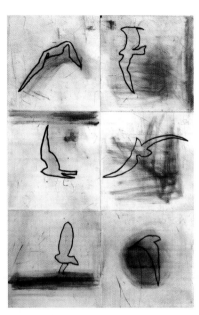

MARTIN KING *Study for the crossing and back* 2007
etching with graphite and encaustic,
unique state, 89.0 x 59.5 cm

MARTIN KING

South Georgia
Sub Antarctica

recent paintings and works on paper

20 JUNE – 14 JULY

IAN PARRY *Blackwood Tree, East Coast, Flinders Island* 2007
oil on canvas, 91.5 x 122.0 cm

IAN PARRY

From the Island
of the Day Before

recent paintings

26 JULY – 18 AUGUST

JEREMY KIBEL *Southern Alps* 2007
oil and enamel on linen, 150.0 x 50.0 cm

JEREMY KIBEL

Shadow to the Eye

recent paintings

23 AUGUST – 15 SEPTEMBER

JAMES
MAKIN
GALLERY

716 High St. Armadale Vic. 3143
T: 03 9509 5032 **F:** 03 9509 5043
Tuesday–Friday 10:00am–5:30pm
Saturday 11:00am–5:00pm
E: info@jamesmakingallery.com
W: www.jamesmakingallery.com

TIM MAGUIRE

Now at leading bookstores
$99.00

Piper Press
02 9660 0364

ISBN 978 0975 1901 28

Wirnpa (our country)

Yulparija Artists from Bidyadanga inlcuding
Jan Billycan, Alma Webou, Donald Moko,
Daniel Walbidi, Spiderman, Weaver Jack,
Mary Meribida and others

Wirnpa 2006, photograph David Batty

7 Short Street Chinatown
Broome WA 6725
ph/f: 08 9192 2658
w: www.shortstgallery.com

SHORT ST. GALLERY

rachel ellis

russell + havannah st cnr, bathurst 2006 oil on board 36.5x41cm

rachel ellis at hill end 2006

king street gallery on burton
102 burton street darlinghurst
nsw 2010 australia
tel 612 93609727 fax 612 93314458
tuesday–saturday 11am–6pm
email: kingst@bigpond.com
www.kingstreetgallery.com.au

king street gallery
613 king street newtown
nsw 2042 australia
tel / fax 612 95190402
email: kingst@bigpond.com
www.kingstreetgallery.com.au
hours by appointment

Engraved poem, linocut on magnani paper, 71.5 x 102cm

81 Denison Street, Deakin Canberra ACT 2600
Open seven days 10am–5pm T 02 6282 5294 F 02 6281 1315
E mail@beavergalleries.com.au W www.beavergalleries.com.au Exhibitions can be viewed online
Directors: Martin & Susan Beaver (ACGA)

beaver galleries

TIM OLSEN GALLERY

Bird in the Hand, 2007, oil on linen, 170 x 245cm (diptych)

GUY MAESTRI

10 - 28 July 2007

TIM OLSEN
QUEEN STREET
GALLERY

80a QUEEN STREET, WOOLLAHRA NSW 2025 TEL 61 2 9362 4300 FAX 61 2 9360 9672
EMAIL info@timolsengallery.com www.timolsengallery.com GALLERY HOURS Tuesday - Friday 10am - 6pm, Saturday 11am - 5pm

Arthur Boyd *Bride and Bridegroom with rainbow* (1960)

DEALING IN THE BEST AUSTRALIAN ART

WILLIAM MORA GALLERIES
EXHIBITING AT CORNICE
VENICE INTERNATIONAL ART FAIR
6 - 10 JUNE 2007

PADDY BEDFORD
PAINTINGS COURTESY OF JIRRAWUN ARTS
JOHN MAWURNDJUL
BARKS AND LORRKON COURTESY OF MANINGRIDA ARTS AND CULTURE
ANDREW ROGERS
BRONZE SCULPTURES AND PHOTOGRAPHY OF THE
"RHYTHMS OF LIFE" GEOGLYPHS

WILLIAM MORA GALLERIES
60 TANNER STREET RICHMOND
VICTORIA AUSTRALIA 3121
TEL +61 3 9429 1199 FAX +61 3 9429 6833
MORA@MORAGALLERIES.COM.AU
WWW.MORAGALLERIES.COM.AU

WILLIAM
MORA
GALLERIES

CELEBRATING 20 YEARS

AUSTRALIAN COMMERCIAL GALLERIES ASSOCIATION

Queensland Centre for Photography at

the 16th International Los Angeles

Photographic Art Exposition, 2007

photo los angeles

MARIAN DREW

RAY COOK

MARTIN SMITH

PAUL ADAIR

RENATA BUZIAK

NATHAN CORUM

This project was proudly supported by:

Australian Government | Queensland Government

THE VISUAL ARTS AND CRAFT STRATEGY

Queensland Government
Department of State Development and Trade

Griffith UNIVERSITY
Queensland College of Art

DAVID RANKIN

Three Crossings - Drawing V (2005)

The Crossings Paintings | Exhibited Andre Zarre Gallery | New York | October 06 | Sold Out

Visit website for the latest arrivals from New York
Sydney | Brisbane | Melbourne viewings

New York Exhibition | Andre Zarre Gallery | October 07

Australian representative for David Rankin

adrian slinger galleries

PO Box 458 Noosa Heads Qld 4567
Ph (07) 5473 5222 Fax (07) 5473 5233
adrian@adrianslingergalleries.com www.adrianslingergalleries.com

PORTRAITS BY JOHN BRACK

23 AUG – 18 NOV 2007   JOHN BRACK AUSTRALIA, 1920 - 1999 *FRED WILLIAMS* 1958, MELBOURNE OIL ON CANVAS 112.7 X 90.8 CM
A.M. RAGLESS BEQUEST FUND 1963 ART GALLERY OF SOUTH AUSTRALIA, ADELAIDE 0.1976

Subscribe

Subscribe for 2 years and be entered into the draw to WIN Louise Weaver's Artist Edition 1 of 50, valued at $550.

LOUISE WEAVER Out on a limb, 2006
Comprises a screen-printed Belgian linen bag with cotton lining,
containing various found and constructed elements, with slight variation,
including a full-colour lithograph poster, a CD and a hand-stitched zine.
Edition 1 of 50, signed with a numbered certificate.

Subscription rates
2 years (8 issues) AU$130 inc. GST
1 year (4 issues) AU$76 inc. GST

Entry into the draw is open for new 2 year
subscriptions and 2 year renewals that are
made during the period 1 June – 31 August
2007, within Australia only.

Subscribe online at
www.artandaustralia.com.au

Art & Australia Pty Ltd
11 Cecil St, Paddington NSW 2021
Tel 02 9331 4455 Fax 02 9331 4577
Toll free 1800 224 018 (Australia only)
subscriptions@artandaustralia.com.au

[AA 44/4]

Subscription details

Australian and New Zealand subscription price
☐ 1 year (4 issues) for only AU$76.00 (incl. GST)
☐ 2 years (8 issues) for only AU$130.00 (incl. GST)

Overseas subscription price
☐ 1 year (4 issues) for only AU$135.00
☐ 2 years (8 issues) for only AU$240.00

Subscription to commence
☐ current issue ☐ next issue

Payment details

Please debit my
☐ Mastercard
☐ Visa

Card Number

Expiry date

Signature

OR find enclosed
☐ Cheque
☐ Money Order for AU$
payable to Art & Australia Pty Ltd (ABN 84 103 767 228)

My details

Title _____ Initials _____
Surname _____
Address _____
_____ Postcode _____
Country _____
Tel _____
Fax _____
Email _____

Gift recipient's details

Title _____ Initials _____
Surname _____
Address _____
_____ Postcode _____
Country _____
Tel _____
Fax _____
Email _____

If you would prefer to conceal this form in an envelope, you can copy the reply paid address (see reverse) onto your own envelope. No stamp required if mailed within Australia.

Subscribe

Subscribe for 2 years
and be entered into the draw to WIN
Louise Weaver's Artist Edition 1 of 50,
valued at $550.

Delivery Address:
11 Cecil Street
PADDINGTON NSW 2021

Art and Australia
Reply Paid 78663
PADDINGTON NSW 2021

No stamp required
if posted in Australia

AUSTRALIA Au3

VENICE BIENNALE 2007

susan norrie
daniel von sturmer
callum morton

Australia at the Venice Biennale
Exhibition dates: 10 June – 21 November 2007
www.australiavenicebiennale.com.au

Australian Government

Australia Council
for the Arts

BETWEEN

Rex Butler on the art
of Rosemary Laing

AND

HEAVEN

EARTH

opening pages, detail
Rosemary Laing, bulletproofglass #3, 2002, type-C photograph, metallic photographic paper, 120 x 193 cm, courtesy the artist and Tolarno Galleries, Melbourne. © The artist.

opposite, top
Rosemary Laing, groundspeed (Red piazza) #2, 2002, type-C photograph, 110 x 205 cm, courtesy the artist and Tolarno Galleries, Melbourne. © The artist.

opposite, bottom
Rosemary Laing, groundspeed (Harrogate flower) #10, 2002, type-C photograph, 110 x 205 cm, courtesy the artist and Tolarno Galleries, Melbourne. © The artist.

Despite the patriotic song celebrating our 'radiant Southern Cross', how many artists here have actually depicted our skies? Where are Australia's Turner, Constable and Claude? There are glimpses in Streeton, atmospheric effects in the impressionists, and a number of contemporary artists have finally turned to it, but throughout the great nationalistic period of Australian art the sky as subject matter seems to have been forbidden. In Frederick McCubbin's claustrophobic bush, we are lost, unable to do much more than look for a way out. In the steeply rising wheatfields and deserts of Sidney Nolan and Fred Williams, the horizon is barely there, a mere compositional device to prevent the canvas from becoming flat.

It is perhaps only with the end of this landscape tradition that the sky as such can begin to be depicted. Until then, Australian painters concentrated on what was real, what was underfoot, what precisely marked them as Australian. There is perhaps no more interesting an exercise than to go through the history of Australian art, dividing painters up into those who produced landscapes and those who looked to the sky. The two different subject matters correspond to two opposed conceptions of art, two antithetical traditions: the first, of course, being Australian, and the second what we might call 'UnAustralian'.

For what is it that the sky represents? By definition, that which cannot be bounded or delimited. The horizon that marks the edge of our own territory also leads over it, is necessarily that border that touches upon our neighbour. The sky is what we all live under, what joins us all in one interconnected, unimaginably complex system, as we are daily reminded by storms, airborne pollution and the phenomenon of global warming. It is what we individually or even as nations have no control over, which is why the heavens are also the hiding place of the gods, whom we attempt to engage with astrological predictions, the steeples of churches and telescopes trained to outer space.

Rosemary Laing's recent series 'weather', 2006, is aware of all this. Appropriately enough for work about location and its loss, the work itself is subject to a certain loss of location. Before its first Australian showing at Melbourne's Tolarno Galleries, it had already been seen in Düsseldorf and New York, and after its Australian exhibition it will go on to Tennessee and to a variety of other venues in the United States. We can absolutely imagine the idea for this series coming to Laing as she sat in an international airport lounge waiting for the weather to clear while she accompanied the equally peripatetic 'flight research' and 'bulletproofglass' series on their own extensive tours. (And one of the fascinating things about these works is the way they are allegories of the 'take off' of Laing's own career.)

What is 'weather' about? Laing's earlier landscape-based work, all the way from 'Natural Disasters', 1988, through to 'greenwork', 1995, was in a sense involved in long-running questions of national identity. In the series for which she first became known, 'Natural Disasters', we have a number of blown-up and abstracted newspaper images of the 'typical' calamities of nature that befall Australia. The works in the 'Natural Disasters' series are named after iconic paintings of the Heidelberg School. Thus in Laing's *The artist's camp (cyclones)*, 1988, named after Tom Roberts's painting of him and Arthur Streeton pitching a tent en plein air, we have an image of the twisted wreckage left behind after a cyclone. In *Still glides the stream and shall forever glide (droughts)*, 1988, after Streeton's painting of a creek bending languidly towards the horizon at dusk, we have an image of a cracked and parched riverbank in drought. In *Departure of the Orient Circular Quay (floods)*, 1988, after Charles Conder's painting of a steamer leaving Circular Quay, we have, by contrast, an image of raging floodwaters.

Of course, through the upsetting or overturning of the scenes depicted in the Heidelberg originals, Laing is suggesting that it is not the events depicted in her work that are 'disasters' as much as the view which constructs them as such. It is only for a settler culture that attempts to master nature that flood, drought and cyclones are anything out of the ordinary. It is this European gaze that introduces a fatal imbalance, for which there is never the right amount of water, but always either too little or too much. Laing, in showing the 'details of these colonial masterpieces, reminds us that these 'natural disasters' are in fact the necessary flipside to their vision of order and progress.

Something like this is also to be seen in Laing's later series 'brumby mound' 2003, and 'burning Ayer', 2003. In 'brumby mound', we have what appears to be a forest of IKEA furniture planted in the outback and covered with a layer of red dust. Then, in 'burning Ayer', this furniture is amassed in a pile to resemble the famous profile of Uluru or Ayers Rock. The pile has been set alight and left to burn. It is almost a definitive image of the rejection of 'Australianness', here revealed to be an illusion brought about by the misperception of a collection of European bric-à-brac. At the end of the series, when the last of the furniture has burnt away, we have a sense of the country being restored to its 'original' state, before the arrival of European culture.

However, the issues at stake in Rosemary Laing's work are perhaps more complicated than they first appear. Undoubtedly, Laing's efforts to overturn or displace the prevailing European categories of thought can lead to a kind of satire. In *one dozen unnatural disasters in the Australian landscape #2*, 2003, a car is stranded and then set alight in the desert, as though we are literally witnessing Australia's European occupiers bog down and run out of gas when confronted with the harsh realities of the place. And in Laing's series 'groundspeed', 2001, a variety of heavy domestic carpet laid down in the landscape can be read as a commentary on the making over of nature as a kind of 'second nature', but also, much more ambiguously, as an image of the re-assertion of this nature through the cracks in our living rooms and imaginations.

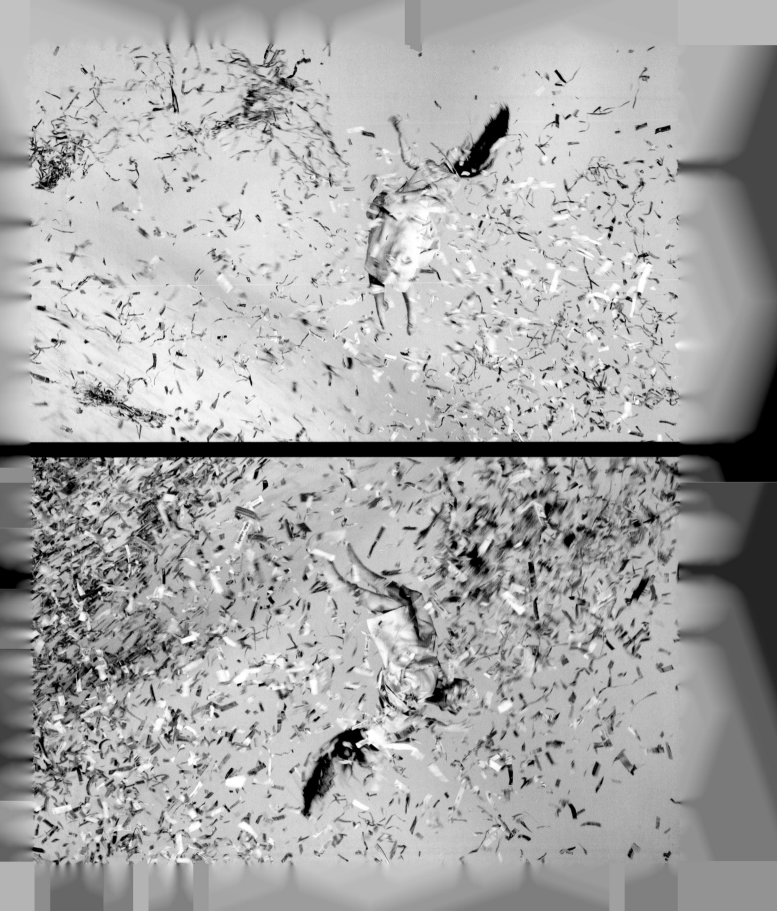

In all of this there is a critical, didactic edge to Laing's work. There is a clarity or legibility to her images, for all their subversive intentions. The work is involved in a re-reading of the colonial past, asserting the 'reality' of the country against the various projections onto it. And there is a geographical specificity to the work, with critics able to demonstrate that the location in which a particular photograph was shot is crucial to its meaning. All this is to say that Laing's work is in fact part of the long tradition of Australian landscape, and does not simply reject it.

But there is another tonality in Laing's work that is not so much critical as utopian, not so much empirical as idealistic. It would operate not by the gravity-bound inversion of categories but by a kind of weightless moving beyond them, in which all conceptual orientations are lost. The subject of this work would no longer be the earth beneath our feet but the clouds over our heads. Its dominant colours would no longer be red and green but blue and white. It would no longer be Australian, but global or international. The questions it would deal with would be bigger than those of national identity, and accordingly the answers it could provide would be less clear and certain.

We first see this other dimension in Laing's series 'brownwork', 1996, which features athletic exercises being staged in an airport: a ball thrown across an empty tarmac, a javelin poised about to be thrown, an abseiler clambering down the roof of an empty cargo carrier. The images are composed with wide, flat horizons, or even with vertiginously tilted angles, as in baroque ceiling painting. Here there is no longer a satire upon nature, but a surpassing of it. The various performers are like quasi-mythological beings, mediating between heaven and earth, as though suspending for a moment the concerns of this world.

Lift-off is finally achieved in Laing's series 'flight research', 1999, in which a woman dressed in what looks like a wedding dress swoops and dives through the air. Her actions do not appear entirely effortless. There is often a stiffness of pose about her, as though she were steering herself or holding herself aloft like a bird. And yet she does achieve that weightlessness only gestured at in 'brownwork'. There is no need for technical prostheses (ball, javelin, the climber's rope and tackle, ultimately the aeroplane) as the woman for a moment floats free. It is a poignancy heightened by the sense that in the performance of the work she is caught at the top of an arc, at the exact moment when her ascent has come to an end and before she begins to fall.

It is a moment that is brief indeed, for in Laing's series 'bulletproofglass', 2002, we see the bride shot down out of the sky. In the first image of the series we watch her looking up in shock, beginning to register what is happening to her. Then, in the images that follow, she tumbles down amidst a flutter of birds' wings, plunging stricken to the ground. Her dreams of transcendence, of breaking her ties to this world are over. (Is it any coincidence that this series came in the wake of the defeat of the referendum for an Australian Republic and the refusal of the Australian Federal Government to say sorry to the country's original inhabitants, two acts that might have helped us break with our colonial past?)

It is at this point that we might turn again to 'weather'. Laing says of the series:

I think we have been through a period when nothing the individual can do will make any difference. We are at the mercy of external forces, events exist outside of individual control.

And certainly in a number of images from the series, in which a child-like figure is held up limply in the air or thrown around in a maelstrom of coloured paper, we have a sense of the human as a frail and vulnerable object subject to greater forces. She is a foil to the bride, whom we see fly through an act of will – this again is why it is so important that it is a real body in space and not computer manipulation – there is a sense of forces superior to us, of events that cannot be navigated or steered through.

In other works from the series we have a leafless and flattened melaleuca forest, as though it exists in the aftermath of an enormous storm or has been trodden on by a giant. There is an eerie stillness to these images, brought out by the monochromatic rendering of the bush and the skein of red fishing net that finds itself snagged on a branch like a trickle of blood. It is a reminder that, for all our emphasis on drawing boundaries around ourselves (and thus excluding others), we are all caught up in phenomena that go beyond us, that cross over every boundary or territorial division we could ever hope to draw. Before the incomprehensible forces of nature we are all as innocent and unknowing as children.

The 'weather' series, returning to the geographical specificity that characterises Laing's earlier work, is shot in part around the biblically named southern New South Wales coastal town of Eden. The place is known both for being an early whaling station and for its preponderance of severe thunderstorms. It is perhaps too much to suggest that the storm Laing depicts is a judgment by God, a form of retribution for past crimes against nature. She is not suggesting a directly interventionist God in this sense. Whatever causes these storms remains firmly off-camera. But the heavens have always been the symbol of what is not known, what cannot be controlled by us, what remains forever out of reach. They are that place where the future is born, the heavens stand for the fate that more and more seems to be approaching and also for the slim possibility that something may arise before this to save us.

Rosemary Laing is represented by Tolarno Galleries, Melbourne, Galerie Lelong, New York, and Galerie Conrads, Düsseldorf.

opposite, detail
Shaun Gladwell, Pataphysical man, 2005, production still, performer Daniel Esteve Pomares, videography Gotaro Uematsu, courtesy the artist and Sherman Galleries, Sydney.

pages 572–73, detail
Shaun Gladwell, War Memorial sessions (Michael mid-session), 2005, production still, performer Michael Steingraber, videography Gotaro Uematsu, photography Josh Raymond, courtesy the artist and Sherman Galleries, Sydney.

Shaun Gladwell
Public space, translation and beauty

Daniel Baumann

There have always been beggars and flâneurs. Modern cities spawned them and banished them. They don't produce anything, they simply occupy space and differ from other city dwellers in their speed; compared with the bustling passers-by and the hurrying workers they move in slow motion. In a time before cars dominated our cities, children and young people played outdoors in streets and lanes. Soon they were transferred into playgrounds and sporting fields, which were then made desolate when funding was withdrawn, or when parks were privatised and turned into advertising space. In the course of the last four decades cities have been covered in concrete in order to speed up product flow and consumption. There has been a merciless process of optimisation and displacement. Still there are ongoing attempts to re-conquer urban space and to use it in a self-determined fashion. A more recent example of this are street climbers, free runners and practitioners of *Parkour* – extreme physical disciplines that engage with the urban environment and which are documented on the video-sharing portal YouTube.

The development of the skateboard, of rollerblades, BMX bikes, street ball and breakdance, can be understood against this background: as a gesture of reclaiming public urban space – although, taking into consideration the actual situation, there is no reason to idealise the re-conquest. The last forty years have seen street culture infiltrate and influence magazines, fashion, film and music; and it has found its way into public institutions such as museums, universities, or galleries.[1] Just like pop culture, street culture thrives on live action and vitality, and both tend to dissolve in the process of being documented and institutionalised. To prevent self-reflection turning into self-dissolution, pop culture developed its own style of writing, which has now grown a bit long in the tooth. On the visual level, the achievements of experimental cinema were co-opted, perfected and commercialised by MTV: fast paced, loose hand-held camerawork, extreme camera angles and seduction through trash aesthetic.

opposite, left, details
haun Gladwell, **Calligraphy and slowburn**,
006, production still from Busan diptych, 2006,
pe-C photograph, 76 x 76 cm, performer Jeong
yu-tae, videography Gotaro Uematsu, sound
yu Hankil, sculpture featured is **Kim Jiyoung,**
What's the purpose of this war?, n.d., courtesy
he artist and Sherman Galleries, Sydney.

haun Gladwell, **Woolloomooloo night**
er hair), 2004, production still, performer
mma Magenta, videography Gotaro Uematsu,
ound Kazumuchi Grime, photograph Josh
aymond, courtesy the artist and Sherman
alleries, Sydney.

opposite, right, details
Shaun Gladwell, Storm sequence, 2000,
video still, videography Técha Noble, sound
Kazumuchi Grime, courtesy the artist and Sherman
Galleries, Sydney.

Shaun Gladwell, Tangara, 2003, production
still, videography Gotaro Uematsu, photograph
Josh Raymond, courtesy the artist and Sherman
Galleries, Sydney.

One interesting thing (there are many others) about Shaun Gladwell's films on breakdancers, BMX riders and skateboarders is how he handles this culture, how he documents it, what risky translations he ventures and where they end up. An older generation may smile and dismiss his films as 'Yoof Culture'. By doing this they ignore the fact that Gladwell deals with a youth culture which shapes the younger generation in the same way that older generations were moulded by jazz clubs, Mozart or Latin lessons.

Storm sequence, 2000, shows a skateboarder on the shore of a stormy ocean, executing his pirouettes on wet ground. Totally absorbed in himself and concentrating on his task, he confronts the roaring sea with the beauty of his movements and the control of his board, and for a few moments his elegance rivals both the landscape and the ballet dancer. In *Storm sequence* Gladwell breaks with the tradition of the restless hand-held camera, which had become the dominant style of the skateboard movie genre. His camera is mounted in a fixed spot, creating a rigid frame in which the skater performs his freestyle manoeuvre. *Storm sequence* surprises the viewer by lifting the skater out of his usual urban surroundings and placing him into a natural and dramatic setting. We get to watch beauty on wet ground, since in the end the skater's performance has nothing to equal the strength of natural forces and his efforts suddenly appear absurd to us. The film both honours and makes relative the performance, an ambiguity which is enhanced by Gladwell's merciless use of slow motion.

The splendid invention of the Austrian priest and physicist August Musger, slow motion is and remains a seductive and dangerous tool. In sport and in science it allows precise studies of motion sequences; in mainstream movies it is used to suggest profound meaning and to gloss over inconsistencies. In art films, slow motion is of interest in places where it's used self-reflectively, as in Douglas Gordon's *24 Hour Psycho* (1993) and where it concentrates on its original purpose: tracking body movement. Some outstanding examples of this are Yoko Ono's *Eyeblink* (1966)[2], and Werner Herzog's *The Great Ecstasy of Woodcarver Steiner* (1974), a magnificent portrait of the ski jumper Walter Steiner. Both films were made using special cameras capable of recording up to 200 exposures per second. They were then shown at normal speed (that is, at twenty-four frames per second), so that the tiniest of movements – for example the blink of an eye – gets drawn out at high resolution to last 35 seconds.

In addition to *Storm sequence*, Shaun Gladwell has used slow-motion technique in *Tangara*, 2003, and *Pataphysical man*, 2005. *Tangara* shows a man hanging by his hands, head downwards like a bat, in a train carriage, *Pataphysical man* documents the breakdancer Daniel Esteve Pomares doing spins on his head. In both films the artist has turned the image 180 degrees, so that the performers are not on their heads anymore, but rather float from the ceiling – an impossibility which triggers a conflict between seeing and knowing. In this way, both *Tangara* and *Pataphysical man* place emphasis on gravity as it is instrumental in even the body's tiniest movement. We observe what singular beauty the movements of the body can engender, how gravity's inevitability and the city's hard edge can produce new movements, and how young people reintroduce elegance, accomplished movements, and dance to the urban landscape. The same is made clear in *Woolloomooloo night,* 2004, in which we watch Emma Magenta perform a long Capoeira dance at an inhospitable petrol station in a nocturnal city.

In *Calligraphy and slowburn*, 2006, Gladwell complicates the setting. Jeong Kyu-tae, a BMX trick rider, presents himself not outdoors in an urban environment, but in a museum, in front of a calligraphy wall. The rider calmly mounts his bike, finds his balance, goes up into some sort of handstand and then returns to the floor. As in *Storm sequence*, *Calligraphy and slowburn* takes the performer out of his usual context to isolate him in an unfamiliar surrounding. The film makes us realise that we are watching a language and its visualisation: the movements performed by Jeong Kyu-tae are like drawings; they are signs which on first glance appear just as abstract as the calligraphy in the background. In both cases, we have to learn a language which is the result of precise and controlled movements. By establishing an analogy between BMX acrobatics, sign and drawing, Gladwell connects in a light and laconic way traditions and cultures which seemed impossible to bring together. *Double linework*, 2000, uses a similar approach: a double projection shows a skateboarder from above, running along the white line in the centre of a road. *Double linework* appropriates the international system of road line marking with ease and concentration, and transforms it into a global drawing.

All the films mentioned here are based on formal rigour. They focus on one single location, actor and moment, they choose a fixed camera angle, and avoid any tricks such as zooms and fast cuts. Gladwell's concentration is equal to the performer's total concentration on his or her act. By doing so, these films make comprehensible the core and the ambiguity of street culture: its search for presence through total immersion and its attempt to re-conquer urban space by getting lost.

1 See for example Aaron Rose and Christian Strike (eds), *Beautiful Losers: Contemporary Art and Street Culture*, exhibition catalogue, Contemporary Art Center (CAC), Cincinnati, 2004.
2 Yoko Ono's work *Eyeblink*, 1966, can be viewed online at www.ubu.com/film.

Shaun Gladwell is represented by Sherman Galleries, Sydney. Translated from German by Anglo-German Communications in Sydney (Bianca Maclean and Fergus Grieve).

Ann Stephen

The
Ungrammatical
Landscape of
Narelle Jubelin

opening pages
Narelle Jubelin, 'Ungrammatical Landscape', 2006,
installation view of murals on the third floor, Centro José Guerrero, Granada, courtesy the artist.

right, detail
Narelle Jubelin, 'A landscape is not something you look at but something you look through', 2006,
petit point renditions, first floor, Centro José Guerrero, Granada, courtesy the artist. Page 580 shows reverse side of the same petit points.

Driving down the A-44 autovia from Madrid to Granada, the wide sky and open plains of La Mancha give way to olive-lined hills, and then massive granite outcrops on the approach to Andalusia, or *al-Andalus* as it is known in Arabic. A different kind of journey, one that nevertheless touches on these vistas, is mapped by 'Ungrammatical Landscape', a recent installation in Granada of petit points and murals by Madrid-based Australian artist Narelle Jubelin. Its curious borrowed title, after Ian Burn, hints at how the work turns the genre of landscape against itself to plot geographies of displacement. Jubelin's multilayered narrative was woven through four floors of Granada's Centro José Guerrero and called forth memory and contingency. In tracking the discontinuous bilingual conversation that Jubelin's work makes with other artists, the viewer finds herself shadowing these contingencies across old and new worlds, beginning in Granada, shifting to New York and Marfa, Texas and then out to the far periphery before finally returning to Spain.

The Centro, a contemporary art centre which opened five years ago in the refurbished newspaper publishing house of *La Patria*, aims to 'wake Granada up from its sleepy provincialism' as part of 'Spain's progression towards democracy'. It honours the Granadian artist José Guerrero (1914–1991), who became a second-generation abstract expressionist and mural painter in New York during the 1950s. In a remarkable homage to this native exile, and with the assistance of two local artists, Paloma Gámez and Domingo Zorrilla Lumbreras, Jubelin recorded Guerrero's exhibited works in some ninety rectangular monochrome murals, each painted to scale with non-expressive brushstrokes and then inscribed with a title, date and dimensions. Jubelin relinquished the role of selecting a colour scheme, preferring a readymade palette given to her by one of Guerrero's friends and contemporaries, the Bauhaus-trained Berta Rudofsky (1910–2006). The top floor of the Centro was left empty but for a series of ghostly blue and red overlaid rectangles, doubled in reflection on a glazed wall which overlooked the neighbouring cathedral. On the floor below, empty murals painted in another colour register surrounded a vast late canvas by Guerrero entitled *Reconciliation*, 1991, laid out flat in the middle of the gallery. For an abstract expressionist following in the footsteps of Pollock,

painting was done on the ground. To display the unstretched canvas horizontally implies incompleteness, not the incompleteness of the painting as much as the unfinished business of reconciliation, a subject with quite specific but different meanings for Spain and Australia. To lay a painting low is also a nod in the direction of minimalism, indexing among other things low visibility and formlessness.

Jubelin reproduced a horizontal canvas in her own miniature petit point rendition of Guerrero's New York studio. The canvas, a tabula rasa ready for action, rendered in creamy pink and mottled grey threads, occupies almost the entire space of the petit point; a tubular steel chair and a painter's work table can just be made out, jammed into the far corner. It was one of five petit points in the entrance gallery based on Guerrero's snapshots from his life in exile as well as glimpses of his native land, set against the backdrop of the Sierra Nevada, the mosaics of the Alhambra dissolving in light. Viewing Jubelin's installation required the viewer to shift between the architectural scale of the blank atmospheric murals to focus on the internally complex miniatures. These exquisite stitched pieces, synonymous with Jubelin's work for over two decades, are for the first time released from the finish of a frame, with each rectangle simply suspended in the centre slit of an otherwise solid glass block, and displayed along an iron ledge strapped between the building's iron pillars. The effect is to reinvent them as double-sided objects with the normally hidden back now exposed. This verso side also serves as a ground for words on glass. Facing the loosely brushed murals, their threads loop, twist or thicken into dense clumps, aping in miniature Jackson Pollock's skeins of paint.

On the floor above, this unlikely dialectical play was heightened by configuring the petit points so that the messy outward-facing side is initially all that is seen. The three iron ledges strung between pillars this time defined a schematic courtyard within the gallery. While both sides of the petit points share thread and a common grid, they cannot be seen together (except in reproduction). Like the visual paradox of 'two faces or a vase' that Jubelin has previously rendered, one must choose either to see the finely worked views or read the words on the

verso against the threads. Language literally turns its back on the image. Such a divided viewing opens up what Slovenian philosopher and sociologist Slavoj Žižek has described as the action of a parallax view in which:

the minimal 'empty' distance between two things produces its object … to discern these mechanisms of power clearly, we have to abstract not only the democratic imaginary … but also the process of economic reproduction.[1]

By walking around the perimeter from left to right, the viewer could pick out a sentence against the unruly rectangles of painterly threads: 'A landscape is not something you look at but something you look through.' Like the exhibition title, 'Ungrammatical Landscape', the words are those of artist Ian Burn, a friend and mentor to Jubelin in the late 1980s. She was one of a younger generation who had sought him out, intrigued by how his minimal and early conceptual art connected to contemporary practices. Jubelin's installation adapted the phenomenological interests of minimalism, which mobilise an embodied rather than an optical seeing. The spectator becomes aware of herself as a perceiving subject through work that articulates the institutional architecture.

Only after stepping inside the spare open-ended space and moving and bending backwards and forwards between the thirteen small blocks spaced along the beams did a fragmented panorama unfold of mostly plain built structures in landscape settings. Visual correspondences ricochet in slow motion between the glass blocks, stirring memories of another site. For instance, two almost abstract squares at either end of the space bracketed the sequence like bookends, their speckled surfaces in fact representing shallow photographic foregrounds; one focuses on the 'footprint' left when a rock is removed, the other literally frames undergrowth through means of a symmetrical white stick frame. Clues to the locations are given in annotations, an indispensable part of all Jubelin's intensely researched work. Both annotations are taken from the documentation of installations: the former, a detail from Robert Smithson's anti-picturesque travelogue *Incidents of mirror-travel in the Yucatan*, 1969; the other, for Mel Ramsden's *Locations* of 1964; installed in a Melbourne park.

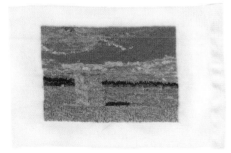

Both of Jubelin's works fix on incidental and nondescript features in order to overturn received conventions of seeing and framing landscape.

These far-flung sites frame five renditions of Don Judd's Chinati Foundation at Marfa, West Texas – an old army base converted in the 1980s into a personal museum for his industrial-scale work. Jubelin introduces Judd's specific objects that are 'neither painting nor sculpture', stitching three open concrete units aligned to the horizon and swamped by their surroundings. Her attention shifts from the geometric structures that stud the horizon to his architectural projects for the Chinati Foundation. When writing about reconstructing this Texan landscape, Judd reveals something of its troubled history, dating back to when:

> airplanes patrolled the border since it was the time of the revolution in Mexico and it wasn't clear or accepted as to where Mexico stopped and the US began. It still isn't clear … Military landscape overlain with a landscape of consumer kitsch is hard to defeat … I hired legal workers from Mexico to make adobes and lay them. The reason for the neglect of the technique is that everyone, Anglo-Americans always and Mexican-Americans now, consider the material unstylish … to both it is not upwardly-mobile.[2]

In the mid-1960s Judd's objects were upwardly mobile, in another way, as they shifted from the cutting edge into the modernist canon. To discern their power, Jubelin's work suggests we have to abstract not only his imagery but also the process of its reproduction and circulation. At the centre of Jubelin's installation in the centre's inner courtyard was a single interior view, based on a photo of fifty-two aluminium works permanently installed in Judd's refurbished artillery sheds. The repeated modular forms dissolve in reflections cast by a grid of windows that frame the gold and blue views of the Texan landscape. The effect is to deflect attention from the work onto the surroundings, not dissimilar to how Jubelin's murals on the Centro's top floor meld the interior view with the exterior.

The petit points render Judd's grand scheme diminutive and intersect his architectural work with the brazen mirror placements at Marfa by the Mozambican-Portuguese artist Ângela Ferreira who mimics the work of both Judd and Smithson, reflecting back the ex-military surroundings. The stitched grid makes Ferreira's temporary

installations – including a Judd-like structure exposed on the exterior wall of an adobe hut – equivalent to the vast North American showrooms. Jubelin conspires with Ferreira's disruptive acts by inserting several readymade minimalist objects in the form of highway snaps of haystacks and adobe buildings, reworking them into the same scheme of speckled blonde foregrounds halved by a horizon of deep blue cloudy skies. They resemble the geometric order of Seurat's unnatural landscapes, also built up by a surface of tiny points of colour. Their pastoral mood is broken by Jubelin's accompanying annotations indicating that they were photographed on highway N-630, opposite the Centro Penitenciario (prison), notoriously alleged, in the wake of the Atocha train bombing of 11 March 2004, to be the location for discussions between members of ETA and presumed Islamic extremists.

A final sequence of three panels shifted the action to the blunt terrain of urban street politics threaded, in Jubelin's quixotic way, through a little-known photograph taken for Judd in 1991, and subsequently turned into an exhibition poster. Passing through Madrid during the first Gulf War, Judd's old anarchist sympathies were struck by the graffiti slogan, 'Saddam Es Malo Bush Es Peor' (Saddam is Bad Bush is Worse). Jubelin connects this with examples of more recent graffiti directed at the current Bush government and 'the coalition of the willing', and another piece from a wall in Redfern, Sydney. The overt politics of the slogans is almost obscured in the stitching, which blurs the blunt immediacy of the speech. This effect of thread has been observed by the art historian Svetlana Alpers:

> a tapestry is difficult to make out. The problem in legibility results from the piecemeal nature of its making and the assertiveness of the threads that shape and describe a world.[3]

Nothing is more piecemeal than the small stitched flecks of colour which constitute a single petit point. A fragmented form of weaving informs Jubelin's entire working process, as she assembles, bit by bit, her tiny nets out of various tenuous connections. The thread and cotton grid pulls together the unlikely combination of Guerrero and Burn, whose work has no more in common than that of thousands of other modernist exiles drawn to New York in the 1950s and 1960s. Along the way Jubelin channels Judd's various interlocutors across

four decades and manages to temporarily hold the fields of abstract expressionism and minimalism in equilibrium.

Yet there is a profound ambivalence about tangling with minimalism for artists such as Jubelin and Ferreira. A fascination for its powerful aesthetic of cool detachment sits awkwardly with practices based on an ethics of engagement. Such unease is not new, though it is now more common than it was in the 1970s when Ian Burn, with fellow Art & Language vigilante Karl Beveridge, began interrogating the politics of minimalism by asking 'Don Judd is it possible to talk?' in reaction to the imperial language of that almost sacrosanct figure.[4] In fact 'Ungrammatical Landscape' takes its name from one of Burn's Xerox works of 1968. He had photocopied a kitsch mountain scene, doubled in reflection to form a diamond, to make a series of estranged minimalist objects. One of these readymade landscapes recently cropped up in four panels of Imants Tillers's 'Diaspora' series of 1992, as both a memento mori and a souvenir patched into a vast landscape about displacement. By chance it was on the shores of that very Swiss mountain lake that José Guerrero spent his first years in exile before arriving in New York.

For all her borrowings, the Granada installation is probably one of the most intensely autobiographic of Jubelin's work. She writes in an introduction to the connotations of it:

> marking the accumulation of time which I have taken to understand … to begin to unravel living in this context … to grapple with the ethics of my own displacement.

Isabel Carlos, the Portuguese curator who directed the 2004 Sydney Biennale, observed that the work's title denotes a way of speaking without the rules of grammar. Like a foreigner searching for some common ground, it also resonates with the desire to negotiate (if not reconcile) differences and to hold out for the possibility of conversation across the fragmented landscape of what is left of modernism.

1 Slavoj Žižek, *The Parallax View*, MIT Press, Boston, Mass., 2006, p. 56.
2 Don Judd, *Don Judd: Architektur*, Westfälischer Kunstverein, Munster, 1989, pp. 48, 72, 82.
3 Svetlana Alpers, *The Vexations of Art*, Yale University Press, New Haven, Conn., 2005, pp. 168–80.
4 Karl Beveridge and Ian Burn, 'Don Judd', *The Fox*, no. 2, 1975, p. 129.

GEORGE TJUNGURRAYI

Judith Ryan

If the first Papunya boards that emerged in 1971 affronted viewers with what Marcia Langton has termed 'the shock of the ancient'[1] – condensed symbols of unknowable secrets unlocked from the ceremonial ground – George Tjungurrayi's linear abstractions are inscrutably modern in their rigorous reduction. But, like the 1971 boards, his more recent canvases conceal far more than they disclose. His pared-down style plays on subtle variations of tone, width and straightness of line, and mirror the extended lines of parallel sand ridges, deeply emblematic of Tjungurrayi's Dreaming country and of his identity.

Tjungurrayi has risen to prominence only in the past decade, forging a bichrome style of scintillating optical stripes articulated with impeccable precision. To understand the evolution of the artist's singular way of conceptualising country in alternating lines and colour, we need to examine his personal history and the canvases that preceded his first solo exhibition at Utopia Art Sydney in 1997. This, moreover, needs to be considered against the constantly changing style and potential of fellow Pintupi artists.

A younger brother of senior artist Naata Nungurrayi, Tjungurrayi was born at Murmu in the Gibson Desert on the western side of Wilkinkarra (Lake Mackay) in about 1943. Here he spent most of his childhood and teenage years, and developed his inner knowledge of significant sites associated with the Tingari cycle, including Wala Wala, Mamultjulku, Kulkurta, Karku and Ngaluwinyamana, which often figure in his work. Also significant was his first encounter with *kartiya* (non-Aboriginal people): in March 2006, at the Papunya Tula painting studio in Alice Springs, he gave a stirring account of his journey on foot out of the Gibson Desert as a seventeen-year-old boy.[2]

Knowing that some of his relatives had moved to government settlements, Tjungurrayi's curiosity was aroused when he discovered that kartiya were grading a road. More mysterious to him were the shoe prints in the sand which caused him to question whether they were left by humans. Apparently kartiya had thrown food to the side and he picked up some bread and took it back to camp, cooking it on the coals to make a kind of damper. He did not see any kartiya, only their shoe prints and excrement, which he covered up. Returning to Mukala, west of Kiwirrkura, where he had been living, Tjungurrayi left his older relatives and began the long walk east with three other Pintupi companions. They survived on food and water found on their journey (Tjungurrayi has spoken about his hunting prowess and bushcraft). They dug for water at Kulpunya, where they slept for the night, then continued to walk east, where charismatic elder Nosepeg Tjupurrula waited ahead. Leaving the others behind, Tjungurrayi saw and followed a kangaroo and chased it over two sandhills and beyond until both he and the kangaroo grew tired, enabling him to strike, kill and cut the kangaroo open, pulling out its internal organs. He put the carcass in the fire, whereupon he saw many emu tracks and discovered plenty of large emu eggs which he carried back to the fire in a *palaja* (container). He cooked the eggs on the coals, cut up and distributed the roasted kangaroo and the eggs, taking the tail and receiving heartiest congratulations from the rest of the party.

Next they walked to Lapi Lapi, meeting George Tjapanangka and his family before trekking further to a site south of Mount Doreen in Warlpiri country, Northern Territory. They walked alongside the graded road and caught sight of a truck going past at intense speed, stirring up a huge amount of dust. Tjungurrayi saw his first white skin and thought it just like baby's skin – like that of a newborn. Kartiya offered him tinned meat, flour, jam and a big container of sugar which Tjungurrayi tasted, relished and soon devoured. West of Mount Doreen, he saw and chased a bullock, speared it in the stomach and feasted on its fat. Kartiya came in two huge trucks to transport people to Yuendumu, splitting up the men and women and shooting all the dogs with scabies,

in preparation for this move. Tjungurrayi hopped in the back of one of those trucks and was frightened by the way it moved and unprepared for the large number of men and women at Yuendumu, some of whom were fighting.

Soon after, Tjungurrayi walked into Papunya to join his relatives in west camp, and in June 1962 he was taken by Jeremy Long, a young officer of the Northern Territory Welfare Branch, to Jupiter Well, a site west of Mukala from where his journey out of the desert had originated. As a young man at Papunya Tjungurrayi learnt to ride horses, wore a stockman's hat and travelled constantly. He also encountered Christianity and still carries his Bible with pride.[3] He remembers seeing the murals at the Papunya School and commented that the founding artists started a little fire which carried the painting movement everywhere, to every community. He was encouraged to start painting by Nosepeg Tjupurrula, in west camp, Papunya, in about 1976, and has painted at other locations since, including at Yayayi, Mt Liebig and now at Walangurru (Kintore), the Pintupi outstation established in 1981.

During these formative years, Tjungurrayi began to lay the groundwork for his current practice, undergoing a gestation period of around two decades before he found his own direction in 1996, the year before his first solo show. When he first started, he painted in what he termed a 'cheating way, dotting quickly' rather than in his measured linear style, and he showed a penchant for concentric circles, meandering snakes and decorative effects.[4] He soon gravitated to an iconography, palette and style not dissimilar to that developed by Pintupi founding artists Charlie Taruru Tjungurrayi, Yala Yala Tjungurrayi, Anatjari Tjampitjinpa and their younger male relatives. His late 1980s and early 1990s canvases adhere closely to the classic iconography of Pintupi visual art that encodes Tingari stories of continuous travel to place to place, symbolised by concentric circles (sites), parallel lines formed of joined dots (paths) and geometric mazes or mosaics of dots (ground designs). He allowed himself few flights of fancy, limiting his palette to red, yellow, black and a sparing amount of white, which he mixed into sombre autumnal tones that resonate with Pintupi sacred geography.

Tjungurrayi's work first came to notice when his *Kunia, the quiet snake at Karrilwarra,* 1990, was selected for inclusion in Dick Kimber's 'Friendly Country Friendly People' exhibition at Araluen Arts Centre, Alice Springs, of the same year.[5] The artist's earlier interest in dotted infill had transformed into a more graphic iconography evident in the striped body of the snake ancestor surrounded by interlinked sets of concentric circles with strong outlines that represent the rock catchment waters.

The curled body of Kunia who created the site Karrilwarra, where the snake is eternally present, is dramatically represented in the central section of the canvas, looking out at the viewer from his ancestral home. This work – vigorously blocked in rather than meticulously finished in layers – is characteristic of Tjungurrayi's other works from the late 1980s and early 1990s, which are also dominated by images of power snakes and dark brown colouration.

Later, evidenced in *Artist's country at Mamultjulku,* 1994, a transition occurred towards a tighter geometry devoid of figurative allusion which is comparable in its hard-edged formalism to the work of Joseph Jurra Tjapaltjarri. Mamultjulku, marked by a long flat hill stretching east-west on the edge of Wilkinkarra near Tjungurrayi's birthplace, is associated with a spear that travelled an extraordinary distance in the *Tjukurrpa* (Dreaming). The concentric circles indicate trees that grow in this area, where two grains, *mungilypa* and *lukara* proliferate. The work is composite and contrapuntal, if primarily linear, and invokes liturgical rhythms congruent with those engraved on *tjurunga* (stone objects). Within this dominant grid of linked roundels, bichrome mazes of shapes create a subtle optical

opening pages, detail
**George Tjungurrayi, The claypan site
of Mamultjulkunga, 2005,** acrylic on
Belgian linen, 183 x 244 cm, courtesy the
artist and Gallery Gabrielle Pizzi, Melbourne.

below
**George Tjungurrayi, Claypan site at
Mamultjulkunga, 2005,** acrylic on canvas,
183 x 244 cm, collection the artist, courtesy
Papunya Tula Artists, Alice Springs. © The artist.

George Tjungurrayi, Snake dreaming at Nguntalpalungu, 2002, acrylic on canvas, 183 x 122 cm, National Gallery of Victoria, Melbourne, presented through the NGV Foundation by Ian and Dorothy Hicks, 2002. © The artist.

background that hint at Tjungurrayi's future direction, which he pursued single-mindedly through 1996 in search of a new, simpler iconography.

Seeking to find himself in the acrylic medium, Tjungurrayi looked at the work of other experienced artists, notably Mick Namarari Tjapaltjarri, Ronnie Jampitjinpa and Charlie Tjapangati, who had already effected a change in the language of Pintupi painting.[6] He saw that to achieve recognition as an artist he needed to reinvent himself and paint in another way, one that sat comfortably with his vision of country, law and self.[7] A new pathway, distinct from that of the aforementioned artists, appeared 'quite suddenly' as Tjungurrayi devised near compositional ideas in a succession of small canvases.[8] In *Tjikarrna*, 1996, and three or four similar works, Tjungurrayi carefully applied herringbone parallel lines in subtle complementary tones and subdivided the designs with vertical lines.

During this exploratory period the artist's palette lightened and diversified, perhaps in response to the spirited and vibrant works of Pintupi women artists who had just begun to paint on canvas for Papunya Tula after the Kintore/Haasts Bluff Canvas Project of 1994–95. He took delight in mixing unusual shades of colour and aligned them in alternating sequences. Daphne Williams recalls that 'George, when mixing the colours, would occasionally seek an opinion as to whether or not they were "pretty"'.[9] He also experimented with four-panelled squares and two-panelled rectangles, formulating many schemata, but kept returning to transverse parallel lines with an elbow or dogleg in square or portrait formats. Synchronous with Timmy Payungka's black-and-white, key-pattern compositions of multiple interlocking parts, Tjungurrayi eventually succeeded in expanding and simplifying the scroll meander so that it is one element only, undulating and sweeping across a horizontal expanse of canvas. This he achieved in his first daring minimal work of significant size (1.8 x 1.5 metres), which focused on the site of Mamultjulku.

Paul Sweeney, a field officer for Papunya Tula during this period, recalled that Tjungurrayi saw himself as the equal of Mick Namarari Tjapaltjarri, Turkey Tolson Tjupurrula and Ronnie Tjampitjinpa and kept asking to paint a 1.8 x 2.4 metre canvas, regarded as a definitive scale then reserved for eminent Papunya Tula artists. This opportunity eventually came in September 1996 when he produced a masterwork, *Tingari dreaming*, 1996, now in the collection of the National Gallery of Victoria, Melbourne. Here Tjungurrayi reached a conceptual distillation of elements that intersected when he thought of Mamultjulku, a site that recurs in his oeuvre. The gently brushed pale mauve and plum lines create tonal reflections and visual sensations, like reverberations in a lake. To achieve this optical effect in two colours of equal emphasis on a foundation of black or other dark priming, Tjungurrayi worked in four layers, first laying in each colour separately, then going over each series of linear arabesques again – one colour at a time – to ensure that the lines ran exactly parallel and their edges were immaculate. In building up the layers, different pigment densities were achieved which gave the work an optical frisson created through the endlessly repeated quivering lines in two shades of subtle colour. Once crystallised, on a monumental scale, the 1996 composition became a template for a stirring series of variations in which colour, nuance and rhythmical pulse are often the keynote. A decade later, in his *Claypan site at Mamultjulkunga*, 2005, the finest horizontal striations of sandstone and cream create an ethereal mirage in which heat and shadow oscillate.

I first glimpsed the artist's seriousness of purpose when he was working on the underlayers of his *Snake dreaming at Nguntalpalungu*, 2002, a painting which began with a freely painted cartoon in colours of purplish red ochre and yellowish beige. At this stage, prior to the latter layers of both colours, the design was raw and vigorous whereas the finished work is a polished production with multiple serpentine lines that gyrate and dazzle the eye. The animated configuration of a myriad of meanders conjures up the journey of a poisonous snake from Nyinmi to Wilkinkarra and the many snakes that sprang from its body and which now inhabit the country around Wilkinkarra, leaving numerous winding tracks. Its maze-like optical effects – dense rather than sparse – differ from compositions of single elongated scroll meanders, which issue from the same vision and painting method. His largest work to date, the equally complex *Untitled (Tingari at Mamultjulkunga)*, 2005 – an optical dance of diamonds, triangles and irregular geometry – reveals his assured orchestration of lines that constantly change direction. This angular, brick-red maze meander retains Tjungurrayi's ascetic purity of palette and crisp articulation of line.

Once he found himself as an artist in 1996, Tjungurrayi's work became instantly recognisable for its rigour of conception and execution and its resonant chords of vibrancy. On the surface, his signature style – devoid of dots and restricted to rhythms of straight, wavering or angled lines – accords with that of his peers, Ronnie Tjampitjinpa and Kenny Williams Tjampitjinpa. But his painting method – built up in four considered layers with carefully mixed nuances of colour – is matched by no other contemporary Pintupi artist. Tjungurrayi sees his work as different and is proud of the remarkable achievements that have stamped him with 'Number One' status in his own mind. His master works – monumental vistas of sandhill country resonant with inside layers of meaning, in light and dark tones of mauve, sandstone, brick, cream or orange – do not come out of a vacuum, but have their place within the trajectory of the Papunya Tula movement and his own quest to make his mark as an artist of consequence. His paintings of parallel linear currents in dual tones of one colour, which may also change direction or fracture into key pattern and maze meanders, are exceptional.

George Tjungurrayi's work of the past decade is sustained and serious, and it sits proudly alongside that of the late visionary innovators Mick Namarari Tjapaltjarri, Rover Thomas and Emily Kame Kngwarreye, artists who were intent on paring down their vocabulary of forms, images and glyphs, until the viewer is left with a special form of visual music. Tjungurrayi's conceptual abstractions condense particular places where he and his ancestors lived and walked not as literal maps, diagrams or notations but as metaphors infused with depth of tonality and rich vibrancy through being inside this country in all its minutiae. His masses of beautifully drawn lines evoke dense rhythms of visual sensations and are the antithesis of western minimalism.

1 Marcia Langton, 'Sacred geography: Western Desert traditions of landscape art', in Hetti Perkins and Hannah Fink (eds), *Papunya Tula: Genesis and Genius*, Art Gallery of New South Wales, Sydney, 2000, p. 265.
2 George Tjungurrayi interviewed by Papunya Tula Field Officer Sarita Quinlivan and author in Papunya Tula studio, Alice Springs, 10 March 2006, on which this account is based.
3 Luke Scholes, personal communication to author, May 2006.
4 Tjungurrayi, op. cit.
5 This work is illustrated in the exhibition catalogue, Richard Kimber (ed.), *Friendly Country – Friendly People*, Araluen Arts Centre, Alice Springs, 1990, n.p.
6 Tjungurrayi, op. cit.
7 ibid.
8 Daphne Williams, quoted in Hetti Perkins and Hannah Fink, 'Genesis and genius: The art of Papunya Tula artists', in Perkins and Fink, p. 181.
9 ibid.

This essay would not have been possible without the generous assistance of Paul Sweeney, Luke Scholes and Sarita Quinlivan of Papunya Tula Artists. The staff and field officers of this Aboriginal-owned company have patiently nurtured and continuously supported George Tjungurrayi's art production over the past three decades. His serious commitment to the practice of painting and his stellar career would not have happened without the magnificent support of Papunya Tula Artists.

The
Renaissance
of Venice

Rachel Spence

Photographs Mark Smith

opening pages
A. Scrocchi, Venezia – Ponte di Rialto, c. 1920s,
original Venetian postcard.

left
Lilli Doriguzzi, 2007.

Don't listen to those who tell you that the Venetian contemporary art scene starts with the biennale and ends with the Palazzo Grassi. During the Venice Biennale of 2005, the art critic of the *Financial Times* claimed that setting the world's most important contemporary art fair in this 'too-serene and aged city' was like 'having a great-grandmother who suddenly announces at a family christening that she is about to breakdance. We smile and hope it will not be too embarrassing.'[1]

It's not just cultural commentators who think *La Serenissima*'s golden days ended with the death of heroic master Francesco Guardi in 1793. Social and environmental scientists warn that the city is sinking under the weight of rising tides and floods of tourists.

It's true that there are grounds for concern: the number of residents has declined to just 62,000, while St Marks Square floods ten times more frequently than a century ago. But there is life in the old dame yet. All over the city, people – artists, gallerists, restorers, collectors – are leading vividly creative lives.

Take Lilli Doriguzzi, a contemporary artist who has been based in Venice for five years. Her lofty fourth-floor studio looks directly onto the Benetton shop windows in Campo San Bartolomeo near Rialto.

This modish vista suits Lilli perfectly, for fashion is one of her chief sources of inspiration. 'In Venice, traveller clothes predominate. You could be in Africa. You could be anywhere', she says somewhat forlornly. For as much as she loves the city she describes as her 'point of reference', she misses 'the amazing attention to fashion' she discovered on the streets of Ravenna, a southern Italian port city on the Adriatic coast.

Born in the Dolomite Mountains, Lilli studied foreign languages and literature at the University of Venice before moving to New York in 1984, where she enrolled at the Art Students League, an old-fashioned school of art where the emphasis was on learning to draw. 'I took a course in anatomical drawing and became fascinated by the architecture of the body', she recalls. 'But I was never interested in the nude.'

The move to Ravenna in 1990 was pragmatic. 'My husband, a ships captain, was made commander of the port there.' Provincial in other respects, the city's embrace of cutting-edge fashion – 'the shop windows were full of Dries Van Noten and Margiela, at a time when no-one outside Milan was stocking them' – acted as a catalyst for her artistic vision.

'I decided to go beyond the classical tradition which studies the proportions of the nude and interrogate the idea of the body dressed.' Now we live in an epoch where Giorgio Armani exhibits at the Guggenheim in New York but in the days when few were making conceptual links between fashion and art, Lilli was ahead of her time.

Her subsequent series of performances and exhibitions included *Corpo profano*, 2001, in which she wrapped five people, whom she considered to be 'fascinating characters', in grey fabric to create a toga-like effect. 'The body had to work to hold up the drapery. And each individual was wrapped differently to

emphasise their personality', she recalls. 'To cover the body like this was to render it more than nude.'

Her most daring intervention was *mettere a nudo* in 2001, which opened with a one-day performance in which she persuaded retailers on Via Cavour, Ravenna's equivalent of Rodeo Drive, to let her cover up their shop windows with white paint. Above the street she suspended 24 metres of cloth on which she had sewn the outline of a coat of armour with metallic thread. 'Clothes are our quotidian protection', she comments.

Naming pop art, and Warhol in particular, as her chief influence, Lilli's work emerges out of a querulous inner dialogue with what it means to live in an image-obsessed age. She describes the act of getting dressed variously as 'our daily war with ourselves' and 'an artwork we do with our own bodies'.

Her tall, well-proportioned frame makes her the ideal clothes horse for the bold looks of Belgian designer Dries Van Noten. Yet even as she extols the virtues of her favourite designer, she frets that a natural human desire to dress up is being contaminated by rampant consumerism. 'I worry that my son watches *The Devil Wears Prada* so often and has such huge respect for certain brands.'

Fortunately, her best work arises out of a sense of ambiguity; nowhere more so than when it comes to representing Venice. 'This city is a tempest', she declares, as she carefully inserts her latest work, *Apparente*, 2006, into a glass presentation case. A transparent, wafer-thin crescent of glass, mounted against a grid of charcoal vertical lines daubed with horizontal violet-grey streaks and bordered with three blood-red tracks on one side, the work both evokes and undermines the image – iconic, clichéd, exquisite – of the gondola.

'In Venice, you are always looking at something very beautiful, very strong, very colourful', she continues. 'This can be distracting.'

The number of artworks both finished and in progress in studio suggest that Lilli has had no trouble maintaining concentration. She puts this achievement down to her decision to base herself initially in a studio at Marghera, the industrial port on the mainland whose edgy, docklands-style ambience has attracted a small colony of contemporary artists. Only after three years in Venice did she feel she could work in the city 'without being suffocated'.

Distance also permitted her to confront the challenge of representing the city itself. 'I was in Istanbul, a city with strong historical links to Venice, when the idea of *Venezia* came to me.' Conceived in 2003, the artwork consists of the word 'Venezia' written in a clean capital font in transparent neon glass. Produced in two series of fifty – one wall-mounted, one a stand-alone sculpture – it is presented in a white polystyrene box.

'I suddenly realised that to write Venice was the way to represent her', recalls Lilli. 'The city has been so over-represented, you have only to read her name and you see her.'

Venezia was first exhibited at Michela Rizzo, an innovative contemporary gallery near St Marks, where it was a notable success, particularly with local collectors who were thrilled to see an artist subvert, rather than be seduced by, their hometown's ubiquitous image.

Among those to be impressed was Contessa Marie Brandolini D'Adda. 'I like the way Lilli never takes anything for granted', she observes, gesturing at the *Venezia* discreetly mounted on the wall of her sitting-room overlooking the Grand Canal. 'She has found a way of working in the city without being devoured by it.'

The Parisian-born Contessa, whose auburn-haired aquiline beauty caused people to notice a resemblance to Françoise Gilot during the recent Picasso exhibition at the Palazzo Grassi, also struggled to find equilibrium when she first arrived in the city.

The daughter of Baroness Béatrice de Rothschild and Armand Angliviel de la Baumelle, she had worked in publishing in Paris and as a banker in New York. However, when she fell in love with Count Brandino Brandolini d'Adda, whose family had lived in their Gothic palazzo since the fifteenth century, she knew that her home from then on would be Venice.

'I had been an active girl', she says with a smile as she recalls the years she spent trying to accustom herself to the leisurely pace of life. 'At first I found Venice difficult, almost like a rival woman!' Salvation arrived in the form of her stepfather, Pierre Rosenberg. Formerly the director of the Louvre, he had a house in Venice and collected glass as a hobby. 'One day, he came home with a *goto*,' remembers Marie. 'And I fell in love. Poum!'

Unlike her husband, the new object of her affections came from humble origins. '*Goti* are beakers made by the glassblowers on Murano with leftover fragments at the end of the work day. They were designed for drinking beer at break time.'

Thanks to Marie, goti now grace some of Europe and the United States's most sophisticated dining tables. 'I reinterpreted what the glassmakers were doing', she explains, holding up a chunky, claret-red tumbler adorned with sunbursts of colour. 'They left the pattern to chance whereas I compose each glass using canes and murrines' (forms of glass rods). Marie's flair for design was instinctive. 'As soon as I arrived at the furnace I felt at home.'

It took the glassworkers a little longer to accept the *Contessa-vetraia* (glassmaker countess) as they later affectionately nicknamed her. 'At first, they didn't believe I was serious. I would get there in the morning and they would say, "Sorry, we have another production scheduled today".' Marie refused to be cowed. From 7 am to 5 pm, she worked in the furnace alongside glassmaster Davide Salvadore. 'I cut canes and swept the floors. In that heat, it was very hard physical work, but I loved it.'

Within months, the new-look goti started to sell. Commissions from Gump's, a luxury homewares store in San Francisco, Bergdorf Goodman and The Conran Shop followed. By then the glassworkers had taken Marie to their hearts, and she in turn had found a place for herself in the city she has come to love.

Today her collection, Laguna B, encompasses two other ranges: Berlingot,

based on a Venini design to which Marie has added carnivalesque stripes, and Laguna Flowers, which are traced with a delicate spiral and blown in pastel hues inspired by Venice's lagoon.

Her innate sense of style and colour is present in every aspect of her life. A local fashion icon, she cuts a striking figure around town, her russet tresses set off to perfection by the vivid hues and sensual prints that are the core of her wardrobe – Laudomia Pucci is a good friend as well as one of her favourite designers.

Meanwhile at home in her light-filled sitting-room, eighteenth-century gilded tables and chairs blend effortlessly with modern furniture. Either side of an antique Murano mirror hang two wall sculptures, a luminescent, rose-red circle and an off-white, bubble-textured cross, by quirky Italian architect-designer Gaetano Pesce.

Cute as a soft toy, a floppy-eared plaster dog by Nikki de Saint Phalle shelters beneath the tapered gilt legs of an antique table. Below Lilli's *Venezia* hangs a semi-abstract vision of the Ducal Palace in shocking pink by French avant-garde artist Charles Lapicque. There is a pastel drawing by Miró, and lithographs by Alexander Calder hang in the kitchen – 'his patterns remind me of murrhines', comments Marie. As for the Diego Giacometti sculpture of a tree, its fragile branches, she says, tempt her to use it as a coat rack.

Later, as we stand on the terrace overlooking the serpentine curve of the Grand Canal, the steel-blue domes of San Marco in the distance, Marie declares that she is full of optimism for the future of Venice. 'Interesting new people are coming to live here from outside. They aren't Venetians yet but they will become Venetians and that's what Venice has always been: a city of *passage*.'

Then she refers to one of her favourite paintings, an early acrylic by Lilli Doriguzzi. 'It is a pop Byzantine view of the Basilica of San Marco. It really gives it pep! And that is how I like to see Venice.'

Bold and forward-looking yet respectful of the city's heritage, Marie's vision chimes with that of contemporary art collector Marino Golinelli who owns a *piano nobile* (the first floor above ground-floor level – literally the 'noble floor'), in Palazzo Barzizza, a thirteenth-century palace close to Rialto on the Grand Canal.

Assisted by the curatorial flair of his wife, Paola Pavirani, Golinelli has transformed the palazzo into a showcase for his collection. In the *sala nobile* (noble hall), an abstract rug by arte povera exponent Alighiero e Boetti lies beneath an antique Murano chandelier. Running frieze-like beneath the painted ceiling beams, a photo-scroll by the rising Chinese star, Wang Qingsong, portrays decadent banquet scenes that reference Velázquez, Duchamp and Rauschenberg.

On the opposite wall hangs *Paintant blue*, 1998, a typically angry explosion of colour (drips and spillages of cobalt, emerald and purple oil stuck with sackcloth) from Argentinian-American artist Fabian Marcaccio, whose work was once described in the *New York Times* as possessing 'the pumped-up subtlety of a Sylvester Stallone movie'.

From Mexican painter Guillermo Olguin comes *Sensa virgenes y santos*, 2001, an oil depicting two deer heads rising out of a blurred female figure. Installed in a corner is Chen Zhen's *Cocun du vide*, 2000, an installation comprising a baby's wooden high-chair inside a curvaceous cage made from Chinese oak beads.

The global reach of this collection is one of its strengths. 'Art helps us to understand a world that is changing around us. I look for pictures that give an insight into the culture of the places where I go to buy them', observes Marino Golinelli as we sit chatting across his desk, the surface of which is covered in a Plexiglass case enclosing *After Goya*, a battlescene montage complete with helicopters and mosques, by American bad-boy artist Alfredo Martinez.

Although close to eighty, Golinelli's acute gaze is still that of the brilliant chemistry student who, some sixty years ago, founded pharmaceuticals firm Alfa Wasserman. From a poor farming background, Golinelli built up the company from scratch. By the 1960s he had enough money to start collecting the modern artworks that had become his passion. 'The first one I bought was a Hans Hartung', he recalls. As the company grew to become a major international force, his collection kept pace. Although most of his modern pieces have been sold to make space for the contemporary works that later bewitched him, he still possesses a fine landscape by British painter Graham Sutherland and a canvas by Roberto Matta that hangs above the bathtub.

Although no longer involved in Alfa Wasserman, chemistry still plays a crucial role in Golinelli's life. From his hometown of Bologna he oversees a not-for-profit education project, the Golinelli Foundation, whose international programs introduce young people to the wonders of science. Furthermore, he traces his fascination for modern art directly to his work as a chemist. 'Chemistry gave me a vision of the world that was abstract', he explains. 'The structure of the atom, proteins – all these are abstract constructions.'

Realising that 'our synapses are physically excited by art', he embarked on an intensive study of colour theory. 'Colour is a physical force. It exists as electromagnetic waves, and according to whether they are short or long, you see yellow, or green or red. As the waves get longer, the colour gets deeper.'

Now he has added 'Art and Science' courses to the Golinelli Foundation curriculum, with the aim of showing how these two disciplines, too often seen as parallel lines that never meet, are intimately entwined. Yet there is nothing cold-blooded about Golinelli's attitude to art. 'I only buy art that arouses my emotions. It must touch on the profound questions of our existence.' He is convinced that art has made him a more open, less conservative person. 'It makes one curious to understand things that one might not have experienced but do exist.'

Right now, several of his favourite painters come from the flourishing artistic colony in the town of Oaxaca in southern Mexico. One is Guillermo Olguin, who, as well as the anthropomorphic figure in the salon, is also responsible for two paintings in the basement of the palazzo.

The powerful *Mujer ardiendo*, 2000, shows a sharp-taloned bird grappling with a woman whose bowed spine is dissolving into terracotta fumes.

'I love the idea of a woman burning up for love', comments Golinelli before ushering me past a stunning Richard Long installation, *Cornwall slate line*, 1990, to Olguin's *Luxurius*, 2000, an oil painting of a jaguar's head emerging out of an abstract turquoise and yellow background. The picture, Golinelli explains, references ancient Mayan belief systems. 'Today, our theory of evolution is based on Darwin. But they worshipped maize and animals. This painting reminds me that the world has changed.'

Other Oaxacan works include *10 emigrantes*, a group of ten ceramic Mayan-style figures by Alejandro Santiago, the totemic quality of which does not prevent them exuding an air of forlorn vulnerability. 'You can see that they have been constrained to leave their homeland', observes Golinelli sadly. Yet his own globetrotting lifestyle suits him. In 2006 he visited, among other places, the biennales of Shanghai, Singapore and Gwangju in Korea. He also loves to spend time in New York, which he perceives – à la Lucio Fontana – as Venice's reverse mirror. 'New York is the city of competition, of conflict, but also of life. While Venice is somewhere you come to cut yourself off from the outside world. A place where you can think.'

Yet when I ask him if he concurs with Thomas Mann's view of the city, he denies it. 'Oh no. Venice is somewhere to live. My bed in Venice is where I sleep best. Then I wake up and do my stretches on a rug by Chilida', he smiles mischievously. 'And that makes me very happy.'

1 Peter Aspden, 'Venetian reflections', *Financial Times Weekend Magazine*, 25 June 2005, p. 46.

Restoration Comedy

Only a princess with punch would promise to restore a run-down Renaissance palazzo in record time

Rachel Spence

'I'm an Aries. We always think somehow we'll get the job done.' Princess Bianca di Savoia Aosta presses a button on a remote control and the room floods with light. The proof of her determination lies before us. Under the gaze of lofty mirrors and pastoral frescoes, a lozenge-tiled wooden floor stretches to tall windows overlooking the Grand Canal. Sculptural stucco carvings wreathe and swirl around the frescoed ceiling and marble door pediments. In the centre of the room, three chandeliers glitter like vast, gilded sea anemones. 'We had to take each one to pieces, clean each part separately and then put it back together again', the Princess confides. 'Our electricians, Francesco and Michele Rado, are geniuses.' Later, she shows me a photograph of the ballroom in mid-restoration, the dingy floor covered in rows of grimy glass tentacles.

Ever since the palazzo's long-term tenants gave notice in October 2004, Bianca has known that restoring the *piano nobile* was going to be a marathon task. Built in the sixteenth century by architect Giangiacomo dei Grigi, Palazzo Papadopoli was originally owned by the Coccina family, who commissioned paintings by Veronese. These paintings were hung over the majestic stone staircase (and are now installed in Dresden). Subsequently the palazzo, which was painted by Canaletto, passed into the hands of the Tiepolo family. In 1864 it was bought by Counts Nicolò and Angelo Papadopoli, from whom Bianca's husband, Gilberto Arrivabene Valenti Gonzaga, is descended.

Originally from Corfu, the Papadopoli family arrived in Venice in the early eighteenth century. So wealthy that Venetians joked they owned 'their own wave on the sea!', the brothers commissioned the innovative interior decorator Michelangelo Guggenheim to transform the palazzo with 'new examples of old-fashioned styles'.

Embracing the neo-rococco tendency that had become fashionable in grand villas across the Veneto, Guggenheim commissioned painters Antonio Paoletti (1834–1882) and Cesare Rotta (1847–1882) to adorn the palazzo with mythical frescoes and Arcadian scenes.

Particularly stunning is *Divinita*, Paoletti's neo-Tiepolesque vision of winged gods, heroes and cherubs disporting themselves against a tender blue sky. There are two real Tiepolos on the floor above, which is still awaiting restoration.

It is interesting to observe the way in which the painters reinterpret rather than repeat their eighteenth-century predecessors. The figures in Rotta's pastoral scenes, in the palazzo ballroom, for example, while full of airy space and delicate colour, also exhibit precise nineteenth-century realism. Rotta is also responsible for the neo-Veronese frescoes that decorate the staircase.

During the restoration process, Bianca found herself confronting the ghosts of her predecessors. 'Look', she says, pointing at a tiny red cat and cockerel painted on the skirting board. 'These are the signatures of Guggenheim's artisans. We found them when we were washing the panels by hand.'

Once the palazzo was shipshape, the next challenge for the Princess was its decoration. The sumptuous wallpaper and curtain fabrics were sourced from Caserta, a town near Naples famous for textile manufacturing. A noted designer himself, Bianca's husband Gilberto created a faux-antique Murano mirror and a vast wooden bench.

A full-length portrait of Princess Maddalena Aldobrandini, one-time mistress of the house, by nineteenth-century painter Antonio Zona, presides over the salon Bianca refers to as the Yellow Room. With her creamy bust and grandiose dress, she cuts a splendid neo-baroque figure, but even finer is the seventeenth-century portrait of an Italian prince whose handsome yet awkward form recalls Velázquez.

So hectic was their schedule, there was no time for Bianca and her team to leave their own imprint. 'The day before the gala dinner [marking the completion of the renovation process], the scaffolding was still on the facade', she admits.

Yet photographs of the gala night show contented diners basking in glittering lamplight – 'When our electrician Francesco finally lit them all up, I was in tears' – smiles Bianca. Since then, she has hosted parties for numerous august clients, including the Larry Gagosian Gallery. For this year's biennale the palazzo will serve as a venue for an exhibition of Ukrainian art.

As for the Princess, she is quietly proud of the part she has played in restoring the palace to its former glory. 'It is a tiny *granolino* for the city I love.'

'**There are days when I barely notice it**. But on a summer day when the window is open and the sun shines on the water', Alessandro Zoppi gestures through his sitting-room window at the Grand Canal, its forest-green water glimmering beneath the polychrome marble facade of the adjacent Palazzo Dario, 'then the reflection of the water hits the ceiling and the fresco seems to move. It's an extraordinary sensation.'

Alessandro, his wife Alessandra, myself and the photographer, Mark Smith, gaze upwards to meet the baleful glare of an elderly, bearded gentleman, a precisely feathered wing sprouting from his fleshy shoulder. Sprawled on a cloud, the God of Time has his left arm around a plump, bare-breasted lady while his other hand is lost between her creamy thighs. Above them, a scumbled blue sky is streaked with rosy clouds. Below, a cherub dances on a sickle.

It is over 150 years since Giovanni Battista Tiepolo (1696–1770) painted *Cronos che incontra la Verità* and this simmering incontro between sex and death still has the power to shock. Little wonder that the painting's flagrant carnality was too much for prudish Victorian sensibilities. Towards the end of the nineteenth century, Verità was discreetly veiled. She remained in this state until two years ago, when Alessandro, an antiquarian and glass collector who has lived in the seventeenth century Palazzo Barbarigo since 1979, received a restoration grant.

'We had never seen the fresco like this', says Alessandra, her eyes shining beneath a halo of dark curls. 'She had always been covered in a sheet from her neck to her knees, so you couldn't see her breasts or pearl necklace or belt.'

It was Cronos's disrespectful right arm which gave the game away. After masking the original with Veritàs's sheet, the nineteenth-century decorators had painted in a new limb that rose to the lady's shoulder. When the latter-day restorers started to clean the fresco with acid, the more recent layer of paint melted away. 'That's when we realised something lay beneath', recalls Alessandra.

Watching the original fresco come back to life was thrilling. 'I couldn't resist climbing up to peek beneath the scaffolding every now and then', admits Alessandra, adding that she encouraged her ten and fourteen-year-old sons, Ascanio and Adriano, to join her. 'You see the pencil marks that Tiepolo made to sketch out the design. It's almost as if you are watching him work.'

Tiepolo is also responsible for the allegorical panels that adorn the corners of the room. In monochrome sepia-pink, their delicate chiaroscuro and languid character are in marked contrast to the colour-saturated drama of the central canvas.

Of course Tiepolo, who was commissioned by the Barbarigo brothers on the occasion of a family wedding in 1760, possessed the majestic range of his Renaissance forebears. His skill as a draughtsman permitted him to handle large-scale, classical religious works, such as the *Road to Calvary*, 1740, which adorns the Venetian church of Sant'Alvise. Meanwhile his whimsical imagination and sensitivity towards space and colour made him the first choice for Venetian nobles looking to decorate their palaces.

As someone lauded for his ability to satisfy demanding aristocrats, it is intriguing that Tiepolo chose such a darkly potent subject for the Barbarigo palace. In stark contrast, for example, is his *Marriage of Ludovico Rezzonico and Faustina Savorgnan* which was painted in 1758 to adorn the Palazzo Ca' Rezzonico for the marriage of its eponymous owner. Cherubs, trumpet-blowing angels and a nuptial chariot tugged by impetuous steeds make this an unmistakable celebration of passion.

Whatever the story behind its commission, the *Cronos* fresco has not only been restored to its full glory but also basks in a fittingly glorious backdrop. The trompe l'oeil shadows painted on the ceiling – 'at first I thought they were real because they are exactly where the light falls' says Alessandra – are once again limpid. The mythical birds inlaid into the mosaic floor are free of blemishes.

'There's always something new to see. Some little detail you haven't noticed', says Alessandra enthusiastically. 'When the room was empty during the restoration, we put a divan in here and I spent a lot of time just staring.'

Virginia Cuppaidge, 1970.
Photograph Clement Meadmore.

Australian artists in the United States of America

Ingrid Periz

Their assumption was, I had come to New York City to make my name, that I had arrived at the centre of the universe and so I must want to suck up to a gallery, get a show, meet Frank Stella or Lichtenstein. Nothing could have made me feel worse. It is in any case, a ridiculous proposition, to arrive at thirty-seven years of age. It simply can't be done. Peter Carey, *Theft* (2006)

In Peter Carey's recent novel *Theft*, New York is the setting for a series of criminal machinations – forgery, theft, murder – that eventually establish the genius of Michael 'Butcher' Bones, an Australian painter whose career is on the skids. Butcher does eventually arrive, but in Germany before New York, and the novel makes clear that this 'arrival' is independent of merit. Carey's view is blackly funny; but do the terms of Butcher's parochial disdain – the smug insularity of New York, the sycophancy of the gallery system, artists' hunger for proximity to current art stars – ring true?

Any survey of Australian artists currently living and working in New York, as opposed to those on short-term studio visits or, like Tracey Moffatt, dividing their time between the city and Australia, must acknowledge an earlier grouping. Drawn in part by the international force of post-painterly abstraction and Greenbergian formalism, this would include sculptor Clement Meadmore (in New York from 1963 until his death in 2005), and painters Robert Jacks (1969–78, a period in which he also spent time in Canada) and Michael Johnson (who spent time in New York from 1969 to 1978). Painter, conceptual artist and writer Ian Burn lived in New York for a decade from 1967, joined intermittently by other members of the Art & Language Group, Mel Ramsden and Terry Smith. Two non-artists deserve note: gallerist and pioneer Soho dealer Max Hutchinson (who lived in New York from 1967 to 1999), and critic Robert Hughes (in New York since

Judy Cotton, c. 1977, courtesy the artist.

Denise Green, 1974, courtesy the artist.

970).[1] The legacy of this earlier grouping extends to the present, not only in the continuing interest in Burn's work, which was indelibly marked by his time outside Australia, but also in the individual careers of long-term New York-based Australian painters Virginia Cuppaidge, Denise Green and Judy Cotton.

Cuppaidge arrived in New York in 1969, wanting to see 'the best abstract art and jazz'.[2] She spent a year visiting museums before beginning to paint and recalls a Piet Mondrian retrospective at the Guggenheim that was 'life changing'. Cuppaidge's painterly assurance and toughness were praised early and she continues to show regularly in New York and Australia but she was shocked when American critic Corinne Robbins, who had never visited Australia, said of her work 'It's so Australian'. Cuppaidge describes her painting as 'self-consciously international – I wanted to shed all that. It took me a good twenty years to understand the parochialism of New York and its art world enclaves.' As an example, she recalls that when she moved from Soho to the Upper East Side her New York friends thought she was no longer a serious artist.

To the teenage Cuppaidge reading *The New Yorker*, the city seemed 'the most intellectual, sophisticated place in the world'. Its occasional limitations have not disturbed her nonchalant take on New York's continued prominence: 'This is where the art world is', she says. Bristling at Robbins's description thirty years ago, she now thinks it correct, if for different reasons. 'New York has forced me to fall back on my Australian roots more than I thought possible.'

A short New York visit while studying in France in 1969 convinced Denise Green of the city's artistic energy. Arriving that year, Green was an 'artist in New York' when she first drew critical attention, a distinction enabling her inclusion in the important 1978 Whitney exhibition 'New Image Painting' at a time when the Whitney did not knowingly show the work of non-Americans.

(Ian Burn also slipped through this gate.) Green was recently the subject of several touring retrospectives in Europe, the United States and Australia, and she continues to exhibit regularly on three continents. Profoundly influenced by Aboriginal art as a mode of thinking, she recalls being taken by Daniel Thomas to Ku-ring-gai Chase National Park outside Sydney to see Indigenous rock art on her first return trip and realising 'something is happening here that's not happening in contemporary western art'. She explains: 'My first ideas about art were shaped in Australia and that remains part of my identity, a really important part.'

'The key to New York', Green says, 'is the huge financial market. You may not like a lot of things about it, but it's a fact. And it's a centre from an ideas point of view … the magazines, critics and curators.' For artists, she adds, 'you want to be in a place where your ideas can be pushed and that means being a player in a bigger arena'.

'The ceiling is high, and you can reach', is how painter Judy Cotton expresses the same sentiment. Arriving in 1971 when 'the New York art world was where it was happening', and the ruling ethos was Greenbergian abstraction, it was, she recalls, 'a very macho art world'. After she had a dispute with Clement Greenberg, 'there were difficulties for me but I persevered. My generation had a little convict taskmaster saying "you're not good enough".' She discarded abstraction after a trial period and resisted the pressure to paint only Australian themes. Later, when incapacitated with Lyme disease, Cotton took up the difficult medium of encaustic, with which she continues to work.

For the Broken Hill-born, Blue Mountains-raised Cotton, landscape is at the core of her aesthetic. 'That horizontal line is always there', she notes. For the last decade and a half, Cotton has worked with aquatic themes, paying special

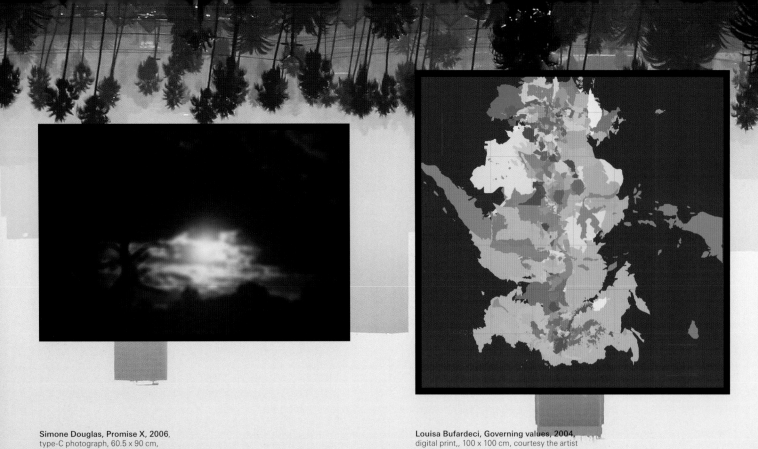

Simone Douglas, Promise X, 2006,
type-C photograph, 60.5 x 90 cm,
courtesy the artist and Artereal, Sydney.

Louisa Bufardeci, Governing values, 2004,
digital print,, 100 x 100 cm, courtesy the artist
and Anna Schwartz Gallery, Melbourne.

attention to the American luminist painter Martin Johnson Heade. A ten-year survey of her paintings travelled Australia in 2002–2003.

Cuppaidge, Green and Cotton arrived in New York as young women beginning their artistic lives, and they would have used the word 'career' at this point. When painter David Rankin arrived in New York in 1989, he was an established artist in mid-career and anxious to avoid repetition. He acknowledges 'a dream I had no right to dream' and that he was in need of a challenge: 'By the time we were forty we were on our way [with wife Lily Brett, author of a writer's appreciation of Rankin in this issue]. It's a little late, but still we did it.' He expands on New York's challenge to painters. Seeing the historical aggregate of paintings in the flesh at institutions like the Metropolitan Museum of Art changed his perception of painting as a cultural practice, and of his place within it. While it inevitably gave him a sense of robustness and clarified his painterly concerns, it also confirmed his sense of living, in Australia, 'on the periphery of western civilization, at the back end of the planet'. New York, that 'immense engine' of a marketplace, makes available the best and the worst and gives a painter, in Rankin's view, the opportunity to pitch himself against a wider field of contemporaries.

Although many art-school-trained younger artists reject Rankin's notion of Australia's ass-endedness, they would not deny the authority of New York's institutions. Photographer Simone Douglas, teaching at New York's Parsons, The New School for Design since 2003, observes:

In New York, you see how much American work is as locally specific in its reference as some Australian work. But the difference is that having a work in the Museum of Modern Art collection puts it in an international context, which having a work in the National Gallery of Victoria, for example, does not.

She notes that distinctly American work is often called international, while work 'which is attached to a place is perceived to lose something'.

Douglas also contrasts the more conceptual approach of the photography courses she taught at Sydney College of the Arts with the medium-based orientation of Parsons. This may account, in part, for the greater conservatism she sees in her New York students. She adds:

In Australia students know it will be a very hard slog. American students are more confident. There are so many galleries; they reasonably expect that they will be able to exhibit. The pressure is still there but there is a sense that there is enough space for everyone. This can be double-edged. They stick to what they do; they are perhaps less willing to push the boundaries of their practice.

Relocation to New York not only brings with it greater opportunities – for Douglas, this is 'purely a population thing' – but inevitably a distancing and separation from established support structures in Australia. Louisa Bufardeci received a Samstag Fellowship that took her to the School of the Art Institute of Chicago (2004–06). Now living in Brooklyn, she explains: 'Often I find the distance very liberating but I feel very far away from Melbourne and all that I set up for myself as an artist before coming to Chicago. I don't want to squander the work of those earlier years.' Being in New York, Bufardeci notes, 'stops me from getting in a rut with a particular approach. Without feedback, I can't rely on the success of one project to make the next. It keeps me constantly questioning and re-evaluating my practice.' Douglas echoes this comment: 'Being away made me see how Australian my work was. I wouldn't have considered myself an Australian artist until I went to New York. This made me seriously reconsider my practice, which I'm still doing.'

Bufardeci works across media, focusing on systems and statistical

Justine Cooper, HAVIDOL, 2007, print ad, 30 × 40 cm,
part of a fictional marketing campaign involving a website,
advertising, paintings and sculpture, assisted by the
Australia Council for the Arts. Courtesy the artist and
Daneyal Mahmood Gallery, New York.

James Angus, Seagram Building, 2000,
spruce, MDF, Plexiglas, 45 × 240 × 75 cm,
courtesy Roslyn Oxley Gallery9, Sydney.

representation. She is sceptical about New York's continued claim to central importance: 'New York feels like an inwardly facing city where simply getting a gallery and making sales is the priority of artists who come to make it here. In other cities – particularly Melbourne and Chicago – there are artists working with the most remarkable and progressive ideas about art and aesthetics.'

Justine Cooper, a new media artist with an interest in science, has lived in the United States since the age of eight, with extended periods working and studying in Sydney in the 1990s. Moving fluidly between the two countries, Cooper considers herself an Australian artist out of an 'allegiance to the country which has supported the work I've made and the fact that I spent most of my twenties in Sydney when new media arts were being nurtured and they flourished'. She too notes the downside of scale: 'While being here gives me more visibility and access to venues and opportunities within the United States, what is lost here is a sense of closeness in the community of artists – there are so many artists here.'

Cooper works largely outside the commercial gallery system, with pieces either commissioned or funded. She was the first artist-in-residence at the Museum of Natural History in 2001; her work-in-progress while undertaking a Lower Manhattan Cultural Center residency at the World Trade Center was destroyed in the terror attacks of September 11. Cooper's recent project, HAVIDOL, 2007, featured a fake pharmaceutical product for a fake anxiety disorder. Its website presentation attracted enormous attention.

The internet's connectivity of like-minded individuals – targeted so ably by Cooper's HAVIDOL project – does constitute a new community of sorts. But just as an earlier generation needed to be in physical proximity to works by artists important to their own practice, some younger artists understand that the web cannot replace the real space-and-time contingencies of artmaking. For them, even the extended stays of overseas residencies and graduate programs keep one essentially transient. Sculptor James Angus remained Australia-based while spending long periods away, studying at the Yale School of Art, Connecticut, through a Fulbright scholarship and working at the Australia Council's Paris Cité Studio. Feeling himself always a visitor, he reversed the situation and now bases himself in New York. Says Angus:

> I think art is a real-time activity, and it is fundamentally a social activity. It's about looking, working and talking with people in real time and space. You need to actually be where you are. Ideas get distorted over long distances, which can be interesting as a phenomenon, but can also be very frustrating at times. Visiting wasn't quite enough.

For sound artist and abstract painter Michael Graeve, New York presents greater opportunities to build an audience and support for his work. A participant in New York's International Studio and Curatorial Program in 2005, he later relocated to the School of the Art Institute of Chicago on being awarded a Samstag Fellowship, 'the platform', as he puts it for his continued stay. Graeve was instrumental in the 1996 establishment of Melbourne's artist-run gallery Grey Area Art Space, and his remove from that scene was not without anxiety. Elissa Sadgrove, Graeve's partner and 2003 artist-in-residence at Bundanon, reiterates Bufardeci's comment about relocation's costs. 'What tends to be lost', she says, 'is a network of Australian contacts and colleagues that one has associated with and worked with for the past decade.' At the same time Sadgrove acknowledges the general hustle of the market or, as she puts it, the 'entrepreneurial, optimistic and opportunistic attitudes of American gallerists'.

Elissa Sadgrove, Passage 2, 2005,
archival digital print on bonded aluminium,
25 x 30 cm, courtesy the artist.

Michael Graeve, c&s, 2006, 3 wall paintings in
acrylic, 4-channel sound composition, dimensions
variable, installation view at Enemy, Chicago,
courtesy the artist. Photograph Tom van Eynde.

In New York Graeve found a supportive community of artists and with it, a 'sense of possibility' that suggests 'the much higher likelihood that my work will resonate with people. Not that it will resonate more or better, but the likelihood of finding kindred spirits here – be they colleagues or supporters – is so much higher.' Consequently he has found it easier to generate European exhibition opportunities from the United States and has several forthcoming shows in Germany.

Relocation can prompt a surprising and belated recognition of Australian-ness, as it has done for Cuppaidge, Cotton and Douglas. Jessica Rankin, daughter of painter David, presents a different case. Rankin makes large-scale embroideries, layered with text, imagery and abstraction and is currently working towards her second solo show. Based in New York since 1990, and after studying in the United States and Melbourne, her sense of Australian identity is self-defined rather than the result of a new perception forged in a different cultural context. 'I do consider myself an Australian artist', she says, 'but when someone asked me recently what I meant by that I couldn't really come up with a coherent explanation. I think my work probably wouldn't qualify as "Australian" or as belonging anywhere in particular. I feel very connected to Australia and maybe I just feel the need to assert that.' Noting the art world 'has shifted so much since my father started working, and that encompasses more than just location', her comments suggest how the claim of identity might serve as a means of self-definition for an artist coming of age in a 'a post-national way of working'.

Natalie Jeremijenko, when asked whether her work might be called post-national, answers no, describing it as 'tactical, Ukrainian, aboriginal, technical,

even sometimes Australian if it works'. The artist, who is also a scientist and engineer, uses these labels interchangeably, 'whichever serves the project best'. Brought to the United States as a research scientist by the Xerox Palo Alto Research Center fifteen years ago and now based in New York, her work explores the social change accompanying technological development. It's work that could be done anywhere, but the United States provides more funding opportunities than Australia.

Many of Jeremijenko's projects are remediative or interventionist: her *FishFingers,* n.d., project develops a food for fish (and humans) that would allow both to process PCBs and heavy metals harmlessly; particulate-sensing *Clear Skies* masks for bicyclists reveal air quality; robotic dogs sniff out environ-mental toxins; and her on-going project *OOZ* radically revises the concept of the zoo. In the most recent *OOZ* work, a high-density avian environment, installed on the rooftop of Postmasters Gallery in Manhattan in 2006, was accompanied by built-in observational and testing mechanisms for the human participants. Not all of Jeremijenko's work appears in an art world context, but for selected projects she chooses the openness of art's participatory invitation, over the authoritative context of science. As she puts it, art licenses opinion in a way science does not. Her projects have been shown at documenta, the Whitney Biennial, and the Stedelijk Museum, Amsterdam.

Kristian Burford and Janaki Lennie, two artists based well outside New York, offer different views on the city's continuing position in the art world. Burford lives in Los Angeles, brought there by a Samstag Scholarship in 1999 which allowed him to study at the Los Angeles Center College of Design. Luck played its part in this choice of venue. Says Burford: 'Los Angeles appealed to me

Janaki Lennie, Provisional view 4, 2002,
oil on canvas, 152 x 182 cm, courtesy the artist.

Kristian Burford, Kathryn is staying at her grandparent's house. It is nine o'clock
on a November evening. She has escaped the company of her grandparents to play
with her grandmother's cat, a queen named Lucy, by moving into the sunroom
of the house. After some minutes of happily petting the cat it has turned on Kathryn,
penetrating the skin of her left index finger with its fangs and raising three lines
of skin on her left wrist with the claws of its left paw. In response to Lucy's attack,
Kathryn has grabbed at the cat in an effort to disentangle herself from it. She has
been fortunate enough to find the cat's collar with three fingers of her right hand.
This has allowed her sufficient purchase on Lucy's slippery form to remove the cat
to the carpeted floor of the sunroom. Kathryn has placed her injured finger in her
mouth so as to contain the pain and her blood. She has then recognised that she
has wet herself, and has, simultaneously, taken the finger from her mouth, 2004,
cibachrome print (agfa superchrome), 50 x 60 cm, courtesy the artist and Sullivan + Strumpf
Fine Art, Sydney.

or reasons that I had no way of substantiating. It turned out to be a fairly ideal place for me to work.' Burford is known for his resin-cast figures installed in life-sized domestic scenes staged to engage a viewer's voyeurism. 'Los Angeles is a city full of people from elsewhere', and Burford sees in this the kind of openness he wants from a prospective audience. Audience development is currently his central concern.

For Burford, Los Angeles is like New York, one of a number of art world centres, but the idea of a physical centre may no longer hold. He says: 'New York is part of the centre but the centre is not geographical, it's a network of communications which is better defined by a publication like *Artforum* than a city.' Melbourne-born Janaki Lennie sees New York's continuing draw for artists and the purview of its art journals a little differently from the vantage point of Houston, Texas where she has lived for thirteen years. Studio space in Texas is relatively inexpensive, unlike New York City. In addition, Texans' pride in their distance from New York, and the East Coast generally, helps underwrite a thriving local art scene where Lennie has found support from collectors, gallerists and institutions. Texas, with the same population as Australia, offers much more opportunity to show and develop a profile amongst a very enthusiastic audience that can transcend the regional. I think one can build an international reputation from here more easily than in Australia.' Lennie's first European show takes place in Germany this year.

At the same time, Texan pride in regional identity and local artists doesn't come without what Lennie calls a 'provincial paranoia in regard to New York'. There is a sense of regional neglect on the part of New York-based journals and consequently Texan artists 'are very strongly oriented towards making

inroads into New York since there is so much more attention paid to artists there'. Lennie is happy to work from where she is, finding in Houston, a 'huge city with vast concrete freeway systems; flat land without defining geography' – a corollary dislocation to the one she experienced as a child moving from Melbourne to Perth, where she was raised. Profoundly influenced by Perth's palette and its spatial orientation, Lennie's landscape paintings mine that disconnection from the other side of the world.

Denise Green describes the condition of being an Australian and a New York artist as 'bi-cultural', and compares it to a writer from Trinidad going to London, where 'they combine their origins with this new thing they find'. In New York, or Chicago, Los Angeles or Houston, Australian artists find different 'new things': a belated sense of identity, or the need to claim one, a familiar dislocation in a different environment, a new community of like-minded peers, a wider arena, a potential audience. While there are distinct generational differences between them, they all trust in the promise of what they might find.

1 The Melbourne-born painter Mary Cecil Allen (1893–1962), who moved to New York in 1926, is an earlier expatriate. In addition to painting, writing, and lecturing at a number of institutions, Allen also arranged 'the first New York exhibition by Australian artists, at the Roerich Museum' in Manhattan, according to her biographer Frances A. M. L. Derham. See her entry under Allen in *Australian Dictionary of Biography*, vol. 7, Melbourne University Press, Melbourne, 1979, pp. 46–47.
Born in the United Kingdom, Mel Ramsden travelled to New York in 1967. He is occasionally listed as an Australian artist in some curatorial contexts. Art & Language sought to undo Clement Greenberg's critical apparatus.
Max Hutchinson also famously brokered the sale of Jackson Pollock's *Blue poles*, 1952, from collector Ben Heller to the National Gallery of Australia, Canberra, in 1974.
2 All quotes are taken from interviews or email correspondence with the artists.

New York, Los Angeles and Houston skyline photographs sourced from iStockPhoto.com.

David Rankin, September 11 2001, 2001,
acrylic and charcoal on linen, 250 x 441 cm,
courtesy the artist and Adrian Slinger Galleries,
Queensland.

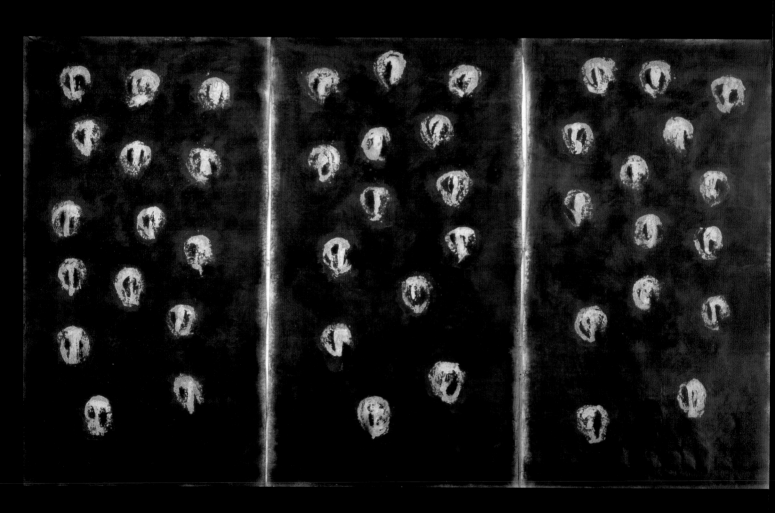

Writer's Choice

Lily Brett on David Rankin

David Rankin and Lily Brett.
Photograph © Bettina Strauss.

e man I love paints every day. This man, the man I am married to, has a
orious sense of humour and can dance up a storm. He has a laugh that can lift
u up in the air. Yet, every day, on canvasses, on large sheets of paper and in
nall notebooks, he grapples with questions of mortality, and struggles with the
tion of what it means to be human.

He is always painting. I envy him. I can scribble notes when I'm on the road,
t I need silence and a routine to write. I envy his ability to draw, paint, sketch
nerever he is. And he does. I've come back to hotel rooms to find he has
pended the bed and there is a canvas on the floor. I've watched him draw and
en paint on trains. On buses. And on planes. When I am on a plane I can't
nk of anything but how uncomfortable I am.

He looks happy when he paints. He has music on in his studio and sometimes
nces between brushstrokes. He can be painting the most moving, almost
artbreaking, almost heart-stopping painting, and he looks calm. I look
nerved and uncomfortable and possibly unkempt even when I am writing
mething hilarious. Something that will later make a lot of people laugh.

We are quite different. I am more reserved. And I can't really dance. But
r work and our lives are intertwined. We have overlapping preoccupations,
rallel themes. We are both looking for answers. Answers to unanswerable
estions.

He was always serious. He was thinking about Leonardo Da Vinci when he
as ten. In the middle of a childhood marked by poverty, violence and alcoholism,
was thinking about Leonardo Da Vinci. And reading books on Buddhism.

While he was reading books on Buddhism and admiring Giacometti's
orkday routine, I was standing in front of a mirror, backcombing my hair to see
w high I could get that beehive to go. Or I was eating. I staved off the many
xieties that threatened to engulf me with chocolate frogs and Violet Crumbles.

I grew up with few relatives. Almost all of my mother's and father's parents,
others, sisters, aunties, uncles, cousins, nephews and nieces were murdered
efore I was born. I spent a lot of my childhood wondering where they were.
ere they in our house? I felt as though I could feel them. Were they in the sky?
the air? In me? Where are we when we're no longer here was a question that
othered me from the time I was small.

The man that I love believes in the indestructibility of the human spirit. In a
988 painting that at first made me cry every time I looked at it, he has painted
e scrappy remains of a family of brothers. The painting is called *The brothers*.
u know that they have endured horror. This family group, set against burnt-
ut beams of architecture in a brown, glazed indeterminable space, are painted
white, spindly lines, a fragile, vulnerable calligraphy. They could be dead or
ey could be alive. What is very present is their spirit. An inextinguishable spirit.

It was that inextinguishable spirit that was to surface, and still does, in most
of his work. He has painted souls in pain and torment. And souls in repose. In
his 'Donna Nobis Pacem' paintings, begun in 2000, he has painted, in abstract
black, radiant markings or planes, groups of people, families, neighbours, friends.
The planes are like faces. Faces that are familiar. I recognise the communities.
I see expressions I have seen before. And I see their peace. The peace seems
eternal.

On 11 September 2001 I was talking on the phone to a friend in Australia
when the sound of the first plane crashing into the World Trade Center ricocheted
through our downtown New York loft.

Soon all of downtown New York was covered in smoke and debris. Everyone
was in a state of shock. It was hard to think. Hard to see. And hard to breathe.
The air remained thick with debris for days. Small bits and pieces that looked
as though they had been torn from wherever they had formerly belonged, filled
the air. The pieces looked lost, disturbed, disconsolate and displaced.

Just walking outside made people cough. The man I am married to couldn't
walk a block without coughing. As though particles and parts of other people's
lives had lodged in his lungs. I felt worried about him. He is a sturdy man.
Broad-shouldered and strong. We left the city but neither of us wanted to stay
away. We came back.

Everything in our loft was coated with the dense, acrid smell of burning.
Burning objects, people and buildings. I felt numb. The man I am married to began
to paint. Bent low or standing high on a ladder, he painted for days. I don't recall
him eating or pausing. He painted a large triptych. Roughly 3 metres by 5 metres.
He called it *September 11*.

In this triptych, flattened, orb-like shapes are rising, ascending. They could
be skulls or stones. But they are souls. I can see them. Some ash is still there.
Small scorch marks are evident. There is a reddish flame-like glow that also
contains the deep, promising pink of an early-morning, dawn light.

Parts of some of the souls are missing, not visible. But they are not in pain.
And they are not alone. They are surrounded by others. Bound together. Unified.
They are firm and whole. And at peace.

Lily Brett was born in Germany and came to Melbourne with her parents in 1948. Her first book,
The Auschwitz Poems, won the 1987 Victorian Premier's Award for poetry, and both her fiction
and poetry have won other major prizes, including the 1995 NSW Premier's Award for Fiction
for *Just Like That*. Her books of essays, *In Full View*, *New York* and *Between Mexico and Poland*,
were critical successes, and her novel *Too Many Men* was a bestseller in Australia, Germany
and the United States. Lily's fifth novel, *You Gotta Have Balls*, followed in 2005 to similar success.
She is married to the Australian painter David Rankin, and lives in New York.

bookshops

The Bookshop

Art Gallery of South Australia
North Terrace Adelaide SA 5000
Tel 08 8207 7029 Fax 08 8207 7069
agsa.bookshop@artgallery.sa.gov.au
www.artgallery.sa.gov.au
Daily 10–4.45

Adelaide's only specialist visual arts
bookshop – stocking books,
magazines, merchandise and gifts.
We specialise in the publications of
the Art Gallery of South Australia –
including exhibition catalogues,
reproductions, postcards and greeting
cards from the Gallery collections.

The Gallery Shop

Art Gallery of New South Wales
Art Gallery Road Sydney NSW 2000
Tel 02 9225 1718 Fax 02 9233 5184
galleryshop@ag.nsw.gov.au
Daily 10–5

The gallery shop carries Australia's
finest range of art publications.
Art books without boundaries:
prehistory to postmodernism,
Australian and international, artists'
biographies from Michelangelo to
Bacon, art movements and histories.

The National Gallery Shop

National Gallery of Australia
Parkes Place Parkes ACT
GPO Box 1150 Canberra ACT 2601
Tel 02 6240 6420 Fax 02 6240 6529
1800 808 337 (during business hours)
Bookshop@nga.gov.au
www.ngashop.com.au
Daily 10–5

Australia's premier art bookshop,
with a range of National Gallery of
Australia merchandise, gifts and art
objects. We cater for everyone, from
the visual arts scholar to the first-time
gallery visitor. Mail orders and special
orders welcome.

Modernism & Australia: Documents on Art, Design and Architecture 1917–1967

Reviewed by Joanna Mendelssohn

This monumental effort is a worthy successor to Bernard Smith's pioneering *Documents on Art and Taste in Australia* (1975), and it is a new publication which will long remain an essential tool of trade for students, teachers and early researchers in the fields of art, architecture and design history. To parallel it to Smith's book is not to denigrate the text; as the authors Ann Stephen, Andrew McNamara and Philip Goad know, their work is hardly the last word on the field, and it easily fulfils its aim to introduce authors and texts that shaped an Australian understanding of modernism.

Smith's work is acknowledged in the introduction, and the selection of documents is very much in the academic tradition he pioneered. There is an awareness of the sociopolitical context of art and an understanding that the visual includes design, architecture and material culture. On the negative side, the modernist/anti-modernist progressive/conservative opposition is preserved in all its crusty glory. It could be argued that this is appropriate in a collection of historic material which documents that unproductive debate, but I expected to read a more nuanced commentary.

There is only a hint in Leonhard Adam's essay 'Has Australian Aboriginal art a future?' of the contempt that many 'progressives' felt for Albert Namatjira's art. It would have been appropriate to have at least mentioned R. H. Croll's contribution to Charles Mountford's pioneering work, *The Art of Albert Namatjira* (1944). Croll was the secretary of the Australian Academy of Art, the enemy of all that was modern. The endorsement of Namatjira by politically conservative anti-modernists meant that he was for many years regarded as an Indigenous equivalent of Pro Hart, by those who judge artists by the company they keep.

This ossified mindset is also present in the commentary on the 1967 essay by Laurie Thomas, 'The only thing anyone could hope for is a change of government', which attacks the Commonwealth Art Advisory Board for appointing an exhibitions officer instead of building a national gallery. This is not one of Thomas's better pieces of writing, so presumably it was included for the content alone. The commentary describes the Commonwealth Art Advisory Board as 'notoriously conservative' and as a part of Menzies's 'shadow', citing the presence of Daryl Lindsay as evidence. Whoever researched this missed the main story. The person appointed as exhibitions officer was James Mollison, a protégé of Daryl Lindsay. When Mollison later became interim director of the Australian National Gallery in Canberra, the *Australian* thundered in an editorial that the appropriate appointment would have been another applicant, its art

critic Laurie Thomas. By any measure Mollison's appointment was a triumph, while Thomas was yesterday's man.

There are so many old friends among these documents that Australian art historians will now feel free to purge some of our yellowing photocopies and notes gathered over the years. *Art and Australia* and its ancestor *Art in Australia* are present as reminders of their place in the history of ideas in this country. Material from Elwyn Lynn's Contemporary Art Society broadsheets of the 1960s, which were first published as typed stencilled sheets, are given the dignity of print they have long deserved. But I wish there had been at least a mention of Rod Shaw's SORA (Studio of Realist Artists) bulletins of the 1950s, which show that at least in Sydney the Communist left could be surprisingly inclusive.

Some of the retrievals are wonderful. Grace Crowley's notes are a reminder that she was a brilliant teacher and thinker as well as an artist. It is a joy to read the original version of Tony Tuckson's 1964 essay on Aboriginal art, a document recovered by the late Richard McMillan. Basil Burdett, the diplomat of modernism, has a delightful 1938 essay on 'Modern art in Melbourne', praising among others 'A. L. Tucker' and 'G. R. Drysdale' as young artists to watch. The editors indicate that they did not include material from the 1939 'Herald' exhibition, curated by Burdett, even though it is central to this period, as it was covered in Eileen Chanin and Steven Miller's *Degenerates and Perverts* (2005). It is a surprise therefore to see the inclusion of texts by Ian Burn, who was the subject of a recent monograph by one of the editors (Stephen), even though his work would more properly fit into a late-twentieth-century anthology.

The beauty of this book is that the documents are creatures of their time. They can be used to show how much has changed, but also how much has stayed the same. A. A. Phillips's 1950 essay 'The cultural cringe' discusses attitudes that are still depressingly familiar. The only difference is that now we cringe to the strut of the United States, when once it was the United Kingdom.

Ann Stephen, Andrew McNamara and Philip Goad, Modernism & Australia: Documents on Art, Design and Architecture 1917–1967, Miegunyah Press, Melbourne University Publishing, Melbourne, 2007, 1039 pp., $65.

Craig Walsh, Cross reference, 35:27:02N/139:39:36E, 2005,
installation view at Yamishita Pier, Yokohama, warehouse no. 3 model,
2-channel digital video projection, 60 min duration, model with
surveillance camera, MDF, plastic, acrylic, led and halogen lighting,
160 x 500 x 300 cm, courtesy the artist.

detail
Simryn Gill, 'May 2006', 2006
series of 778 black-and-white photographs,
12.5 x 18 cm each, courtesy the artist.

BANGKOK
SHAUN GLADWELL AND CRAIG WALSH
David Teh

Although it maintains a huge
embassy in Bangkok, Australia's
official footprint in Thailand doesn't
include a dedicated cultural bureau.
Nevertheless, the Australian Embassy
has earned a reputation for promoting
new media art, through exhibitions such
as 'Streetworks: Inside Outside Yokohama',
touring Southeast Asia in 2007.

'Streetworks' featured works created
for the 2005 Yokohama Triennale. Craig
Walsh's *Cross-reference 35:27:02N/
139:39:36E*, 2005, centred on an
architectural model of a Yokohama
warehouse which housed footage of
viewers encountering it in Yokohama,
alongside real-time imagery from
a surveillance camera. To peer into
its half-open roll-a-doors is to begin
a chain of spatial inversions which
confound the distinctions between
here and there, inside and outside.
This folding ramifies through inversions of scale: peering figures, live
and recorded, mingle with tourists
and passers-by.

Shaun Gladwell's *Yokohama
untitled*, 2005, has the rhythm of early
virtual reality and 'first-person shooter'
video games. The camera follows
breakdancers as they saunter through
generic urban spaces, their passage
punctuated by outbursts of acrobatics.
Critical praise surrounding Gladwell's
work often revolves around the
physical poetry of what David Broker
calls the 'diversionary activities' of
subcultures. But more compelling is
the window they open on public space.
While the setting is generic and the
subcultures global, these glimpses
are often locally specific: witness the
resolute indifference of Japanese
commuters, so at odds with the
breakdancers' bodily histrionics.

A similar tension binds Gladwell's
Storm sequence, 2000, a work
celebrated as much for its prodigious
market value as for its neo-romantic
intensity. In slowed video time, the
impatient flux of the surf becomes a
constant, behind the dancer's controlled
pauses. *Yokohama linework*, 2005,
is an exhilarating study in moving-
without-seeing. Gladwell's performative
mappings of public space highlight
as many differences between places
as similarities. Despite this concrete
city's vibrant street cultures, such
a trajectory is unthinkable in Bangkok,
so patchy and treacherous are its
urban surfaces.

TOKYO
SIMRYN GILL
Michael Condon

In early 2007 the new National Art
Center in Tokyo hosted the exhibition
'Living in the Material World – "Things"
in the Art of the Twentieth Century
and Beyond', which featured an
installation by Simryn Gill. In a series
of photographs titled 'May 2006',
2006, the expiry date of Gill's twenty-
nine rolls of Kodak black-and-white
film, the Sydney artist examines her
city's inner-west suburbs through a
personal lens. Slippers lie on a
cement path, a jet flies over a fenced
backyard, an orange tree hangs full of
fruit over an unkempt garden.

Although there are signs of human
activity – locals gather in front of
a Liquorland – the camera rarely
becomes intimate with the people
that inhabit Sydney's inner west.

Reminiscent of Gill's photo series
'Power Station', 2004, and 'Dalam', 2001,
Gill examines people through their
context and environment. 'Dalam',
a collection of 258 photographs of
people's living rooms taken along the
Malay Peninsula, focuses on interiors,
while 'May 2006', is about the view
from the street, sneaking glimpses
through wire fences, at cement
footpaths and faux Italian pillars.
A dog looks away from the camera;
we see empty soccer fields and
motionless swings.

The exhibition, which included
works from Picasso and Tom Wesselman,
traced how people deal with the
advent of material possessions. Gill's
contribution was an examination of
the material that makes up a Sydney
suburb: multilingual shop signs in a
mixture of English, Chinese and
Vietnamese are a sign of ethnicity;
posters displaying upcoming, now
long-gone, rock concerts are the only
sure mark of time.

Gill's 'May 2006' photographs are
not a kind of street photography, but
rather, a portrait of the people through
the weatherbeaten wooden planks
of their fences and the dirt on their
footpaths.

**Streetworks: Inside Outside Yokohama,
Shaun Gladwell and Craig Walsh,**
The Art Center, Chulalongkorn University,
Bangkok, Thailand, 1 February – 7 April 2007;
Valentine Willie Fine Art, Kuala Lumpur,
25 April – 12 May 2007; Substation, Singapore,
30 May – 18 June 2007.

**Simryn Gill: Living in the Material World –
'Things' in the Art of 20th Century
and Beyond,** National Art Center, Tokyo,
21 January – 19 March 2007.

etail
arah Ryan, sun, 2006, digital lenticular photograph,
) x 60 cm, courtesy Gitte Weise Galerie, Berlin.

Stephen Bush, Bimblebox poplar, 2005,
oil and enamel on linen, 167.6 x 198 cm, courtesy SITE
Santa Fe, Santa Fe, and Sutton Gallery, Melbourne.

BERLIN
SARAH RYAN
Galeria Schulte-Fischedick

et's get straight to the point: the
ew exhibition of photographs by
ustralian artist Sarah Ryan, on view
t Gitte Weise Gallery, Berlin, in early
007, was nothing short of magic.
nd while their enchantment worked
lowly, viewers were inevitably
pellbound.

Ryan's black-and-white photographs
ocus mainly on nature with an elaborate
se of light. Ryan has refined her
se of digital lenticular photography
o develop her signature style. This
articular technique, best known from
opular three-dimensional postcards,
lows her to create subtle compositions
vith overlapping images, suggesting
novement and a cinematic effect.

Works such as *sun*, *second sun*,
remonition, *breeze* and *in the garden*,
ll 2006, provide a fairytale view into
reetops and branches. They capture
noments of pure beauty, distilling a
eculiar atmosphere reminiscent of
ne films of Ingmar Bergman. Similar
o a slightly unreal daydream, in which
ight and day have merged, Ryan's
lurry, twilight zone images induce a
vide range of feelings in the observer.

Indeed, her technique provokes a
very physical perception. It's as though
one can hear the leaves rustling or feel
the sunlight on one's skin. And while
the subject here is the artist's hometown, Toowoomba in Queensland,
the imagery is universal. Ryan shows
us what we've all seen before, yet
she manages to enrich these common
images with memory, emotion and
a distinct sense of déjà vu.

During my visit the gallery owner,
Gitte Weise, turned off the lights. The
effect was striking: the light in *sun* and
second sun seemed to keep glowing –
an effect generated by the lenticular
technique. But far from indulging in
theatrical effects – as is the case with
so many works involving new media –
Sarah Ryan enlarges both the field of
perception and the possibilities
inherent in the medium.

SANTA FE
STEPHEN BUSH
Zane Fischer

Like Merlin, the famed wizard of
Arthurian legend, the painter Stephen
Bush may actually be living backwards
through time. In his exhibition 'Gelderland'
at SITE, Santa Fe, something of a
survey introduction to the Australian's

work for audiences in the American
southwest, Bush weaved between
past and future in a wobbly, unpredict-
able and expert dissection of cultural
values and painter's technique. The
earliest works on view, the 'Caretaker'
series from the late 1980s, rely on
an Albert Bierstadt-like fixation of
romanticised landscape as an offset
backdrop for quixotic beekeepers
at work among symbolically broken
branches, curious disco apparel
and dizzying terrain. The works
progress through to Bush's current
output, wherein a lexicon of arche-
typal figures, architecture and objects
spill out, rootless, atop a foundation of
poured paint swirls. In this primordial
ooze of plastic future materiality,
rendered in confrontational greens,
pinks, yellows and blacks, Bush
manages to effuse the same grandeur
and scale through abstraction.

It is the degree of deconstruction
and pure composition that Bush
overlays on his haphazard swirls,
which gives the impression that he
is somehow remembering the future.
Ignoring horizon and toying with
proportion, he nonetheless carefully
infuses moments of meaning – such
as the cavern which represents the
psyche, the contemplative interior –
onto opportunistic pockets of his

paintings. In one demonstrative work,
Bimblebox poplar, 2005, his timeless
philosopher's cave opens out into an
overhead view of a series of swampy
lagoons, like a view from space,
complete with the earth's rotund
underbelly rotating gamely at the top
of the picture plane, while disembodied
elements hover inexplicably in the
foreground: a catamaran, a mech-
anical wheel, a carefully arranged
stack of poplar logs.

In 'Gelderland', Bush's precise
command of both art – and world –
history finally, inexorably collided with
postmodernity's casual but desperate
search for meaning. As a painter,
he is dutifully chronicling the iconic,
emotional triggers that confound and
inspire us at that point of intersection,
something that he's eyeing with the
benefit of his long view from out of
the ooze.

Sarah Ryan: Like Never Before, Gitte Weise
Gallery, Berlin, 2 February – 17 March 2007.

Stephen Bush: Gelderland, SITE Santa Fe,
Santa Fe, 10 February – 13 May 2007.

Ron Mueck, Spooning couple, 2005, mixed media, 14 x 65 x 35 cm, private collection, London, courtesy Brooklyn Museum, New York.

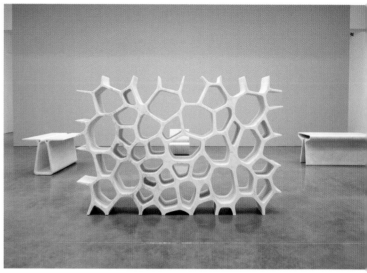

Marc Newson, Voronoi shelf, 2006, white Carrara marble, 178.1 x 276.2 x 37.5 cm, courtesy Gagosian Gallery, New York.

BROOKLYN
RON MUECK
Paddy Johnson

It is much to sculptor Ron Mueck's credit that, while visiting his early 2007 show at the Brooklyn Museum, New York, I did not find myself comparing his realistic sculptures to those at Madame Tussauds Wax Museum. Not that I thought I necessarily would, but the inevitable question a viewer has to ask of hyper-realistic work is whether it transcends representation. Photorealism, for example, has frequently failed this test in recent years, which may explain why I haven't seen an exhibition of this kind in New York for some time. Sculptors such as Mueck, however, rarely seem to run into this problem. Why?

I obviously can't speak for the artist, but it seems clear that the redundancy in simply replicating an object verbatim reduces the appeal of the practice. Known for his skilful use of scale and technical virtuosity, Mueck's exhibition avoids the pitfalls of representation by imbuing his sculptures with tenderness and vulnerability. Taking up the majority of the entrance to the museum, a giant

newborn, titled *A girl*, 2006, complete with slightly bloodied skin and wet hair, rested still on a plinth. While the sculpture may well have been the weakest in the show, as Mueck's choice of scale feels uncharacteristically obvious, the child still elicits enough paternal feelings that you have to give the work credit for its emotive qualities.

On the second level of the museum, a number of the artist's better-known works filled the space. While no literal interpretation can be drawn from *Man in a boat*, 2002, and *Wild man*, 2005 – sculptures depicting a small nude on a fishing boat and a Christ-like figure respectively – they unquestionably draw biblical references to temptation and the search for God. By contrast, *Big man*, 2000, a 2-metre tall sculpture reminiscent of Lucian Freud's paintings of the Australian performance artist Leigh Bowery, and *Spooning couple*, 2005, a small sculpture that does as the title describes, make no such claims. As a whole however, the works demonstrate sensitivity and grace that goes beyond the function of allegory. And managing this is far more than a wax sculpture of Whoopi Goldberg could ever hope to do.

NEW YORK
MARC NEWSON
Ingrid Periz

Marc Newson's aluminium *Lockheed lounge*, 1986, made history in 2006 when it attracted the highest price at auction for the work of a living designer. Its hourglass 'orgone' shape lingered for a while in Newson's designs but was nowhere apparent in his first solo exhibition in the United States at New York's Gagosian Gallery in early 2007. Here he concentrated on objects worked in a single, seamless shape worked from a range of materials.

Carrara marble, nickel and Micarta (an obscure laminate that is a footnote in the history of Bakelite), are favourites. From the marble, Newson wrests the cellular *Voronoi shelf*, 2006, a 183 by 275 centimetre airy web that is clearly designed as a stand-alone object, commanding Gagosian's central gallery space. Also shaped from single blocks of marble are two 'extruded' tables, variations on a theme, with one shaped like a T and the other its inverse, and a similarly 'extruded' chair. Extraordinary craftsmanship underwrites the joke of making stone behave like metal,

or like breathable tissue. Newson uses a mirror-like type of nickel for a surfboard designed specially for tow-in surfing, and for a simple chair that has the sexiness of a 1940s woman's high heel. Micarta gives him a warmer medium to work with, producing amber stripes with a woody feel which, thanks to the material's light sensitivity, will darken over time. A Micarta table with hollowed legs and a single-dimpled top, like a belly button, is notable.

Throughout his career Newson has produced small editions of beautifully crafted furniture. Now, as the overheated American art market looks to design, or what is increasingly called design-art, his work will no doubt find an enthusiastic audience.

Ron Mueck, Brooklyn Museum, New York, 3 November 2006 – 4 February 2007; National Gallery of Canada, Ottawa, 2 March – 6 May 2007.

Marc Newson, Gagosian Gallery, New York, 25 January – 3 March 2007.

Rosemary Laing, weather #1 (Eden), 2006, type-C photograph,
0 x 220 cm, courtesy the artist and Galerie Lelong, New York.

detail
David Noonan, Untitled, 2007, collaged paper, 25.5 x 20.5 cm,
courtesy the artist and Foxy Production, New York.

NEW YORK
ROSEMARY LAING
Ingrid Periz

Laing's third exhibition for Galerie Lelong's New York site comprised a suite of ten photographs made in response to climate change. The 2006 'weather' series continues Laing's signature vein of airborne women, but modifies it in important ways.

Here Laing strips her work of some of its daredevil costume drama touches. Her female subjects have shed the wedding gowns of previous series and wear instead a much simpler garment inspired by nineteenth-century working women and designed by Laing herself. Unlike many of her previous images of suspended females, in 'weather' there is neither ground nor sky. The landscape element is entirely absent from these images; the single subject is surrounded instead by a whirlwind of paper strips. Rather than appearing studio-bound, these works seem instead placeless. Removing the 'wow' factor of Laing's more elaborately contrived series such as 'bulletproof glass', 2002, and 'flight research', 1999, may be a risk the artist can take. Lacking a structuring horizon line, and in a slightly squarer format, these bodies-in-flight have a very different relationship to the aerial ground on which they are positioned. Laing's pictorial interest here seems to be more in the disposition of the body than knockout visual tricks.

'Weather' didn't entirely dispense with Laing's landscape concerns. The show included two photographs of Eden, the New South Wales fishing town. These blasted landscapes suggest a distinctly antipodean gothic which Laing would do well to leave alone. In one image a red plume adorns a tree, a minimal reminder of the more elaborate interventions Laing has staged in other environments. The other image of Eden has none, and is arguably the stronger for it.

PARIS
DAVID NOONAN
Nina Miall

David Noonan's ongoing preoccupation with the artifice of the theatre found its fullest expression at the Palais de Tokyo, Paris, earlier this year. For his first solo exhibition in Paris, the Australian artist created a site-specific installation in which fabric-covered panels and wooden supports produced a series of architectural interventions. Subtly arranged, these walled structures are reminiscent of the screens and flats of set design, and represent a recent development in Noonan's practice. With their stagy self-reflexivity they offer a deconstruction of institutional display strategies; not only those deployed by the museum but, more importantly for the artist, by the theatre.

Within this configured space, Noonan presented a group of large-format silkscreen prints, collages, recent gouaches and sculpture. Noonan's decision to combine a variety of mediums reflects his long-held fascination with the physicality and aesthetics of collage. Fragmentary images sourced from 1970s counter-culture are montaged or superimposed, creating haunting, monochromatic mise en scènes redolent with narrative ambiguity. Ripped or torn linen is often used to delineate the different images, complicating the picture plane and suggesting a depth of field that reverses the flatness of the collaging process.

In creating these composite works, Noonan trawls through all manner of obscure and eclectic material, from album covers to old theatre programs, looking both for formal correspondences between images and for evocative and unsettling juxtapositions. He is attracted to highly stylised and avant-garde forms of performance and their representation through secondary media – from mime to Japanese Kabuki theatre and Indonesian shadow puppetry – and their exaggerated gestures dominate his imagery.

Many of the works featured in Noonan's Palais de Tokyo exhibition have an absurdist bent, appearing as afterimages of Berlin dada or suggesting the influence of playwrights such as Alfred Jarry and Samuel Beckett. Others explore the darker underbelly of cults, carnivals and other ritualistic gatherings, revealing how the spiritually uplifting can also harbour sinister leanings.

Rosemary Laing, weather, Galerie Lelong, New York, 1 February – 10 March 2007.

David Noonan, Palais de Tokyo, Paris, 22 March – 6 May 2007.

Break: Construct

'**Break: Construct**', installation view, featuring **Peter Madden and Seung Yul Oh, Whole of whole, 2006, Pee mung been garden, 2006; Seung Yul Oh, Nectars, 2006;** and **Marnie Slater, Any moment, 2006,** courtesy Govett-Brewster Art Gallery, New Plymouth.

Andrew Clifford

Over the last decade, New Plymouth's Govett-Brewster Art Gallery has secured a significant international reputation that belies its status as a provincial New Zealand gallery. But with a substantial staff turnover in recent years, including the departure of long-serving director Greg Burke, the gallery's ability to sustain that stature could have seemed in question. To his credit, Burke managed to recruit an impressive curatorial line-up from abroad before resigning. And with the appointment late last year of Rhana Devenport, former co-curator and senior project officer of the Asia-Pacific Triennial (APT), and manager of public programs and education for the 2006 Biennale of Sydney, Govett-Brewster's international networks should be in good shape. But how easily can the gallery relate to its local context, showing a sensitivity to the nuances of regional history and culture, as well as demonstrating an intimate grip on the pulse of emerging practice in New Zealand?

As if to rebut any concern over the latter, it was timely that Devenport's first curatorial assignment was 'Break', Govett-Brewster's third biennial survey of emerging artists, as well as more established artists who have made a significant 'break' in their practice. The gallery described 'Break' as 'reviewing the latest developments in contemporary New Zealand art'. Not an easy task for a curator new to the country, but not such a stretch for someone closely involved with the regional research driving the APT, especially after a three-month curatorial residency at Auckland contemporary gallery Artspace in 2005, which included curating their annual 'new artists' exhibition.

'Break: Construct', Devenport's edition of the exhibition, picked up from threads she established with Auckland's Artspace exhibition, 'Compelled'. Two artists exhibited in 'Compelled' – Seung Yul Oh and Sam Morrison – made a second appearance in 'Break: Construct'.

A relative unknown in 2005, Morrison has demonstrably grown in confidence; and his ability to transform found objects into irresistible, interactive installations transcends the crudeness of his equipment. Ping-pong balls, rubber gloves, wooden crates, bottles and bins are brought to life by foot-activated air pumps, which in turn transform his materials into kinetic sound sculptures that are part DIY science experiment and part craft show.

Oh has also gone from strength to strength with regular shows confirming the growing popularity of his cartoonish woodland creatures and free-form, goopy structures. For 'Break: Construct' he was paired with Peter Madden, adding an additional layer through which to negotiate the ways artists manufacture work. Madden's reconstructions of reality through photography and collage blended well with Oh's playful psychedelia and anthropomorphism. Black-and-white blobs of paint on the rear wall suggested googly eyes and cellular soup.

Snakes, caterpillars and toadstools combined Madden's exhumation of *National Geographic* tableaus with Oh's kitset menageries. All this was presided over by a multistorey giraffe with a sensor-triggered tail that pays homage to the kinetic sculptures of Len Lye, which form a central part of Govett Brewster's collection.

Photography played an interesting role in Devenport's exploration of constructs. As well as Madden's discussion of temporality and mortality with his recontextualisation of found imagery, there were also the fakeries of Yvonne Todd and Ben Cauchi. Cauchi's silvery photographs highlight the slippery relationship between photography and documentation, reality and illusion. Working with the painstakingly time-consuming techniques of tintype and ambrotype printing, each image is in fact a one-off and contradicts the assumption that photography is an instantaneous and mass-produced medium for capturing moments in favour of highly crafted illusions that both exploit and reveal their potential for fraudulence. Todd's images play with the glamorous façade of portraiture, hinting at the domestic narratives and suburban escapism that underlie the perfect picture.

Artificial suburban utopias also featured in Simon Lawrence's video flyover of a proposed suburban development. Combined with propped and balanced PVC pipes, programmed lamps and packing tape, he creates fictive domestic environments of possibilities and futility. Simon Denny, on the other hand, uses found materials such as crumpled gift wrap and old blankets to deny his work any sense of grand narrative or association and to focus attention on the art-making process. Scraps are left in seemingly arbitrary configurations as artistic residue, demonstrating nothing but their formal placement in the space and interdependence with other materials.

At the top of the gallery, towering, but only just, above Oh's giraffe, was another site-specific work that made good use of the building's idiosyncratic multi-level layout. Marnie Slater built a new top level for the gallery – a sort of sniper's look-out platform that provided new perspectives on the other works in the gallery, as well as a voyeuristic view of other gallery visitors. Despite the heavy engineering, it had an evasive presence; clad with mirrors, it camouflaged itself by absorbing and reflecting its surroundings.

Devenport assembled a tight selection of fresh work that integrated well with the gallery's spaces and heritage. Govett-Brewster, it would seem, remains a gallery to keep an eye on.

Break: Construct, Govett-Brewster Art Gallery, New Plymouth, 16 December 2006 – 18 February 2007.

Julia Gorman, Julia, 2007, courtesy
the artist and Uplands Gallery, Melbourne.
Photograph Ben Glezer.

Relentless Optimism

Veronica Tello

A work of art supposedly possesses an enigma. If we dig deep, we may obtain a more profound understanding of who we are and the world we live in – without needing to hug a tree. In this game of hypothesis and scenario painting, one might also suggest that art is meant to elicit a revelatory – even cathartic – appreciation of our society and culture. Perhaps, but this seems unlikely. This, however, is precisely what Mark Feary's curated exhibition 'Relentless Optimism' sought to do.

Feary attempted to propel us into a state of self-reflection and asked us to consider the here and now. According to Feary, our era is defined by 'descent and desolation'. He proclaims: 'It is difficult to remain positive in an increasingly negative world. Nothing is really getting better, just more difficult, more complicated, just worse.' Note, 'descent' suggests that there was once a higher plane (a better time or place). This loaded 'Relentless Optimism' with a sense of nostalgia for an elusive past and/or future when 'things' were or will be better. This is confirmed by Feary when he states: 'Relentless optimism, as a concept, counters the despair, isolation and disappointment endemic of contemporary life with positivism, faith and chance.' The exhibition sought distance from over-indulgent narcissism and destructive thought patterns. Paradoxically, Feary contends that the eleven art projects situated in the abandoned rooms of The Carlton Hotel, Melbourne, also embraced the 'doom, loneliness and futility of our lives'.

Indeed, we saw dejection in Ronnie van Hout's work *Anomie*, 2007. Here, a few blankets and a sleeping bag were carelessly sprawled across the floor in one of the hotel rooms to make an ad-hoc bed. A single navy-blue sheet hung lazily from the top of a window pane and blocked out the sun. The only light source came from a television, which sat on a green milk crate. It was a scenario that reeked of depression. This affect was repeated in Tony Garifalakis's *The kids are right for doing it wrong*, 2007, and then inverted in works such as *Julia*, 2007, by Julia Gorman. In her installation, Gorman transformed her decrepit hotel room into a child's room, principally through the arrangement of factory-produced wooden letters to spell out 'JULIA' on the front door. This was a simple but effective gesture to create a warm and safe place within a ruin. 'Relentless Optimism' conflated a number of dichotomies in order to create a space riddled with paradoxes: doom and gloom, happiness and faith, darkness and light.

While the exhibition, to varying degrees and effects, addressed the depressed state of society, the show failed to address a perhaps more relevant stream of apathy – the general lack of curatorial experimentation and innovation in Australia. The show comprised a list of 'trendy' Melbourne artists, which is not to say that the artists are not talented, but notwithstanding, most were poached from just two of Melbourne's formidable contemporary art institutions: Uplands Gallery and Gertrude Contemporary Art Spaces. With its stock of recognisable and popular artists, 'Relentless Optimism' has been described as a veritable 'mini Melbourne biennale'.[1]

In this light, one cannot help but wonder, what is the role of any curated exhibition that attempts to represent a current mood: in this case, the apathetic condition? Is it to 'represent' or to create a space for sincere dialogue about the milieu we live in? The latter has a bias for experimentation and politics, while the former is decidedly more superficial and commercially driven. The distinction is total: innovation or complacency?

As in other areas of life and creative endeavour, contemporary art too often languishes in its comfort zone, content to criticise from a safe distance and without much vigour to propose solutions or actual avenues for change. One might then suggest that as a concept, 'Relentless Optimism' had a blind spot. For, rather than attempting to experiment with aesthetics and curatorship, it was complacent in its standardising and ranking of artists by contemporary public and commercial art galleries. Moreover, while holding the exhibition in a formerly impoverished hotel and brothel (which could be seen as an anti-aesthetic act in itself), in actual fact this venue was renovated and gentrified, and it was within this latter context that the exhibition took place. It is the responsibility of curators to be open to experimentation and to other processes of renewal. Reissuing the familiar was a curious curatorial approach for a show that purported to invert doom into hope.

1 Penny Webb, 'Relentless optimism', *Age*, 14 February 2007.

Relentless Optimism, The Carlton Hotel, Melbourne, 7 February – 3 March 2007.

A Constructed World, Constructed
World plates, 2007, courtesy the artists
and N.O. Gallery, Milan.

M.M.M.

Daniele Balit

M.M.M. (Milano-Melbourne-Milano), a cultural exchange between the sister cities Melbourne and Milan, developed by commissioning curators Max Delany and Natalie King and the Monash University Museum of Art, involved three exhibitions: 'Schifanoia', 'Dolls' and 'Too Near, Too Far'. 'Schifanoia'[1] included the presentation of a mysterious and exclusive event entitled *The Social Contract*.

I would like to reveal the secret of *The Social Contract*. I could have done so in this review of the exhibition 'Schifanoia', but I was not among the ninety-one participants who were allowed inside the Milan apartment in which *The Social Contract* was made public. The lucky few, moreover, are restricted by the contract to keep secret what they have seen, and have subsequently proved impossible to corrupt. I have now given up my idea of revelation, and the secret of *The Social Contract* will remain intact. On reflection, this isn't so bad because it suggests that the work was taken seriously by those who saw it and therefore can be considered a success, of sorts.

The Social Contract was conceived by Jacqueline Riva and Geoff Lowe, aka A Constructed World (ACW), for 'Schifanoia'. The principal focus of the event was not the 'artwork' revealed in the apartment but rather the contract binding the ninety-one participants to keep its existence secret for a period of six months. To reveal the secret, to talk about it with friends, relatives and colleagues, or to write a review, would breach the signed, legally binding pact made with Riva and Lowe. In this way, ACW entrusted the visitors with a great responsibility: they were asked to 'self-manage' the meaning of the work, and not discuss its meaning with anyone. By enforcing these rules, the artists hoped to encourage a reconsideration of pre-established systems of understanding and interpreting art. However, a doubt lurks in the background: which outcome can be considered an indicator of success – the keeping of the contract or its breach?

The 'Schifanoia' exhibition, curated by Ilaria Bonacossa , took place in four Milanese apartments and also in a more traditional exhibition space, the N.O. Gallery, the site for ACW's *Constructed world plate*, 2006–07, which consisted of objects visitors could put together as they pleased, and ACW's video project *Shell and pea*, 2006. In the N.O Gallery, a room filled with layers of black-and-white ink-jet prints explained, through fragmentary images, the history of ACW. With this installation Riva and Lowe contrasted the experiential aspect of the works shown in the apartments with the more detached and conceptualist documentation strategies shown in the exhibition space.

The central role of collaborative practice was also brought to the fore in 'Too Near, Too Far', another exhibition in the M.M.M. program, held in the art centre C/O Careof in Milan. The modus operandi of Australia's new generation of artists in Melbourne appears to be marked by 'peer to peer' interaction and by the sharing of means, resources and ideas, thanks to a strong network of non-profit and artist-run initiatives. The Italian curators of the exhibition, Chiara Agnello and Roberta Tenconi, wanted to emphasise this aspect of the Melbourne creative scene, which they observed during a 2006 residency in Australia. They paralleled this to their experience in Italy, where such interactions occur far less frequently. The exhibition featured artists Alicia Frankovich, Simon Horsburgh and David Rosetzky. The artists' works were exhibited adjacent to documentation regarding the network of independent Melbourne spaces, including Gertrude Contemporary Art Spaces, Clubs project, Conical and West Space. After the close of the exhibition, the body of documentation became a permanent part of the public archive of C/O Careof.

Surrealist tonalities were on show in the third M.M.M. exhibition, 'Dolls' at Milan's Galleria Raffaella Cortese, with the display of works by artists Destiny Deacon, Virginia Fraser, Zoe Leonard, Maria Marshall and Laurie Simmons. As curator Natalie King suggests, dolls induce 'poignant, amusing and eerie scenarios' and, as in the work of surrealist Hans Bellmer, dolls are used as powerful transitional and communication devices. In Deacon's photographs, dolls become elements in a game of representation, sinking a cutting and ironic blade into Australia's fraught Indigenous and non-Indigenous histories.

---

1 'The title 'Schifanoia', as noted by Ilaria Bonacossa in the 'Schifanoia' exhibition catalogue, is inspired by a magnificent palace near Ferrara that hosts the series of frescoes *Ciclo dei Mesi* by the Ferrarese school (1469 –1470). Conversely, in contemporary Italian the word 'schifanoia' sounds something like 'disgusting boredom', therefore making fun of the project, or hinting at what some people think of contemporary art: that it is boring or disgusting.

Schifanoia, A Constructed World (Geoff Lowe and Jacqui Riva), N.O. Gallery, Milan, and four Milanese apartments, 2 February – 9 March 2007; **Too Near, Too Far**, C/O Careof contemporary art centre, Milan, 3 February – 17 March, 2007; **Dolls**, Galleria Raffaella Cortese, Milan, 1 February – 14 April 2007.

Before the Body – Matter

detail
Benjamin Armstrong, Conflict, 2003–05,
blown glass, fabric, steel wood and wax,
101 x 104 x 139 cm, Monash University Collection,
courtesy Monash University Museum of Art,
Melbourne.

Ashley Crawford

The body has been a subject for art for time immemorial: from ancient rock paintings through to the Pietà and the crucifixion, from countless nudes and innumerable portraits. Is there, in this new millennium, room for more on the subject?

Curator Geraldine Barlow most certainly thought so. In an extraordinary selection of sixteen artists, ranging from Hany Armanious to Pat Brassington, Brent Harris to Mike Parr, Barlow discovered an ongoing obsession with the human form in contemporary art, and one far from the usual clichés of figuration.

To be sure, something has happened to the body in recent times. In an article penned for Britain's *Guardian* newspaper in 2005, the English author JG Ballard speculated on the appeal of the television series *C.S.I. – Crime Scene Investigation*. He concluded:

I suspect that the cadavers waiting their turn on the tables are surrogates for ourselves, the viewers. The real crime the C.S.I. team is investigating, weighing every tear, every drop of blood, every smear of semen, is the crime of being alive. I fear that we watch, entranced, because we feel an almost holy pity for ourselves, and the oblivion patiently waiting for us.[1]

Indeed, as Barlow postulates in her introduction to the exhibition, the body presented here is 'rendered as porous, wounded, pathologised and beyond plenitude'. In Barlow's selection the body is 'cut up, reconfigured, dispersed and dissolved'. It is 'prodded, probed and pulled asunder'. Yes, we are in trouble indeed.

And the show proved it. There is something almost pathological about the approach these contemporary artists take to the body. It ranges drastically, from Pat Brassington's weirdly distorted and distended figure in *Rocket*, 2005, in which a pair of white legs seem to plummet downwards interminably, through to Susan Norrie's strangely claustrophobic *Shudder (pathology)*, 1994, in which the figure is so dispersed that we drown in the viscous fluids of extermination.

Hany Armanious, always a master of the macabre, was included with *Basic instruction no. 4*, 2003, and one immediately wondered what exactly we were being instructed to do. If this is an alternative, alien illustration to *The Joy of Sex*, then humanity is going to be hard-pressed to keep up. Like the sex scene in Nicholas Roeg's film *The Man Who Fell To Earth* (1976), Armanious's figures morph and melt in a queasy union. Given the context it is equally hard not to imagine Benjamin Armstrong's *The hour*, 2005–06, as a particularly strenuous and painful bowel movement. An elegant glass and wax sculptural assemblage, the contents of the top bulb of Armstrong's time-glass structure resemble strange excrement as it descends.

Even more evocative of bodily processes was Vera Moller's *ego (relaxed)*, 1996, a bizarre multilayered assemblage of latex gloves that evoke deflated lung sacs or multitudinous deformed condoms. The result is strangely invasive, recalling Barlow's notion of the body being prodded and probed, but here literally by hundreds, if not thousands, of latex-clad fingers.

Something eerily similar in terms of evoking the internal workings of the body occurred with Lauren Berkowitz's *Dystrophy*, 1997, a wall-hanging composed of cricket ball cut-offs. With its deep red hue, the work is suggestive of cellular devastation and mutation.

There were all sorts of extremes of bodily presence in 'Before the Body – Matter', from the powerfully visceral works of Mira Gojak and Mike Parr through to the cool but troubling paintings of Brent Harris. Gojak was presented here with a massive 150 x 100 centimetre texta and felt-tip pen drawing. While suggestive of a morass of tangled human hair, *Something has to go 1*, 2006, is essentially abstract, the body present through the sheer energy and execution of the work. Something similar occurred with Mike Parr's gnarly self-portrait, *Bronze liars*, 1996. This bronze comes from a series Parr executed in which he would plunge his hand into a block of clay and 'sculpt' himself 'blind', working via touch alone. The results are a powerful illustration of self-perception.

Harris's trio of paintings, *Just a feeling*, 1996, also hinted at psychological exploration. Set against a garish pink background, his simple, illustrative images could be read as reducing the body to eye and penis, focal points of desire. Similarly simplified was John Meade's strange sculptural assemblage, *Set of holds*, 1999. Again, given the context, one was tempted to read these as some form of accoutrement for strange sexual foreplay, which would beg the question – holds for *what*?

One of the most powerful works in the show was Dale Frank's *Dirk Diggler*, 2000, a massive acrylic paint and varnish work. With its deep scarlet depths the painting recalls a massive spread of congealing blood.

'Before the Body – Matter' was a massive undertaking, also including powerful works by Donna Bailey, Ti Parks, Simone Slee and Judy Watson. What was remarkable was that almost all the works came from the Monash University collection. Geraldine Barlow evidenced a uniquely imaginative approach to reinterpreting the collection, and created a powerful assemblage indeed.

1 JG Ballard, 'In cold blood', *Guardian*, 25 June 2005.

Before the Body – Matter, Monash University Museum of Art, Melbourne,
30 November – 15 December 2006 and 1 February – 14 March 2007.

ARTARMON GALLERIES

GLEN PREECE
September 2007

NEIL CUTHBERT
October 2007

The Blue Musician 52 x 40 cm Oil on Board

A Fundamental Fork in the Road (detail)

WATERFRONT
DARWIN CITY   TOGART

art

The Toga Group in partnership with the Northern Territory Government will be embedding arts and cultural initiatives into the new world-class Darwin City Waterfront Development through hosting a new contemporary art award and developing a major program of public art commissions.

1st TogArt Contemporary Award
This award will be held at Parliament House in Darwin between the 10th of July and the 1st of August. This non-acquisitive award offers a generous prize of $15,000 to the work considered by judges to be the most outstanding work in the exhibition. A further $5000 will be awarded to the people's choice.

Public Art and the Darwin City Waterfront
The commissioning of exemplary public art within the Darwin City Waterfront will serve to distinguish and enhance the unique world-class precinct by integrating artworks into its fabric and enhancing the lifestyles of current and future generations.

'Our challenge is not to develop a 'formulaic' waterfront, a style that is already prevalent around Australia, but rather to stamp this project with the quality that will serve to distinguish Darwin in a global context, to set it apart, exhibiting the unique characteristics of our city, by drawing on our rich cultural past, our dynamic present, and our promising future.' Chief Minister—Hansard 23 August 2005.

An initiative of:

Northern
Territory
Government

TOGA GROUP

www.darwincitywaterfront.com.au

Please direct all enquiries to Felicity Green, Public Art Manager—Darwin City Waterfront Toga Group, GPO Box 882, Darwin NT 0801 **Telephone** (08) 8942 0523 **Facsimile** (08) 8981 6688 **Email** fgreen@darwincitywaterfront.com.au

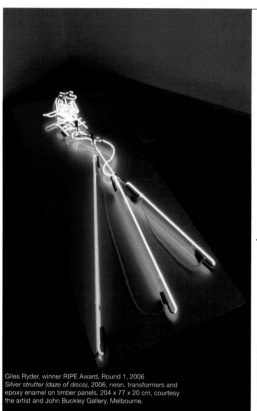

Giles Ryder, winner RIPE Award, Round 1, 2006
Silver strutter (daze of disco), 2006, neon, transformers and
epoxy enamel on timber panels, 204 x 77 x 20 cm, courtesy
the artist and John Buckley Gallery, Melbourne.

ripe

**Art & Australia/
ANZ Private Bank
Contemporary
Art Award**

for emerging
professional artists

closing date
1 August, 2007

For applications and
guidelines, visit
the NAVA website
www.visualarts.net.au

NAVA

**NATIONAL ASSOCIATION
FOR THE VISUAL ARTS LTD**

Small Quiet Gestures

1 June – 1 July 2006
Chris Bond, Barbara Campbell, Aleks Danko, Danielle Freakley, Rosemary Joy, Linda Sproul
Curated by Jan Duffy and Linda Sproul

Linden
CENTRE FOR CONTEMPORARY ARTS

www.lindenarts.org

image: Chris Bond *3rd June 2006* (installation detail)

ELWYN LYNN

A Selection of Works
30 June – 17 July 2007

The Milk Factory Gallery
& Exhibition Space
31 Station Street
Bowral NSW
Ph: 02 48621077

the milk factory gallery
www.milkfactorygallery.com.au

TIWIART

Now you

can purchase

Tiwi Art

online

www.tiwiart.com

Tunga Pumupuni Jilamara
by Roslyn Orsto ©

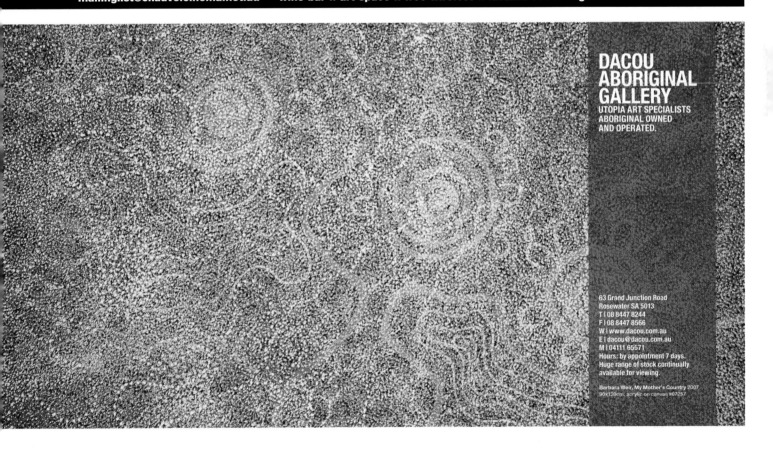

Cairns Regional Gallery

To 8 July

Jorg Schmeisser: Elsewhere
Japanese textiles and prints
An exhibition by Jorg Schmiesser featuring
finely executed, exquisitely coloured etchings
of ancient ruins and past life
A Cairns Regional Gallery Curated Exhibition

15 June – 29 July

Papuwah: The art of Nuigini
A collection of contemporary visual material
produced by craft practitioners and artists from our
nearest international neighbour, Papua New Guinea.
Works included in this exhibition range from fibre
basketry and weaving to prints and paintings
A Cairns Regional Gallery Curated Exhibition

13 July – 19 August

Art Bank 25 years
Artbank, the Australian Government art rental initiative,
is at the forefront of collecting contemporary art
and craft from Australia's emerging and established
Indigenous and non-Indigenous artists. Celebrating
twenty-five years, this exhibition features artworks
acquired each year of its operation including photography,
sculpture, paintings, glass and Indigenous artworks
A Travelling Exhibition supported by Visions Australia.

Cairns Regional Gallery
cnr Abbott and Shield streets
Cairns QLD 4870
Tel 07 4046 4800
Fax 07 4031 6410
www.cairnsregionalgallery.com.au
marketing@cairnsregionalgallery.com.au

BENDIGO ART GALLERY

To 24 June
The Paris End: Fashion,
Photography and Glamour

2 June – 8 July
Mission Voices

30 June – 5 August
The Arthur Guy
Memorial Painting Prize

From 11 August
Paddy Bedford.

42 View Street, Bendigo VIC 3550
Tel 03 5434 6088 Fax 03 5443 6586
www.bendigoartgallery.com.au
Daily 10–5
Entry by donation

Bendigo
Art Gallery

 TWEED RIVER ART GALLERY

To 17 June
CPM NATIONAL PRINT AWARDS
A biennial prize with an increasing national
profile, organised by Tweed River Art
Gallery and Community Printmakers
Murwillumbah. 2007 Judge: artist and
printmaker Graham Fransella

MULTIPLICITY
Prints and multiples drawn from the
collections of Museum of Contemporary
Art and University of Wollongong,
exploring the development of this art
form from the 1960s to the present

21 June – 12 August
PRIVATELY COLLECTING:
KEN HINDS CULTURAL HERITAGE
COLLECTION
Showcasing a selection of recent
acquisitions which presents a version of
Australian art history to the present day
including Fairweather, Whitely and Tucker

OPERATION ART
An annual touring exhibition by students
across NSW, in appreciation of sick
children and their families at the Children's
Hospital at Westmead

NAIDOC WEEK
An annual exhibition of artwork by artists
of the Bundjalung nation, the traditional
inhabitants of the Tweed Area, scheduled
to coincide with the fiftieth anniversary
of NAIDOC Week, a celebration by all
Australians of Aboriginal culture

From 16 August
2007 OLIVE COTTON AWARD
An annual national award for photographic
portraiture. Please contact the gallery
for entry forms or see our website for
information.

A Tweed Shire Council community facility
cnr Tweed Valley Way and Mistral Road
Murwillumbah NSW 2484
Tel 02 6670 2790 Fax 02 6672 7585
tweedart@tweed.nsw.gov.au
www.tweed.nsw.gov.au/artgallery
Wed–Sun 10–5 / Free admission

Broken Hill Regional Art Gallery

To 17 June

RED Earth / Moon Shimmer
New works by Catherine Parker based on
her Broken Hill artist-in-residence in 2006

22 June – 29 July

Line of Load
A photographic exhibition by Peter Liddy
documenting the historic architecture and
infrastructure along Broken Hill's Line of
Load. The exhibition is based on his
Broken Hill artist-in-residence in 2006

15 June – 22 July

The Naughty Apartment
Nigel Helyer

From 3 August

Living Treasures:
Masters of Australian Craft

 arts|nsw

Broken Hill Regional Art Gallery
404–408 Argent Street, Broken Hill NSW 2880
Tel 08 8088 6897 Fax 08 8088 6956
artgallery@brokenhill.nsw.gov.au
10–5, Mon–Sun, Free admission

Caloundra *Regional* Art Gallery

June – 8 July

Sacred Scarab
An installation by Sally Spencer that interprets ancient Egyptian symbols and animal totems, using ceramic contemporary materials

Telltales
NSW artist Duke Albada presents a series of mixed media works that recount her travel adventures, capturing the essence and energy of each journey

11 July – 12 August

Squeeze '07, Re-ignition
The second biennial art exhibition that encourages the region's art educators out of their classrooms and into their studios to ignite their arts practice

From 15 August

Sunshine Coast Art Prize 07
A national contemporary painting and two-dimensional art prize valued at $20,000, which includes a four-week residency in Maleny on the Sunshine Coast Hinterland. The judge is freelance curator and writer Tim Morrell.

A Caloundra City Council initiative supported by Sajen Legal

22 Omrah Avenue, Caloundra QLD 4551
Tel 07 5420 8200 Fax 07 5420 8292
artgallery@caloundra.qld.gov.au
www.caloundra.qld.gov.au/caloundragallery
Wed–Sun 10–4 Free admission

LATROBE REGIONAL GALLERY

From 7 July
Vivienne Binns
The Vivienne Binns's exhibition will include work from the 1960s to the present. Vivienne has been at the centre of all major developments in Australian art and culture over the last forty years, from wild and groovy happenings to political activism, from late modernist and post colonial critique to community art events. The exhibition will be the first major survey of this important Australian artist. Curated by Merryn Gates. Toured through the Tasmanian Museum of Art.

From 4 August
Godwin Bradbeer
A mid-career survey exhibition of the drawings of Godwin Bradbeer, presented by Shepparton Art Gallery. The drawings in this exhibition span a period from 1975 to 2005, and show the artist's ongoing exploration of psychoanalytic concepts and the body. His work takes a particular interest in the adolescent phase, and has been discussed in relation to androgyny and notions of beauty.

Legends 1 Owen Rye
Owen Rye is an experienced artist and long-term adventurer in the world of ceramics. He achieves magnificent variety in the pots he creates – in scale, colour, shape and surface texture. As an artist Rye is drawn to the mysterious and uncertain; the poetic rather than the scientific, resolving the dilemma between the two through an imaginative process that links the earth's archaeological past with its uncertain future.

138 Commercial Road
Morwell Victoria 3840
Tel 03 5128 5704
Fax 03 5128 5706
Mon–Fri 10–5, Sat–Sun 11–4
Free admission

GLADSTONE REGIONAL ART GALLERY AND MUSEUM

To 14 June
SPORT & WAR
Firing national passions, sport and war has helped shape the Australian identity. Stories told through photographs, and sporting memorabilia.
An Australian War Memorial travelling exhibition funded by the Federal Government's commemorations program *Saluting Their Service*, tour assisted by Australian Sport Commission and *Visions of Australia*, an Australian Government initiative

30 June – 28 July
ARTS NAIDOC
50 years: Looking Forward, Looking Blak: Celebrating NAIDOC 2007
Works by artists of the Port Curtis region presented in conjunction with selections from the permanent collection

2 July – 18 August
WOVEN FORMS
Contemporary basket making in Australia: celebrating the diversity, skill and innovation of both Indigenous and non-Indigenous artists
An Object Gallery touring exhibition supported by BHP Billiton, Gordon Darling Foundation and *Visions of Australia*, an Australian Government initiative

From 4 August
EDUCATION MINISTER'S AWARDS FOR EXCELLENCE IN ART 2006
An annual exhibition featuring the work of Queensland secondary school art students that recognises excellence in visual arts
Toured by Museum & Galleries Services Queensland.

Gladstone Regional Art Gallery and Museum
cnr Goondoon and Bramston streets, Gladstone QLD 4680
Tel 07 4976 6766 Fax 07 4972 9097
www.gladstone.qld.gov.au/gragm
gragm@gragm.qld.gov.au
Mon–Sat 10–5

MOSMAN ART GALLERY

2 June – 15 July
Mosaic Now: Works from Italy and Australia
This truly unique travelling exhibition from the Bundoora Homestead Art Centre presents Italian and Australian mosaics, exploring the history of this ancient practice and its more contemporary expressions. The exhibition includes a selection of works from Scuola de Mosaicisti del Friuli, an internationally acclaimed school of mosaics located in Spilimbergo, Northern Italy, as well as works by noted Australian practitioners

Polarities in Print: New Work from the Print Circle
For the exhibition 'Polarities in Print', twenty-eight members of The Print Circle showcase their creativity and skills by employing contrasting printing techniques and subject matter to create a series of diverse images. The theme encourages the artists to produce images which explore the idea of different polarities such as racial, geographic or personal

28 July – 26 August
Mosman Art Prize 60th Anniversary
The oldest local government art award in Australia, offering an acquisitive painting prize of $20,000, sponsored by Mosman Council, the Allan Gamble Memorial Art Prize of $3000, a Viewers' Choice Prize of $1000, a Commendation Prize of $1000, and a Young Emerging Artists Award of $1000.

Mosman Art Gallery
cnr Art Gallery Way (formerly Short Street) and Myahgah Road
Mosman NSW 2088
Tel 02 9978 4178 Fax 02 9978 4149
www.mosman.nsw.gov.au/
Daily 10–5, closed public holidays, free admission

GEELONG GALLERY

From 8 June
An artist abroad:
the prints of James McNeill Whistler
A National Gallery of Australia Travelling Exhibition

From 23 June
Robert Clinch: urban myths

From 7 July
Contemporary Australian silver and metalwork 2007
A Buda Historic Home and Gardening touring exhibition.

Geelong Gallery's outstanding collection of paintings, sculpture and decorative arts spans Australian art from the colonial period to the present day.

Little Malop Street, Geelong, Victoria 3220
Tel: 03 5229 3645 Fax 03 5221 6441
geelart@geelonggallery.org.au
www.geelonggallery.org.au
Mon–Fri 10–5, weekends and public holidays 1–5
Guided tours of the permanent collection 2 pm Saturday
Free admission

WOLLONGONG CITY GALLERY

To 17 June
Michael Callaghan: A Survey 1967–2006
Prints, posters and paintings spanning three decades
A Manly Art Gallery and Museum touring exhibition

John Vucic-Wolfpup: NPK Orchis
An exploration of the hidden world of soil life and the human body

To 1 July
Mark Tedeschi: Femininity and Other Feelings
Images of universal human emotions and states of being

16 June – 5 August
Tim Johnson and Karma Phuntsok: The Luminescent Ground
A visual narrative that has its roots in Buddhism while referencing other world views

23 June – 29 July
Anita Larkin, 2006 Resident Artist: Object Incognito
Sculptures that explore the secret lives of abandoned objects

Shift
Works by participants in the gallery's Mentor Program for young artists

From 4 August
Andrew Christofides: A Survey
Paintings, prints, and constructions spanning twenty-five years

Yang Xifa: Dawn Dream
Paintings exploring meanings and questions of existence.

Wollongong City Gallery
cnr Kembla and Burelli streets, Wollongong NSW 2500
Tel 02 4228 7500 Fax 02 4226 5530
gallery@wollongong.nsw.gov.au
www.wollongongcitygallery.com
Tues–Fri 10–5, weekends and public holidays 12–4
Closed Mondays, Good Friday, Christmas Day, Boxing Day and New Year's Day

Dear Readers and Subscribers,
It gives us great pleasure to present

The inaugural Art & Australia Artist Edition: Louise Weaver

This new program of Artist Editions celebrates the work of Australian artists and promotes a more accessible, broader form of collecting

far right
Louise Weaver, Out on a limb, 2006 screenprinted Belgian linen bag with cotton lining, 63 x 45 cm. The bag contains various found and constructed elements, with slight variation, including a lithograph poster, a CD (sound made in collaboration with Phil Edwards and Peter Ellis), and a zine bound with hand-stitched cotton thread. Edition of 50, signed with a numbered certificate.

*Orders will be filled on a first come first serve basis.
Price does not include postage and packing.

Exclusive offer
50 editions available from *Art & Australia* and Darren Knight Gallery, Sydney
$550 including GST

To place your order:
Tel 02 9331 4455
Fax 02 9331 4577
subscriptions@artandaustralia.com.au
www.artandaustralia.com.au

'The edition … contains various mysterious objects pertaining to Guido Valdez's mythical and fantastic journeys'
Louise Weaver

Queensland

Adrian Slinger Galleries
3 Hastings Street, Noosa Heads 4567
Tel 07 5473 5222
Fax 07 5473 5233
info@adrianslingergalleries.com
Director: Adrian Slinger
Private consultant.
Sole Australian representative of the
internationally acclaimed painter David
Rankin.
Sat–Wed 10–5

Art Galleries Schubert
Marina Mirage, Seaworld Drive,
Main Beach 4217
Tel 07 5571 0077
info@artgalleriesschubert.com.au
www.artgalleriesschubert.com.au
Representing: Brett Whiteley, Fred
Williams, Arthur Boyd, Sidney Nolan,
William Robinson, Jeffrey Smart,
Charles Blackman, Lloyd Rees, Ian
Fairweather, John Olsen, Sam Fullbrook,
Hans Heysen, John Coburn, Ray Crooke,
Lawrence Daws, Russel Drysdale,
Robert Dickerson, Grace Cossington-
smith, James Gleeson, Albert Tucker,
Gary Shead and Tim Storrier. See also
Schubert Contemporary listing.
Daily 10–5.30

Australian & Oceanic Art Gallery
cnr Grant and Warner streets,
Port Douglas 4877
Tel 07 4099 4494
Fax 07 4099 4417
info@oceanicart.com.au
www.oceanicart.com.au
Directors: Tom and Kerry Colrain
Australian and Indigenous contemporary
and traditional art. Featuring Lockhart
River, Torres Strait and Queensland
Western and Central Desert art.
Mon–Fri 10–6, Sat 10–1, and by
appointment

Crows Nest Regional Art Gallery
New England Highway,
P.O. Box 35, Crows Nest 4355
Tel 07 4698 1687
Fax 07 4698 2995
art@crowsnestshire.qld.gov.au
www.cnnet.com.au
Monthly exhibitions of paintings, sculpture,
photography, ceramics, textiles, jewellery
and much more. Annual acquisitive
competition each July.
Tues–Sat 10–4, Sun 11.30–4

Fire-Works Gallery
11 Stratton Street, Newstead 4006
Tel 07 3216 1250
Fax 07 3216 1251
Mobile 0418 192 845
michael@fireworksgallery.com.au
www.fireworksgallery.com.au
Director: Michael Eather
Themed contemporary art exhibitions,
specialising in Aboriginal works.
Tues–Fri 11–5, Sat 11–4, and by
appointment

Grahame Galleries and Editions
1 Fernberg Road, Milton
P.O. Box 515, Paddington 4064
Tel 07 3369 3288
Fax 07 3369 3021
editions@thehub.com.au
www.grahamegalleries.com
Director: Noreen Grahame
Specialising in fine art prints, works on
paper and artists' books. Organiser of the
Artists' Books and Multiples Fair.
Wed–Sat 11–5, and by appointment

Graydon Gallery
29 Merthyr Road, New Farm 4005
Tel 07 3622 1913
Fax 07 3357 6226
info@graydongallery.com.au
www.graydongallery.com.au
Director: Cath Nicholson
Exceptional exhibition space for hire by
artists in Brisbane's gallery precinct.
Contact Cath Nicholson to discuss your
exhibition requirements and discuss
availability of space.
Tues–Sat 10–6, Sun 11–5

Heiser Gallery
90B Arthur Street, Fortitude Valley 4006
Tel 07 3254 2849
Fax 07 3254 2859
bh@heisergallery.com.au
www.heisergallery.com.au
Director: Bruce Heiser
Representing leading Australian artists
and dealing in modern Australian works
of art.
Tues–Sat 10.30–6

Ipswich Art Gallery
d'Arcy Doyle Place, Nicholas Street,
Ipswich 4305
Tel 07 3810 7222
Fax 07 3812 0428
info@ipswichartgallery.qld.gov.au
www.ipswichartgallery.qld.gov.au
Queensland's largest regional gallery
presents a dynamic program of visual
art exhibitions, social history displays,
educational children's activities and
special events.
Daily 10–5, closed Christmas Day,
Boxing Day, New Year's Day,
Good Friday and Anzac Day morning

Libby Edwards Galleries
482 Brunswick Street,
Fortitude Valley 4006
Tel 07 3358 3944
Fax 07 3358 3947
bris@libbyedwardsgalleries.com
www.libbyedwardsgalleries.com
Monthly exhibitions of paintings, works on
paper and sculpture by contemporary
Australian artists.
Tues–Sat 11–5, Sun 1–5

Logan Art Gallery
cnr Wembley Road and Jacaranda
Avenue, Logan Central 4114
Tel 07 3826 5519
Fax 07 3826 5350
artgallery@logan.qld.gov.au
www.logan.qld.gov.au
Director: Annette Turner
Regular program of local artists' work.
National touring exhibitions. Logan art
collection. Changing monthly exhibitions.
Tues–Sat 10–5
Free admission

Philip Bacon Galleries
2 Arthur Street, Fortitude Valley 4006
Tel 07 3358 3555
Fax 07 3254 1412
artenquiries@philipbacongalleries.com.au
www.philipbacongalleries.com.au
Director: Philip Bacon
Artists include Davida Allen, Charles
Blackman, Arthur Boyd, Rupert Bunny,
Cressida Campbell, Peter Churcher,
Charles Conder, Grace Cossington Smith,
Ray Crooke, Lawrence Daws, Ian
Fairweather, Donald Friend, Sam Fullbrook,
James Gleeson, Gwyn Hanssen Pigott,
Nicholas Harding, Barry Humphries, Philip
Hunter, Michael Johnson, Robert Klippel,
Norman Lindsay, Stewart MacFarlane,
Sidney Nolan, Justin O'Brien, Margaret
Olley, John Olsen, John Perceval, Margaret
Preston, Lloyd Rees, William Robinson,
John Peter Russell, Wendy Sharpe, Garry
Shead, Gordon Shepherdson, Jeffrey
Smart, Tim Storrier, Arthur Streeton,
Roland Wakelin, Tony White, Brett
Whiteley and Fred Williams.
Tues–Sat 10–5

QUT Art Museum
2 George Street, Brisbane 4001
(next to Brisbane City Botanic Gardens)
Tel 07 3864 5370
Fax 07 3864 5371
artmuseum@qut.edu.au
www.artmuseum.qut.com
To 22 July: 'Freestyle', new Australian
design for living
From 27 July: 'Breaking New Ground',
Brisbane women artists of the mid-
twentieth century.
Tues–Fri 10–5, Wed 10–8, Sat–Sun 12–4
Closed Mondays and public holidays

Redland Art Gallery
cnr Middle and Bloomfield streets
Cleveland 4163
Tel 07 3829 8899 Fax 07 3829 8891
gallery@redland.qld.gov.au
www.redland.qld.gov.au
Director: Emma Bain
The Redland Art Gallery showcases a mix
of innovative exhibitions and specialises in
a varied program that looks to define the
cultural identity of Redland Shire.
Mon–Fri 9–4, Sun 9–2
Free admission

Schubert Contemporary
Marina Mirage, Seaworld Drive,
Main Beach 4217
Tel 07 5571 0077
info@schubertcontemporary.com.au
www.schubertcontemporary.com.au
Representing contemporary artists: Dale
Frank, Cherry Hood, Michael Zavros,
Denise Green, Geoffrey Proud, Zhong
Chen, Rhys Lee, Margarita Geogiadis, Sally
Smart, Robert Ryan, Martine Emdur, David
Ralph, George Raftopoulos, Melinda
Harper, Nick Howson, Katherine Hattam,
Anthony Lister, Dane Lovett, Anthony
Bennett, Anwen Keeling, Darren Wardle,
Simon Mee, James Willebrandt, Rod
Bunter, Abbey McCulloch, VR Morrison,
Gordon Richards, Craig Ruddy, Jason
Cordero, Victoria Reichelt, Timothy John,
Melissa Egan, Wayde Owen, Karlee
Rawkins, Susan O'Doherty, Melitta Perry,
Marise Maas, Craig Waddell, Mitchell Kelly,
Mark Gawne, Fran Tomlin, Joanna Burgler,
Mark Gawne, John Cottrell, Mark Dober,
Keren Seelander, Mari Hirata, Deborah
Halpern, Philip Stallard, Annie Herron.
From 8 June: Anthony Bennett, solo
exhibition
From 20 July: Michael Zavros, solo
exhibition
From 17 August: Wayde Owen, solo
exhibition.
Daily 10–5.30

Stanthorpe Regional Art Gallery
Lock Street, Weeroona Park,
Stanthorpe 4380
Tel 07 4681 1874 Fax 07 4681 4021
stanart@halenet.com.au
www.granitenet.net.au/groups/
StanthorpeArtsFestival
Director: Nicole Bryzenski
Monthly program of national touring
exhibitions, local artists' works, permanent
collection of known Australian artists, and
'Music in the Gallery' – local and national
musicians.
Mon–Fri 10–4, Sat–Sun 10–1
Free admission

Suzanne O'Connell Gallery
93 James Street, New Farm 4005
Tel 07 3358 5811
Fax 07 3358 5813
suzanne@suzanneoconnell.com
www.suzanneoconnell.com
Director: Suzanne O'Connell
Specialists in Australian Indigenous art
from Warakurna, Blackstone, Patjarr,
Amata, Yuendumu, Haasts Bluff, Balgo
Hills, Kununurra, Tiwi Islands, Maningrida
and Yirrkala.
Wed–Sat 11–4

Toowoomba Regional Art Gallery
531 Ruthven Street, Toowoomba 4350
Tel 07 4688 6652
Fax 07 4688 6895
artgallery@toowoomba.qld.gov.au
www.toowoomba.qld.gov.au
Director: Diane Baker
15 June – 8 July: 'Home Island, Home
Country', an exhibition of children's art
from remote North Queensland and the
Torres Strait. A travelling exhibition
developed by Cairns Regional Gallery and
toured by Museum and Gallery Services
Queensland
From 29 June: 'Direct Attack: Lionel
Lindsay's Craft and Criticism', metal plates,
woodblocks, sketches, proofs and prints
to review Lindsay's point that 'whether you
draw with pen, pencil, etching-needle or
engraver, the direct attack on your material
is undoubtedly the right one' (1922)
13 July – 19 August: The Blake Prize for
Religious Art, presented by the Blake
Society.
Tues 10–4, Sun 1–4, public holidays 10–4,
closed Christmas Day and Good Friday
Free admission

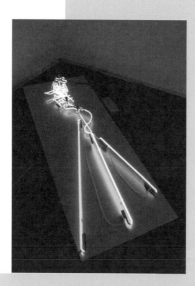

Giles Ryder, Silver strutter
(daze of disco), 2006,
neon, transformers and epoxy
enamel on timber panels,
204 x 77 x 20 cm, courtesy
the artist and John Buckley
Gallery, Melbourne.

New South Wales

Albury Regional Art Gallery
546 Dean Street, Albury 2640
Tel 02 6051 3480
Fax 02 6041 2482
alburygallery@alburycity.nsw.gov.au
www.alburycity.nsw.gov.au/gallery
To 12 June: 'Return to the Scene of the
Crime', Rotary Youth Photography Project
To 3 August: Max Dupain in Albury
1 June – 8 July: 'Constructed Realms:
Photography as Theatre', Albury National
Photography Prize
15 June – 15 July: 'Paper Animals', Anne
Bennett, Euan Heng, Heather Shimmen,
Carolyn Lewens, Neil Stanyer and more
From 6 July: 'Size Matters' – Kidspace
13 July – 19 August: 'Murray Cod: the
Biggest Fish in the River'
20 July – 19 August: Stephen Anderson
From 24 August: Heidi Lefebre; 'Heaven on
Earth: Dream On'.
Mon–Fri 10.30–5, Sat–Sun 10.30–4
Free admission

Annandale Galleries
110 Trafalgar Street, Annandale 2038
Tel 02 9552 1699
Fax 02 9552 1689
info@annandalegalleries.com.au
www.annandalegalleries.com.au
Directors: Bill and Anne Gregory
Australian and international contemporary
art and modern masters. Specialists in
Aboriginal bark paintings and sculpture
from Arnhem Land. 240 metres of space in
three galleries.
Tues–Sat 11–5

Art & Australia Project Space
11 Cecil Street, Paddington 2021
Tel 02 9331 4455
Fax 02 9331 4577
info@artandaustralia.com.au
www.artandaustralia.com.au
The Art & Australia Project Space exhibits
the work of artists selected for RIPE, the
ANZ Private Bank / Art & Australia
Contemporary Art Award for emerging
professional artists. Administered by NAVA,
RIPE is a unique initiative that features
emerging artists on the back cover of
Art & Australia. The selected artists:
Del Kathryn Barton, Nick Mangan, Astra
Howard, Amanda Marburg, Selina Ou,
Jonathan Jones, Christian de Vietri, James
Lynch, Michelle Ussher, Rob McHaffie,
Louisa Dawson and Giles Ryder.
By appointment

Artarmon Galleries
479 Pacific Highway, Artarmon
P.O. Box 62, Artarmon 1570
Tel 02 9427 0322
www.artarmongalleries.com.au
Director: Philip Brackenreg
Recapture the wonder of the world in fine
art viewing presented in major exhibition
continuing for the estate of Joshua Smith
(1905–1995) with Yve Close in June, the
Australian Watercolour Institute Member
in July and Bruce Herps and Judith Ryrie
in August.
Mon–Fri 10–5, Saturdays 11–3, closed
public holidays

Artbank –
national contemporary art rental
Free call 1800 251 651
www.artbank.gov.au
Artbank supports visual artists and
craftspeople by the acquisition of their
work, while stimulating a wider
appreciation of Australian contemporary
art. Artbank offers competitive and tax
deductible rental rates for businesses.
With a collection comprising over 9000
significant works of all sizes, in a broad
variety of styles and media, Artbank is
Australia's largest and most prominent
collection for rental, offering flexibility for
annual change over. Showrooms are
located in Sydney, Melbourne and Perth,
visits by appointment.

**Australian Galleries,
Painting & Sculpture**
15 Roylston Street, Paddington 2021
Tel 02 9360 5177 Fax 02 9360 2361
enquiries@australiangalleries.com.au
www.australiangalleries.com.au
Director: Stuart Purves
Monthly exhibitions of contemporary
Australian painting and sculpture by artist
represented by Australian Galleries.
Mon–Sat 10–6

**Australian Galleries,
Works on Paper**
24 Glenmore Road, Paddington 2021
Tel 02 9380 8744
Fax 02 9380 8755
enquiries@australiangalleries.com.au
www.australiangalleries.com.au
Director: Stuart Purves
Monthly exhibitions of contemporary
Australian works on paper by artists
represented by Australian Galleries.
Mon–Sat 10–6, Sun 12–5

Bandigan Art
39 Queen Street, Woollahra 2025
Tel 02 9328 4194
Fax 02 9326 1259
info@bandigan.com
www.bandigan.com
Directors: Suzanne Lowe
and John Colquhoun
Monthly exhibitions of contemporary
Aboriginal paintings, sculptures, fibre
works and ceramics.
Tues–Fri 10–6, Sat–Sun 11–4

Banziger Hulme Fine Art Consultants
Level 1, 51–53 The Corso, Manly 2095
Tel 02 9977 0700
Fax 02 9977 0690
banziger.hulme@ozemail.com.au
www.faceofasia.com.au
Directors: David Hulme
and Brigitte Banziger
Specialising in international and local
art brokerage, free initial consultation
on purchase and sale of Australian
and international art.
By appointment

Bega Valley Regional Gallery
Zingel Place, Bega 2550
Tel 02 6499 2187
rcameron@begavalley.nsw.gov.au
www.begavalley.nsw.gov.au
Director: Ross Cameron
Changing exhibitions featuring individual
artists and groups from the local area,
plus travelling exhibitions from around
Australia. Artist enquiries welcome.
Tues–Fri 10–4, Sat 9–12

Berkeley Editions
Suite 2, 202 Jersey Road, Woollahra 2025
Tel 02 9328 5288
Fax 02 9328 5277
info@berkeleyeditions.com.au
www.berkeleyeditions.com.au
Publishers of fine art limited editions.
Representing: Jason Benjamin, Charles
Blackman, Arthur Boyd, David Boyd,
Fred Cress, Ray Crooke, Melissa Egan,
Frank Hodgkinson, Colin Lanceley, David
Larwill, Helen Norton, Margaret Olley,
Martin Sharp, Garry Shead and Salvatore
Zofrea. Regular printmaker information
evenings are held at the gallery. Phone
or see website for details.
Tues–Sat 11–4, or by appointment

Bonhams & Goodman
7 Anderson Street, Double Bay 2080
Tel 02 9327 9900 / 1800 099 310
Fax 02 9327 2917
info.aus@bonhams.com
www.bonhamsandgoodman.com.au
Chief Executive Officer: Tim D. Goodman
National Head of Art: Geoffrey Smith
Fine art auctioneers and valuers
specialising in Australian, international
and Aboriginal Art, fine jewellery, furniture
and decorative arts, collector cars and
other collectables.
Mon–Fri 9–5, weekends as advertised

Boutwell Draper Gallery
82–84 George Street, Redfern 2016
Tel 02 9310 5662
Fax 02 9310 5851
info@boutwelldraper.com.au
www.boutwelldraper.com.au
Directors: Susan Boutwell
and James Draper
Contemporary Art – Australian,
international and Aboriginal. Painting,
sculpture, photography, ceramics, video,
installation, holograms and performance.
Wed–Sat 11–5

Boyd Fine Art
Struggletown Fine Arts Complex
Sharman Close, Harrington Park 2567
Tel 02 4648 2424
Fax 02 4647 1911
mboyd@localnet.com.au
Gallery complex including award-winning
restaurant. Monthly exhibition program.
Wed–Sun 10–5

Brenda Colahan Fine Art
P.O. Box 523, Paddington 2021
Tel 02 9328 3137
Mobile 0414 377 227
BrendaColahan@bigpond.com
Member of Art Consulting
Association of Australia
Specialising in the procurement and
resale of modern and contemporary
fine art, investment advice, appraisal
and valuation. Artist representation:
BCFA artists regularly exhibit at Barrack
Gallery, Art Equity L6/16–20 Barrack
Street, Sydney.

Brenda May Gallery
2 Danks Street, Waterloo 2017
Tel 02 9318 1122
www.2danksstreet.com.au
Formerly Access Contemporary Art
Gallery. Currently representing Robert
Boynes, Jim Croke, Sybil Curtis, James
Guppy, Melinda Le Guay, Barbara Licha,
Angela Macdougall, Carol Murphy,
Lezlie Tilley, Peter Tilley and Hadyn Wilson.
To June 23: Barbara Licha, painting,
sculpture; Catriona Stanton, sculpture,
assemblage.
26 June – 14 July: 'I'm as mad as hell ...',
curated group show
17 July – 11 August: Carla Priivald, painting,
prints; Andrew Best, sculpture
From 14 August: Leslie Oliver, sculpture;
Helen Mueller, sculpture, prints.
Tue–Fri 11–6, Sat 10–6

Christopher Day Gallery
cnr Elizabeth and Windsor streets,
Paddington 2021
Tel 02 9326 1952
Fax 02 9327 5826
Mobile 0418 403 928
cdaygallery@bigpond.com.au
www.cdaygallery.com.au
Quality traditional and modern masters
for sale. Sole agent in New South Wales
for Graeme Townsend. Works normally
in stock include Beauvais, Blackman,
Dobell, Forrest, Heysen, Johnson,
Knight, Lindsay, Nedela, Olsen,
Rees and Streeton.
Mon–Sat 11–6, or by appointment

Conny Dietzschold Gallery
Sydney/Cologne
2 Danks Street, Waterloo 2017
Tel 02 9690 0215
Fax 02 9690 0216
info@conny-dietzschold.de
www.conny-dietzschold.de
International contemporary art including
painting, sculpture, installation,
photography, video and new media,
focusing on new tendencies in conceptual,
concrete and constructive art.
Tues–Sat 11–6

Cooks Hill Galleries
67 Bull Street, Newcastle 2300
Tel 02 4926 3899
Fax 02 4926 5529
mail@cookshill.com
www.cookshill.com
Representing Arthur Boyd, Sidney Nolan,
Fred Williams, Charles Blackman, John
Olsen, John Perceval, Russell Drysdale,
Norman Lindsay, Brett Whiteley, Tom
Roberts, Arthur Streeton, Frederick
McCubbin, Ray Crooke, Jeffrey Smart
and Charles Conder.
Fri, Sat and Mon 11–6, Sun 2–6, or
by appointment

Defiance Gallery
47 Enmore Road, Newtown 2042
Tel 02 9557 8483
Fax 02 9557 8485
crswann@bigpond.net.au
www.defiancegallery.com
Director: Campbell Robertson-Swann,
Manager: Lauren Harvey
Sculpture and painting from established
and emerging Australian artists.
Representing: Angus Adameitis, Tim Allen,
Tom Arthur, Blaze Blazeski, Janik
Bouchette, Grace Burzese, Pamela Cowper,
Rachel Douglass, Mark Draper, Rachel
Fairfax, Ivor Fabok, Peter Godwin, Ulvi
Haagensen, Madeleine Halliday, Nigel
Harrison, Debra Headley, Paul Hopmeier,
David Horton, Geoff Ireland, Jennifer
Johnson, Ian McKay, Brian Koerber, Anita
Larkin, Michael Le Grand, Russell McQuilty,
Tony Phillips, Campbell Robertson-Swann,
Tony Slater, Phillip Spelman, David Teer,
Willemina Villari, Jennifer Watson, Cathy
Weiszmann and David Wilson. Please see
website for further information on
individual artists and upcoming exhibitions.
Wed–Sat 11–5

Deutscher~Menzies Pty Ltd
Fine Art Auctioneers and Valuers
12 Todman Avenue, Kensington 2033
Tel 02 8344 5404
Fax 02 8344 5410
sydney@deutschermenzies.com
www.deutschermenzies.com
Managing Director: Adrian Newstead
The leading Australian owned art
auctioneers and valuers.
13 June: Major Fine Art Auction, Sydney.
Mon–Fri 9–5.30

Eva Breuer Art Dealer
83 Moncur Street, Woollahra 2025
Tel 02 9362 0297
Fax 02 9362 0318
art@evabreuerartdealer.com.au
www.evabreuerartdealer.com.au
Director: Eva Breuer
Eva Breuer Art Dealer specialises in buying
and selling museum quality Australian
paintings and works on paper by traditional,
modern and contemporary Australian
artists, such as Sidney Nolan, Arthur Boyd,
John Olsen, Brett Whiteley, Garry Shead,
William Robinson, James Gleeson,
Fred Williams, Ray Crooke, Kevin Connor,
Donald Friend, David Boyd, Brian Dunlop,
Margaret Olley and many more.
Tues–Fri 10–6, Sat 10–5, Sun 1–5

**Galeria Aniela Fine Art
and Sculpture Park**
261A Mount Scanzi Road,
Kangaroo Valley 2577
Tel 02 4465 1494
aniela01@bigpond.com
www.galeriaaniela.com.au
High quality art from leading Australian,
Aboriginal and international artists
including Boyd, Perceval, Blackman, Olsen,
Crooke, Dunlop, Billy Stockman, Petyarre,
Napangardi. Purpose-designed gallery, set
against the backdrop of the magnificent
Kangaroo Valley escarpment on three
hectares of sculptured park. Only two
hours drive south of Sydney, but a world
away from the mainstream of commercial
galleries and the busy city.
Fri–Sun 11–4, or by appointment

Gallery Barry Keldoulis
2 Danks Street, Waterloo 2017
Tel 02 8399 1240
barry@gbk.com.au
www.gbk.com.au
Director: Barry Keldoulis
Very contemporary with a focus on the
best of the emerging generation.
Tues–Sat 11–6

Gallery Gondwana Australia
43 Todd Mall, Alice Springs 0870
Tel 08 8953 1577
Fax 08 8953 2441
alice@gallerygondwana.com.au
www.gallerygondwana.com.au
Director: Roslyn Premont Lali
Representing the best in Aboriginal fine art,
Australian design and arts from the Pacific
region. Established in 1990, the gallery
works exclusively with internationally
acclaimed artists and sources works from
Indigenous artists and communities.
Mon–Sat 9.30–6, or by appointment

Gitte Weise Gallery – Berlin
Linienstrasse 154
Berlin 10115
Germany
Tel 49 (0) 30 280 451 64
Fax 49 (0) 30 308 746 88
mail@gitteweisegallery.com
www.gitteweisegallery.com

Goulburn Regional Art Gallery
Civic Centre, cnr Bourke and Church
streets, Goulburn 2580
Tel 02 4823 4443
Fax 02 4823 4456
artgallery@goulburn.nsw.gov.au
www.goulburn.nsw.gov.au
Exhibitions and public programs cover a
broad range of art and craft media with a
focus on contemporary regional practice.
Mon–Fri 10–5, Saturdays and public
holidays 1–4, or by appointment

Grafton Regional Gallery
158 Fitzroy Street, Grafton 2460
Tel 02 6642 3177
Fax 02 6643 2663
mail@graftongallery.nsw.gov.au
www.graftongallery.nsw.gov.au
Director: Jude McBean
To 1 July: 'The Blake Prize for Religious Art',
was established in 1949 as an incentive to
raise the standard of contemporary
religious art and named after artist and
poet, William Blake. The prize is a unique
and exciting cultural icon, controversy and
debate keep it dynamic and contemporary;
'ArtExpress', the art-making component of
the NSW Higher School Certificate
examination in Visual Arts, 2006; 'Barry
Ridgeway: My Mother's Dream', paintings
exploring the history the Donovans,
members of the Dunghutti tribe of
Kempsey; 'The Cathedral School', artworks
by students from the Clarence Valley
Anglican School
4 July – 12 August: 'Racing', Louise Mann
'as eye see it'; 'Very Real North Coast'; 2007
NPWS Indigenous Art Prize; Digby Moran;
Grafton Art Club.
Tues–Sun 10–4

GRANTPIRRIE
86 George Street, Redfern 2016
Tel 02 9699 9033
Fax 02 9698 8943
info@grantpirrie.com
www.grantpirrie.com
Directors: Stephen Grant and Bridget Pirrie
Contemporary Australian, Indigenous and
international artists. Representing: Peter
Adsett, Lionel Bawden, Lyndell Brown and
Charles Green, Maria Fernanda Cardoso,
Todd Hunter, Alex Kershaw, Todd McMillan,
Selina Ou, Patrick Pound, Ben Quilty,
Caroline Rothwell, Tim Silver, Judy Watson,
Judith Wright and Koen Wastjin.
Representing artists in association with
Warlayirti Arts, Mornington Island Art
Centre and Maningrida Arts and Crafts.
Tues–Fri 11–6, Sat 11–5

Groundfloor Gallery
383 Darling Street, Balmain 2041
Tel 02 9555 6102 Fax 02 9555 6104
info@groundfloorgallery.com
www.groundfloorgallery.com
Director: Jeannette Mascolo
Representing a diverse range of
contemporary visual art, sculpture and
photography by leading Australian and
international artists.
Wed–Fri 11–5, Sat–Sun 12–5

Hardware Gallery
263 Enmore Road, Enmore 2042
02 9550 4595
www.hardwaregallery.com.au
Exhibiting contemporary Australian
paintings and fine art etchings.
Representing: Nicholas Fintan, Ray Firth,
Keith Looby, Rodney Monk, Josonia
Palaitis, Sandi Rigby.
Tues–Sat 11–5

Harris Courtin Gallery
26 Glenmore Road, Paddington 2021
Tel 02 9368 7950
Fax 02 9368 7943
art@harriscourtingallery.com.au
www.harriscourtingallery.com.au
Contemporary original works by emerging
and mid-career Australian artists.
Gallery 1:
5–30 June: Works on paper: Vanessa
Ashcroft, Denis Clarke, Robyn Kinsela,
Sylvia McEwan and Shiela White
3–28 July: Ghasan Saaid (solo)
From 7 August: Barbara Hilder (solo)
Gallery 2:
Changing monthly group exhibitions by
gallery artists.
Tues–Sun 10–6

Harrington Street Gallery
17 Meagher Street, Chippendale 2008
Tel/Fax 02 9319 7378
Artists' cooperative established in 1973.
A new exhibition is mounted every three
weeks throughout the year from February
to December.
Tues–Sun 10–4

Hazelhurst Regional Gallery & Arts Centre
782 Kingsway, Gymea 2227
Tel 02 8536 5700
Fax 02 8536 5750
hazelhurst@ssc.nsw.gov.au
www.hazelhurst.com.au
Director: Michael Rolfe
A major public and community gallery
with changing exhibitions, comprehensive
arts centre, theatrette, gallery shop and
terrace café.
Daily 10–5, closed Good Friday, Christmas
Day and Boxing Day

Hogarth Galleries Aboriginal Art Centre
7 Walker Lane, Paddington 2021
Tel 02 9360 6839
Fax 02 9360 7069
info@hogarthgalleries.com
www.aboriginalartcentres.com
Director: Melissa Collins
First and foremost Aboriginal art gallery
representing Australia's emerging and
established artists and their communities.
Tues–Sat 10–5

Ivan Dougherty Gallery
UNSW College of Fine Arts
Selwyn Street, Paddington 2021
Tel 02 9385 0726 Fax 02 9385 0603
idg@unsw.edu.au
www.cofa.unsw.edu.au/galleries/idg/news
Ivan Dougherty Gallery mounts
approximately ten exhibitions each year,
focusing on twentieth century and
contemporary Australian and international
art of all disciplines.
5–21 July: 'Connections', an exhibition to
coincide with 'ConnectEd', the
International Conference on Design
Education Sydney 2007
26 July – 25 August: 'Echoes of Home:
Memory and Mobility', the art practices of
fourteen Australian-based Asian artists
and craft-makers utilise traditional
techniques to tell their stories about
everything from the Australian landscape
to Asian medicine
From 30 August: 'Papunya Tjupi: A New
Beginning', an exhibition of new work from
emerging artists and established senior
Papunya artists, Michael Jagamara Nelson
and Long Jack Phillipus Tjakamarra, from
the new Papunya Tjupi Art Centre.
Mon–Sat 10–5, closed Sundays and public
holidays

John Gordon Gallery
360 Harbour Drive, Coffs Harbour 2450
Tel 02 6651 4499 Fax 02 6651 1933
info@johngordongallery.com
www.johngordongallery.com
Director: Nicholas Kachel
Contemporary Australian and Aboriginal
art. Sourcing fine Aboriginal art from
Papunya Tula, Watiyawanu, Warmun,
Balgo, Maningrida and Tiwi Islands.
Mon–Fri 9–5, Sat 9–4, Sundays by
appointment

The Ken Done Gallery
1 Hickson Road, The Rocks, Sydney 2000
Tel 02 9247 2740 Fax 02 9251 4884
gallery@done.com.au
www.done.com.au
A vibrant space in The Rocks precinct, with
exhibitions by Australian artist Ken Done,
featuring Sydney Harbour, the beach, reef
and outback. Recent original works on
canvas and paper, limited-edition prints
and posters, bookshop and art related
products.
Daily 10–5.30, closed Christmas Day only

King Street Gallery
613 King Street, Newtown 2042
Tel/Fax 02 9519 0402
kingst@bigpond.net
www.kingstreetgallery.com.au
Viewing of larger-scale works
by gallery artists.
By appointment

King Street Gallery on Burton
102 Burton Street, Darlinghurst 2010
Tel 02 9360 9727
Fax 02 9331 4458
kingst@bigpond.com
www.kingstreetgallery.com.au
Representing: John Bokor, Andrew
Christofides, Elisabeth Cummings, Robert
Eadie, Rachel Ellis, Gail English, David
Floyd (estate), Salvatore Gerardi, Jon
Gintzler, Hardy and Strong, Frank Hinder
(estate), Robert Hirschmann, James Jones,
Ian King, Martin King, Idris Murphy,
Amanda Penrose Hart, Jenny Sages,
Wendy Sharpe, Kim Spooner, Kensuke
Todo, John Turier and John Elliott.
Extensive stockroom selection. Approved
valuer for the Cultural Gifts Program. ACGA
member.
Tues–Sat 11–6

Legge Gallery
183 Regent Street, Redfern 2016
Tel 02 9319 3340
Fax 02 9319 6821
enquiries@leggegallery.com
www.leggegallery.com
Representing: Susan Andrews, Paul Bacon,
John Bartley, Robert Cleworth, Lachlan
Dibden, Brian Doar, Neil Evans, Fiona Fell,
Vivienne Ferguson, Joe Frost, Rew Hanks,
Steve Harrison, David Hawkes, Catherine
Hearse, Bruce Howlett, Annette Iggulden,
Alan Jones, Madeline Kidd, Bryan King,
Steve Kirby, Pat Larter, Richard Lewer,
Peter Liiri, Emma Lohmann, Tony
McDonald, Shelagh Morgan, Glenn Murray,
Derek O'Connor, Kathryn Orton, Peggy
Randall, James Rogers, Kerry Russell, Evan
Salmon, John Smith and Beryl Wood.
Tues–Sat 11–6

Libby Edwards Galleries
47 Queen Street, Woollahra 2025
Tel 02 9362 9444
Fax 02 9362 9088
syd@libbyedwardsgalleries.com
www.libbyedwardsgalleries.com
Monthly exhibitions of paintings, works on
paper and sculpture by contemporary
Australian artists.
Mon–Sat 10.30–5.30, Sat 11–5, Sun 1–5

Liverpool Street Gallery
243a Liverpool Street, East Sydney 2010
Tel 02 8353 7799
Fax 02 8353 7798
info@liverpoolstgallery.com.au
www.liverpoolstgallery.com.au
Directors: James Erskine
and William Nuttall
Representing Rick Amor, Tony Bevan (UK),
Enrique Martinez Celaya (USA), Gunter
Christmann, Kevin Connor, Steven Harvey,
Anwen Keeling, David Keeling, John Kelly,
Jennifer Lee (UK), Kevin Lincoln, David
Serisier, Peter Sharp, Aida Tomescu, Kate
Turner, Dick Watkins, Karl Wiebke and
Magdalena Wozniak.
Tues–Sat 10–6

Maitland Regional Art Gallery
230 High Street, Maitland 2320
Tel 02 4934 9859 Fax 02 4933 1657
artgallery@maitland.nsw.gov.au
www.mrag.org.au
Maitland Regional Art Gallery (MRAG)
hosts a vibrant calendar of ever-changing
exhibitions promoting visual arts and craft
in the region. From the gallery shop you
can purchase unique gifts of original art for
your family, friends or even yourself.
29 June – 5 August: 'Wanderlust', Liz
Jeneid and Alexander Arcus
From 11 August: 'Circus', Joe Furlonger
along with Egg Face, a quirky collection of
children clown faces.
Tues–Sun 10–5, closed Mondays and
public holidays

Manly Art Gallery and Museum
West Esplanade (next to Oceanworld)
P.O. Box 82, Manly 1655
Tel 02 9976 1420 Fax 02 9948 6938
artgallery@manly.nsw.gov.au
www.manly.nsw.gov.au
Director: Therese Kenyon
To 24 June: 'Pamela Thalben-Ball:
A colourful life', a retrospective celebrating
Thalben-Ball's career; Ruth Downes
'FREE LUNCH – Lunch for the trades',
celebrating the often neglected work of
the trades while playing with the language
of modern cuisine
29 June – 29 July: NSW Indigenous Art
Prize, a selection of works from Indigenous
artists from around New South Wales;
Peter Elliston 'Volcano', photographs about
people and the volcanic landscape
From 3 August: 'Celebration', Australian
Ceramics Association presents an
exhibition of ceramics used in
commemoration of important events,
including functional, non-functional and
installation work – curated by Prue
Venables; Peter Battaglene 'Deep Blue',
ceramics resulting from a recent residency
at the CSIRO laboratory in Hobart.
Tues–Sun 10–5

**Marlene Antico Fine Arts
& The Paddington Art Prize**
P.O. Box 1469
Double Bay, NSW 1360
Tel 02 9362 0282
Mobile 0418 167 135
info@paddingtonartprize.com.au
The PADDINGTON ART PRIZE 2007 –
a $20,000 acquisitive prize is awarded
annually for a contemporary painting
inspired by the Australian landscape. This
prize is made possible by the patronage
of Marlene Antico. Congratulations to
John Beard, winner of the Paddington
Art Prize in 2006, and to Rob Bartolo
and Suey McEnnally, joint winners of the
People's Choice Award 2006. To have
your name added to the mailing list, please
contact us at info@paddingtonartprize.com.au
For updated exhibition listings for
Marlene Antico Fine Arts please visit
www.marleneantico.com.au

Martin Browne Fine Art
57–59 Macleay Street, Potts Point 2011
Tel 02 9331 7997
Fax 02 9331 7050
mbfayellowhouse@ozemail.com.au
www.martinbrownefineart.com
Director: Martin Browne
Specialising in contemporary Australian
and New Zealand art. Representing Tim
Maguire, Savanhdary Vongpoothorn,
McLean Edwards, Ildiko Kovacs, Roy
Jackson, Neil Frazer, Christine Johnson,
Paul Dibble, Michael Cusack, A. J. Taylor,
Karl Maughan, Simon Taylor, Linde Ivimey,
Kirsteen Pieterse, Alexander McKenzie and
the estate of Colin McCahon.
Tues–Sun 11–6

**Maunsell Wickes
at barry stern galleries**
19–21 Glenmore Road, Paddington 2021
Tel 02 9331 4676
Fax 02 9380 8485
mw_art@bigpond.net.au
www.maunsellwickes.com
Director: Dominic Maunsell
Specialising in contemporary Australian
painting, works on paper and sculpture.
Changing monthly exhibitions.
Tues–Sat 11–5.30, Sun 1–5

Michael Carr Art Dealer
124A Queen Street, Woollahra 2025
Tel 02 9327 3011
Fax 02 9327 3155
info@michaelcarr.net
www.michaelcarr.net
Sale and exhibition of international
and Australian paintings and sculpture,
representing Ron Robertson-Swann,
Michael Taylor, Pat Harry, Judy Cassab,
Richard Allen, James McGrath, Tony Lloyd,
Stephen Haley and David Harley.
Tues–Fri 10–6, Sat 10–5

Michael Nagy Fine Art
53 Jersey Road, Woollahra 2025
Tel 02 9327 2966
Mobile 0410 661 014
michael@nagyfineart.com.au
www.nagyfineart.com.au
Michael Nagy Fine Art exhibits
contemporary Australian art and modern
Australian and international art.
Tues–Sat 11–6, Sun 12–5

Miles Gallery
Shop 17 Dural Mall, Kenthurst Road,
Round Corner, Dural 2158
Tel 02 9651 1688
sales@waynemilesgallery.com
www.waynemilesgallery.com
Directors: Kelly and Wayne Miles
Digital artworks of Wayne Miles, emerging
artists, Tim Storrier, Reinis Zusters, Robert
Dickerson, works on paper by Barbara
Bennett, Anne Smith, Judy Cassab and
Frank Hodgkinson.
Daily 9–5
Closed first Sunday of each month
and public holidays

Moree Plains Gallery
cnr Frome and Heber streets, Moree 2400
Tel 02 6757 3320
moreeplainsgallery@bigpond.com
www.moreeplainsgallery.org.au
Moree Plains Gallery is in north-western
New South Wales and presents travelling
and local exhibitions, including a
permanent display of Aboriginal artefacts
in the old bank vault.
Mon–Fri 10–5, Sat–Sun 10–2
Free admission

Museum of Contemporary Art
140 George Street, Circular Quay,
The Rocks, Sydney 2000
Tel 02 9245 2400
Fax 02 9252 4361
www.mca.com.au
The Museum of Contemporary
Art is Australia's only museum solely
dedicated to exhibiting, interpreting and
collecting contemporary art from Australia
and around the world. Opened in 1991
on spectacular Sydney harbour, the MCA
has developed a reputation as Australia's
foremost contemporary visual arts
institution.
To 3 June: 'Craigie Horsfield: Relation'
To 12 August: New Acquisitions 2007;
'The Art of Giving: Donations to the MCA
Collection';
From 21 June: 'The Hours: Visual Arts of
Contemporary Latin America'
1 June – 12 August: Matthew Ngui
From 24 August: Primavera 2007
From 30 August: Julie Rrap.
Open daily 10–5, closed Christmas Day
Free admission

Newcastle Region Art Gallery
1 Laman Street, Newcastle 2300
Tel 02 4974 5100
Fax 02 4974 5105
artgallery@ncc.nsw.gov.au
www.newcastle.nsw.gov.au/go/artgallery
The gallery exhibits over twenty-five
exhibitions annually, reflecting the diversity
of contemporary art practice and the
breadth of the gallery's significant
collection of Australian art and Japanese
and Australian ceramics.
Tues–Sun 10–5, closed Good Friday and
Christmas Day

New England Regional Art Museum
106–114 Kentucky Street, Armidale 2350
Tel 02 6772 5255
www.neram.com.au
Home of the Howard Hinton, Chandler
Coventry and NERAM collections along
with regularly changing exhibitions.
Facilities include six gallery spaces,
a café, museum shop, artists' studio,
public art space and an audiovisual
conference theatre.
Tues–Fri 10–5, Sat–Sun 9–4, closed
Mondays and public holidays
Museum of Printing Thurs–Fri 10.30–3.30
or by appointment

Nimbin Artists Gallery
49 Cullen Street, Nimbin 2480
Tel 02 6689 1444
Regular exhibitions featuring artists living
and working in and around Nimbin and the
North Coast. Artists include Christine
Robinson, Ian Pearson, Shirley Miller,
Magpie, Ruth Sutter, Lindsay Hunt and
many more. Paintings, sculpture, ceramics,
engraved glass, prints, jewellery, felt,
furniture and other art forms.
Daily 10–5

Nimbin Regional Gallery
81 Cullen Street, Nimbin 2480
Tel 02 6689 0041
Special exhibitions changing every two
to three weeks. Spectacular venue for
functions and exhibitions, for bookings
contact number above.
Daily 10–5

Peloton
19 and 25 Meagher Street,
Chippendale 2008
Tel 02 9351 1063 Mobile 0414 312 492
info@peloton.net.au
www.peloton.net.au
Directors: Matthys Gerber, Lisa Jones
and Giles Ryder
A program of exhibitions and exchange
projects of national and international
contemporary art and artists.
Wed–Sat 1–6

Rex Irwin Art Dealer
1st Floor, 38 Queen Street,
Woollahra 2025
Tel 02 9363 3212 Fax 02 9363 0556
brettballard@rexirwin.com
www.rexirwin.com
The gallery represents important Australian
and international artists as well as
emerging artists. A changing exhibition
program every three to four weeks and an
impressive stockroom viewable by
appointment.
Tues–Sat 11–5.30, or by appointment

Rex-Livingston Art Dealer
156 Commonwealth Street,
Surry Hills 2010
Tel 02 9280 4156 Fax 02 9280 4060
art@rex-livingston.com
www.rex-livingston.com
Director: David Rex-Livingston
Specialising in dealing museum quality
twentieth-century investment art and the
exhibition of emerging, mid-career and
senior artists.
Tues–Sat 11–5 or by appointment

Richard Martin Art
98 Holdsworth Street, Woollahra 2025
Tel 02 9327 6525
Fax 02 9327 6524
info@richardmartinart.com.au
www.richardmartinart.com.au
Director: Richard Martin
Regular exhibitions of paintings and
sculpture by prominent and emerging
contemporary Australian artists.
Also buying and selling quality
investment pieces.
Tues–Sat 11–6, Sun 1–5

Robin Gibson Gallery
278 Liverpool Street, Darlinghurst 2010
Tel 02 9331 6692
Fax 02 9331 1114
robin@robingibson.net
www.robingibson.net
Established and emerging artists,
Australian and international. Exhibitions
change monthly.
Tues–Sat 11–6

Roslyn Oxley9 Gallery
8 Soudan Lane (off Hampden Street)
Paddington 2021
Tel 02 9331 1919
Fax 02 9331 5609
oxley9@roslynoxley9.com.au
www.roslynoxley9.com.au
Australian and international contemporary
art. Representing James Angus, Hany
Armanious, Robyn Backen, Angela
Brennan, The Estate of Robert Campbell
Jnr, Tony Clark, Bill Culbert, Destiny
Deacon, John Firth-Smith, Dale Frank,
Jacqueline Fraser, The Estate of Rosalie
Gascoigne, Fiona Hall, Louise Hearman,
Bill Henson, Yayoi Kusama, Lindy Lee,
Linda Marrinon, Mandy Martin, Tracey
Moffatt, TV Moore, Callum Morton, Nell,
David Noonan, the Estate of Bronwyn
Oliver, Michael Parekowhai, Patricia
Piccinini, Julie Rrap, Vivienne Shark LeWitt,
Nike Savvas, Kathy Temin, Jenny Watson,
John Wolseley and Anne Zahalka.
Tues–Fri 10–6, Sat 11–6

Savill Galleries
156 Hargrave Street, Paddington 2021
Tel 02 9327 8311
Fax 02 9327 7981
enquiry@savill.com.au
www.savill.com.au
Director: Denis Savill
Exhibiting works for sale by leading
Australian Artists including Boyd,
Blackman, Crooke, Nolan, Dickerson,
Olsen, Shead, Smart, Robinson. Extensive
stockroom.
Mon–Fri 10–6, Sat 11–5, Sun 2–5 during
exhibitions

Sherman Galleries
16–20 Goodhope Street, Paddington 2021
Tel 02 9331 1112
Fax 02 9331 1051
info@shermangalleries.com.au
www.shermangalleries.com.au
Sherman Galleries hosts exhibitions
of contemporary art by leading Australian
and international artists.
1–23 June: Daniel Crooks
23 June – 21 July: Shane Cotton
19 July – 12 August: Michael Landy
From 17 August: Marion Borgelt.
Tues–Fri 10–6, Sat 11–6

S.H. Ervin Gallery
National Trust Centre
Watson Road, Observatory Hill
(off Argyle Street), The Rocks,
Sydney 2000
Tel 02 9258 0173
Fax 02 9251 4355
www.nsw.nationaltrust.org.au
One of Sydney's leading public art galleries,
S.H. Ervin presents an innovative and
diverse program of exhibitions exploring
historical and contemporary themes in
Australian art. Trust Café, Arts Bookshop,
Parking onsite.
To 17 June: Janet Dawson survey,
examining the career of one of Australia's
most accomplished artists from its genesis
in the 1950s through to the present day.
Spanning fifty years, the works range from
abstraction through realism to
expressionism
29 June – 12 August: 'From here to
Eternity', works from the Victorian
Tapestry Workshop. This exhibition
showcases those by Australia's leading
artists including Angela Brennan, Mike
Brown, Jon Cattapan, Alun Leach-Jones,
Reg Mombassa, Gareth Sansom and
Martin Sharp. The exhibition's title is
drawn from Martin Sharp's quintessentially
Sydney tapestry *Eternity*, his graphic
homage to Arthur Stace.
Tues–Sun 11–5, closed Mondays and
public holidays
$6, $4 National Trust members and
concessions

SOHO Galleries
104 Cathedral Street, Sydney 2011
Tel 02 9326 9066
Fax 02 9358 2939
art@sohogalleries.net
www.sohogalleries.net
Director: Nigel Messenger
Innovative contemporary art including
paintings, sculpture, glass and works on
paper by creative Australian artists.
Tues–Sun 12–6

Stills Gallery
36 Gosbell Street, Paddington NSW 2021
Tel 02 9331 7775
Fax 02 9331 1648
info@stillsgallery.com.au
www.stillsgallery.com.au
Contemporary Photomedia.
Representing: Brook Andrew, Narelle Autio,
Roger Ballen, Pat Brassington, Christine
Cornish, Brenda L. Croft, Sandy Edwards,
Merilyn Fairskye, Anne Ferran, Petrina
Hicks, Shayne Higson, Mark Kimber,
Steven Lojewski, Ricky Maynard, Anne
Noble, Polixeni Papapetrou, Trent Parke,
Bronwyn Rennex, Michael Riley, Glenn
Sloggett, Van Sowerwine, Robyn Stacey,
Danielle Thompson, Stephanie Valentin
and William Yang.
To 9 June: Van Sowerwine
13 June – 14 July: Mark Kimber,
Tim Georgeson and Caia Hagel
18 July – 18 August: Merilyn Fairskye
From 22 August: Magnum 60th
anniversary exhibition.
Tues–Sat 11–6

Sturt Gallery
Range Road, P.O. Box 34, Mittagong 2575
Tel 02 4860 2083
Fax 02 4860 2081
mpatey@sturt.nsw.edu.au
www.sturt.nsw.edu.au
Sturt Gallery offers the finest in Australian
contemporary craft and design. Monthly
exhibitions.
Sturt Café: Wed–Sun 10–4
Gallery: Daily 10–5

Sullivan+Strumpf Fine Art
44 Gurner Street, Paddington 2021
Tel 02 9331 8344
Fax 02 9331 8588
art@ssfa.com.au
www.ssfa.com.au
Directors: Ursula Sullivan
and Joanna Strumpf
Representing Sydney Ball, Penny Byrne,
Kristian Burford, Matt Calvert, Nick Devlin,
Marc de Jong, Sebastian Di Mauro, Juan
Ford, Helen Fuller, Therese Howard,
Sherrie Knipe, Joanna Lamb, Alasdair
MacIntyre, VR Morrison, Emily Portman,
Kate Shaw and Darren Sylvester.
Buying and selling contemporary art.
Tue–Fri 10–6, Sat 11–5, Sun 2–5, or by
appointment

Tamworth Regional Gallery
466 Peel Street, Tamworth 2340
Tel 02 6767 5459
gallery@tamworth.nsw.gov.au
Director: Elizabeth McIntosh
Presenting a changing exhibition program
over two galleries comprising touring and
regional exhibitions, permanent
collections, an art studio and gallery shop.
Tues–Sat 10–5, Sun 12–4

thirtyseven degrees
Contemporary Fine Art Gallery
1/2 Danks Street, Waterloo 2017
Tel 02 9698 4499
info@thirtyseven-degrees.com
www.thirtyseven-degrees.com
Director: Dominik Mersch
Focusing on well-established
contemporary artists from Europe's
German-speaking culture, as well as
established and upcoming contemporary
Australian artists.
14 June – 7 July: Caroline Rannersberger
12 July – 4 August: Tracy Cornish
From 16 August: Isidro Brasco,
Ronald & McDonnell, Stefan Mauck.
Tues–Sat 11–6

Tim Olsen Gallery
76 Paddington Street, Paddington 2021
Tel 02 9360 9854
Fax 02 9360 9672
tim@timolsengallery.com
www.timolsengallery.com
Specialising in contemporary Australian
painting and sculpture. Changing
exhibitions by gallery artists including
John Olsen, David Larwill, Philip Hunter,
Melinda Harper and Matthew Johnson.
Tues–Fri 11–6, Sat 11–5

Tim Olsen Gallery Annex
72a Windsor Street, Paddington 2021
Tel 02 9361 6205

Tim Olsen Gallery Queen St
80a Queen Street, Woollahra 2025
tim@timolsengallery
www.timolsengallery.com
Director: Tim Olsen
Tues–Sat 11–5

Trevor Victor Harvey Gallery
515 Sydney Road, Seaforth 2092
Tel 02 9907 0595
Fax 02 9907 0657
trevorharvey@tvhgallery.com.au
www.tvhgallery.com.au
Directors: Trevor and Skii Harvey
Notably eclectic exhibitions featuring a
monthly rotation of contemporary
paintings and sculpture with select pieces
from established and emerging Australian
and international artists.
Tues–Sat 11–6, Sun 12–5

Utopia Art Sydney
2 Danks Street, Waterloo 2017
Tel 02 9699 2900
Fax 02 9699 2988
utopiaartsydney@ozemail.com.au
Representing contemporary Australian
artists including John Bursill, Liz Coats,
Tony Coleing, Helen Eager, Marea Gazzard,
Christopher Hodges, Emily Kame
Kngwarreye, Peter Maloney, Makinti
Napanangka, Walangkura Napanangka,
Ningura Napurrula, Gloria Petyarre, Lorna
Napanangka, Angus Nivison, Kylie Stillman,
Ronnie Tjampitjinpa, Warlimpirrnga
Tjapaltjarri, George Tjungurrayi, George
Ward Tjungurrayi and John R Walker.
Utopia Art Sydney represents Papunya
Tula artists in Sydney.
Tues–Sat 10–5, or by appointment

UTS Gallery
University of Technology, Sydney
Level 4, 702 Harris Street, Ultimo 2007
Tel 02 9514 1652
Fax 02 9514 1228
utsgallery@uts.edu.au
www.utsgallery.uts.edu.au
Curator: Tania Creighton
UTS Gallery hosts a vibrant program of
monthly changing exhibitions featuring
local, national and international art and
design practice.
To 22 June: 'Shinmi Park: Changeability,
the Fashion Trace'
3 July – 3 August: 'The Trouble with the
Weather: A Southern Response', co-
curated by Jacqueline Bosscher, Norie
Newmark and Maria Miranda.
Mon–Fri 12–6

Wagner Art Gallery
39 Gurner Street, Paddington 2021
Tel 02 9360 6069
Fax 02 9361 5492
wagnerart@bigpond.com
www.wagnerartgallery.com.au
Directors: Shirley Wagner
and Nadine Wagner
Wagner Art Gallery has been synonymous
with great Australian art for the past
twenty-seven years and is recognised
mainly for representing the work
of the modern masters – the elite artists.
The gallery is also committed to the
established contemporary artists of the
twenty-first century along with focusing
on the talented but younger and less
exposed – the emerging artists. Monthly
exhibitions showcase the best of
contemporary Australian art and provide
a variety of options for collectors.
Mon–Sat 10.30–6, Sun 1–6

Wallspace Gallery
25-27 Brisbane Street, Surry Hills 2010
Tel: 02 9264 8649
mail@wallspacegallery.com.au
www.wallspacegallery.com.au
Director: Cathy Linsley
Representing and exhibiting established
and emerging artists, view website for
details, artists submissions welcome via
email, CDs, slides and photographs.
Tues–Sat 10–6

Watters Gallery
109 Riley Street, East Sydney 2010
Tel 02 9331 2556
Fax 02 9361 6871
info@wattersgallery.com
www.wattersgallery.com
Directors: Frank Watters, Alexandra
Legge, Geoffrey Legge
To 23 June: Margot Hutcheson, recent
paintings; Mostyn Bramley-Moore,
paintings
27 June – 21 July: Ian Howard and Xing
Jun Qin, mixed media
25 July – 18 August: Ruth Waller, paintings;
Roger Crawford, paintings
From 22 August: Maeve Woods, paintings;
Vicki Varvaressos: paintings.
Wed–Fri 10–7, Tuesdays and Saturdays 10–5

Western Plains Cultural Centre
Dubbo Regional Gallery
Museum and Community Arts Centre
76 Wingewarra Street, Dubbo 2830
Tel 02 6801 4431 Fax 02 6801 4449
gallery@dubbo.nsw.gov.au
www.dubbo.nsw.gov.au
Wed–Mon 10–4

Wollongong City Gallery
cnr Kembla and Burelli streets,
Wollongong East 2500
Tel 02 4228 7500
Fax 02 4226 5530
gallery@wollongong.nsw.gov.au
www.wollongongcitygallery.com
One of the largest regional art museums in
Australia, with a major collection of
contemporary Aboriginal, Asian and
Illawarra colonial art.
To 17 June: 'Michael Callaghan: A Survey
1967 – 2006', a Manly Art Gallery and
Museum touring exhibition; 'John Vucic-
Wolfpup: NPK Orchis'
To 1 July: 'Mark Tedeschi: Femininity and
Other Feelings'
16 June – 5 August: 'Tim Johnson and
Karma Phuntsok: The Luminescent Ground'
23 June – 29 July: 'Anita Larkin, 2006
Resident Artist: Object Incognito',
sculpture; 'Shift', gallery Mentor Program
for young artists
From 4 August: 'Andrew Christofides: A
Survey', paintings, prints, and
constructions spanning twenty-five years;
'Yang Xifa: Dawn Dream', paintings.
Tues–Fri 10–5, Sat–Sun and public holidays
12–4, closed Good Friday, Christmas Day,
Boxing Day and New Year's Day
Free admission

Yuill|Crowley
5th Floor, 4–14 Foster Street,
Surry Hills 2010
Tel 02 9211 6383
Fax 02 9211 0368
yuill_crowley@bigpond.com
Contemporary art.
Wed–Fri 11–6, Sat 11–4.30

ACT

ANU Drill Hall Gallery
Australian National University
Kingsley Street (off Barry Drive),
Acton 2601
Tel 02 6125 5832
Fax 02 6247 2595
dhg@anu.edu.au
http://info.anu.edu.au/mac/Drill_Hall_
Gallery/index.asp
Director: Nancy Sever
Providing link exhibitions developed
in conjunction with the university's
wide ranging academic interests
or to coincide with major conferences
and public events. National and
international exhibitions, and works
from the university's own extensive
collection.
To 24 June: 'Greg Johns: Patterns',
a retrospective of this South Australian
sculptor, surveying the 1970s to the
present
28 June – 5 August: 'Jan Senbergs,
A Singular Vision', works on paper
by Senbergs, whose imagery of our
urban habitat and industrial landscape
contributes to our understanding
of place – curated by Elisabeth Cross
From 9 August: 'ANU Creative Fellows,
Works of Sidney Nolan, Arthur Boyd and
Narritjin Maymuru', three significant
Australian artists awarded an ANU Creative
Arts Fellowship, focusing on the
connection between country and personal
creativity – curated by Mary Eagle.
Wed–Sun 12–5

Matthew Kyme, **Black & white
VI (Cindy)**, 2005, oil on canvas,
82 x 66 cm, courtesy Art Nomad,
Brighton.

Beaver Galleries
81 Denison Street, Deakin 2600
Tel 02 6282 5294
Fax 02 6281 1315
mail@beavergalleries.com.au
www.beavergalleries.com.au
Canberra's largest private gallery. Regular
exhibitions of contemporary paintings,
prints, sculpture, glass and ceramics by
established and emerging Australian
artists. Licensed café.
To 11 June: Meg Buchanan, paintings and
works on paper; Anita McIntyre 'Ancient
land – family lines', ceramics
14 June – 2 July: Marc Rambeau,
paintings and works on paper; Jenny
Orchard, ceramics
2–20 August: GW Bot, prints and paintings;
Nick Wirdnam, glass sculpture
From 23 August: Christine James,
paintings; Caitlin Perriman – drawings.
Daily 10–5

National Gallery of Australia
Parkes Place, Canberra 2600
Tel 02 6240 6502
Fax 02 6240 6561
information@nga.gov.au
www.nga.gov.au
The National Gallery of Australia collection
contains more than 100,000 works.
In 2007 the gallery celebrates its twenty-
fifth anniversary, with new displays of the
Asian art, international art and sculpture
collections.
From 29 June: 'George Lambert',
a retrospective exhibition of one of
Australia's most remarkable artists from
the Edwardian era, particularly notable
for his versatility in different media
To 14 October: 'VIPS: Very Important
Photographs from the European
American and Australian photography
collection', to mark the gallery's
twenty-fifth anniversary, a selection
of some 150 of the most beautiful and
significant works from Europe, America
and Australia will be on display.
Daily 10–5

National Portrait Gallery
Old Parliament House, King George
Terrace, Canberra 2600
Commonwealth Place, Canberra 2600
Tel 02 6270 8236
Fax 02 6270 8181
npg@dcita.gov.au
www.portrait.gov.au
'Giving a Face to the Nation': the National
Portrait Gallery aims to increase the
understanding of the Australian people –
their identity, history, creativity and
culture – through portraiture. There
is always something new to see at the
National Portrait Gallery with an ongoing
program of exhibitions at the gallery's
two exhibition spaces at Old Parliament
House and Commonwealth Place by
Lake Burley Griffin.
Old Parliament House
To 5 August: 'Reveries: Photography
and Mortality'
From 24 August: 'Portraits by John Brack'
Daily 9–5
Commonwealth Place
To 1 July: 'Australia's Creative Diaspora
Photographed by Nathalie Latham'
From 13 July. 'Studio: Australian Painters
and Creativity'.
Wed–Sun 10–5

Solander Gallery
10 Schlich Street, Yarralumla 2600
Tel 02 6285 2218
Fax 02 6282 5145
sales@solander.com.au
www.solander.com.au
Established 1974. Specialising in
collections and investment art. Continuing
exhibitions and in stock prominent and
emerging Australian contemporary artists:
Boyd, Cassab, P. Churcher, Coburn, Crooke,
Cullen, de Teliga, Dickerson, Firth-Smith,
Green, Griffen, Griffiths, Harris, Harry,
Hodgkinson, Jacks, Juniper, Kelly,
Kngwarreye, Leach-Jones, Larter, Larwill,
Lester, Leti, Looby, Lynn, Martin, McInnis,
Nolan, Olsen, Perceval (Celia), Proud,
Schlieper, Shead, Shearer, Sibley, Storrier,
Warren and Woodward.
15 March – 26 April: 'Robert Juniper,
New Works'.
Thurs–Sun 10–5

Victoria

Adam Galleries
1st Floor, 105 Queen Street
Melbourne 3000
Tel 03 9642 8677 Fax 03 9642 3266
nstott@bigpond.com
www.adamgalleries.com
Director: Noël Stott
Traditional to contemporary Australian
paintings, prints, drawings and sculpture.
Selected exhibitions of work by established
artists throughout the year.
Mon–Fri 10–5, Sat 11–4 during exhibitions,
or by appointment

Alcaston Gallery
11 Brunswick Street, Fitzroy 3065
Tel 03 9418 6444
Fax 03 9418 6499
art@alcastongallery.com.au
www.alcastongallery.com.au
Director: Beverly Knight
Exhibiting contemporary Indigenous art –
paintings, works on paper, sculpture,
limited edition prints and ceramics.
26 June – 21 July: Jukuna Mona Chuguna,
In conjunction with Mangkaja Arts
17–28 July: Alcaston Gallery @ Depot
Gallery, 2 Danks Street, Waterloo, Sydney:
Gulumbu Yunupingu, Larrakitj (memorial
poles) and bark paintings, in conjunction
with Buku Larrnggay Mulka Centre,
Yirrkala, Northern Territory
24 July – 18 August: John Bulunbulun,
Tommy Gondorra Steele and Fiona
Jin-Majinggal Mason, in conjunction
with Maningrida Arts and Culture,
Northern Territory
From 21 August: Bentinck Island Mob
and Netta Loogatha, in conjunction
with Mornington Island Arts and Craft,
Queensland.
Tues–Fri 10–6, Sat 11–5, or by appointment

Alison Kelly Gallery
10 Woodside Crescent, Toorak 3142
Tel 03 9824 2583
Mobile 0417 542 691
ak@alisonkellygallery.com
www.alisonkellygallery.com
Specialising in works from remote
communities in the Kimberley, Central and
Western Deserts, Arnhem Land and the
Tiwi Islands.
By appointment only

Anna Schwartz Gallery
185 Flinders Lane, Melbourne 3000
Tel 03 9654 6131
mail@annaschwartzgallery.com
www.annaschwartzgallery.com
Established 1982, Anna Schwartz
Gallery represents and exhibits leading
contemporary artists, and works with a
broad range of public and private
collectors.
Tues–Fri 12–6, Sat 1–5, groups by
appointment

Aranda Aboriginal Art
Hoddle Street, Collingwood 3066
Tel 03 9419 8225 Fax 03 9419 8227
Mobile 0412 55 22 95
Melbourne@arandaart.com
www.arandaart.com
Director: Adam Knight
Modern masters from an ancient culture.
Tues–Fri 10–6, Sat 11–5, and by
appointment

ARC One Gallery
45 Flinders Lane, Melbourne 3000
Tel 03 9650 0589 Fax 03 9650 0591
mail@arc1gallery.com
www.arc1gallery.com
Representing Pat Brassington, Lyndell
Brown and Charles Green, Peter Callas,
Maria Fernanda Cardoso, Karen Casey,
Rose Farrell and George Parkin, Sue Ford,
Adam Hill, Cherry Hood, Guo Jian, Janet
Laurence, Dani Marti, Ross Moore, Vanila
Netto, Robert Owen, David Ralph, Eugenia
Raskopoulos, Jacky Redgate, Julie Rrap,
Wilson Sheih, Phaptawan Suwannakudt,
Imants Tillers, Guan Wei, Gosia
Wlodarczak and Ann Zahalka.
Tues–Fri 11–5, Sat 11–4

Art Nomad
Brighton 3186
Tel 03 9598 5739 Fax 03 9598 8338
info@artnomad.com.au
www.artnomad.com.au
Art Nomad is a virtual art gallery and an
Australian fine art gallery with a
difference! Browse works by emerging,
important and collectable Australian
Artists online, make a selection and we'll
bring them to you for inspection. We stock
works by: Arkley, Audette, Beeton, Blabey,
Blackman, Boissevain, Boyd, Bromley,
Coburn, Connor, Crooke, Curtis, Dickerson,
Ferguson, Ferling, Fisher, Friend, Giardino,
Gleeson, Grigoriev, Hart, Heysen, Hinder,
Kelly, Kyme, Long, McClelland, Neil,
Newton, Nolan, Olsen, Onus, Pugh, Roche,
Sawrey, Streeton and Tucker.
Tues–Sun 10–6 or by appointment

Artistry Galleries
cnr High Street and Glenferrie Road,
Malvern 3144
Tel 03 9509 5599
Fax 03 9509 5799
info@artistrygalleries.com.au
www.artistrygalleries.com.au
Director: John Lagerwey
Buyers and sellers of fine art by Australian
artists, specialising in notable works by
David Boyd, Fred Williams and Pro Hart.
Tues–Sat 10–5, Sun 11–5

Arts Project Australia
24 High Street, Northcote 3070
Tel 03 9482 4484
Fax 03 9482 1852
info@artsproject.org.au
www.artsproject.org.au
Director: Lena Cirillo
Innovative studio and gallery with exciting
calendar of exhibitions and collection of
works featuring the 'outsider art' genre.
Mon–Fri 9–5, Sat 10–1, or by appointment

Australian Art Resources
77 City Road, Southbank 3006
Tel 03 9699 8600
Fax 03 9696 5096
info@artresources.com.au
www.artresources.com.au
Fine Art Consultancy specialising in
collection development and management.
Art Rental service. Visitors welcome to
view work by leading Australian artists.
Mon–Fri 9–6, Saturdays by appointment

**Australian Centre
for Contemporary Art**
111 Sturt Street, Southbank 3006
Tel 03 9697 9999
Fax 03 9686 8830
info@accaonline.org.au
www.accaonline.org.au
Executive Director: Kay Campbell
Artistic Director: Juliana Engberg
The Australian Centre for Contemporary
Art (ACCA) operates as a *kunsthalle*,
a temporary exhibitions space delivering
the very latest and best of Australian and
international artistic practice. Located
in a landmark rust-red monolith within
the new contemporary arts precinct in
Southbank, ACCA is Melbourne's premier
contemporary art space presenting a
changing program of exhibitions, events
and education programs. Please visit the
website for updated information about
exhibitions and other events.
Tue–Sun 11–6
Mon 10–5 by appointment only
Open public holidays except Christmas
Day and Good Friday
Free admission

**Australian Galleries,
Painting & Sculpture**
35 Derby Street, Collingwood 3066
Tel 03 9417 4303
Fax 03 9419 7769
enquiries@australiangalleries.com.au
www.australiangalleries.com.au
Director: Stuart Purves
Monthly exhibitions of contemporary
Australian painting and sculpture by artists
represented by Australian Galleries.
Mon–Sat 10–6, Sun 12–5

Australian Galleries, Works on Paper
50 Smith Street, Collingwood 3066
Tel 03 9417 0800
Fax 03 9417 0699
enquiries@australiangalleries.com.au
www.australiangalleries.com.au
Director: Stuart Purves
Monthly exhibitions of contemporary
Australian works on paper by artists
represented by Australian Galleries.
Mon–Sat 10–6, Sun 12–5

Australian Print Workshop
210 Gertrude Street, Fitzroy 3065
Tel 03 9419 5466
Fax 03 9417 5325
auspw@bigpond.com
www.australianprintworkshop.com
Director: Anne Virgo
Specialising in fine art limited-edition
prints by leading contemporary artists.
Regular exhibitions and a comprehensive
range of prints for sale.
Tues–Fri 10–5, Sat 12–5

Bonhams & Goodman
Level 1, 540 Malvern Road, Prahran 3181
Tel 03 9823 6270 / 1800 099 310
Fax 03 9826 3642
info.melb@bonhams.com
www.bonhamsandgoodman.com.au
Chief Executive Officer: Tim D. Goodman
National Head of Art: Geoffrey Smith
Fine art auctioneers and valuers
specialising in Australian, international
and Aboriginal Art, fine jewellery, furniture
and decorative arts, collector cars and
other collectables.
Mon–Fri 9–5, weekends as advertised

Boscia Galleries
Level 4, 175 Flinders Lane, Melbourne 3000
Tel 03 9639 0399
Director: Michele Boscia
art@bosciagalleries.com
www.bosciagalleries.com
Representing leading Aboriginal artists.
Specialist consultants to investors and
collectors.
Exhibitions held monthly.
Tues–Sat 11–4 or by appointment,
closed January

Bridget McDonnell Gallery
130 Faraday Street, Carlton 3053
Tel 03 9347 1700
Fax 03 9347 3314
bridget@bridgetmcdonnellgallery.com.au
www.bridgetmcdonnellgallery.com.au
Established 1983. Specialising in
nineteenth and twentieth century
Australian and European paintings,
drawings and prints; also featuring works
from St Petersburg 1940 to 1990.
Tues–Fri 10–5, Sat 12–5, Sun 12–5
during exhibitions only

Brightspace
Level 1, 8 Martin Street, St Kilda 3182
Tel 03 9593 9366
bright@brightspace.com.au
www.brightspace.com.au
Directors: Kantor, Greer, Hefner and Owen
To 10 June: RMIT Masters exhibition
14 June – 8 July: Ricky Howell
and Winter Salon
12 July – 5 August: 'A Survey and
Installation', David Waters
21 July – 12 August: 'Rascals from
Ramingining', Bula'bula Arts.
Wed–Sat 12–6, Sundays 1–5

**BVR Arts Management
and Online Gallery**
P.O. Box 3226
Prahan East 3181
Tel 03 9530 3472 / 0409 409 239
ebvr@bvram.com
www.brvam.com
Art advisory, research, curatorial services
for private and corporate collections,
management and marketing for artists and
galleries, online exhibitions and stockroom,
showroom visits welcome by appointment.

Charles Nodrum Gallery
267 Church Street, Richmond 3121
Tel 03 9427 0140
Fax 03 9428 7350
gallery@charlesnodrumgallery.com.au
www.charlesnodrumgallery.com.au
Exhibiting and dealing in a broad range of
modern and contemporary Australian and
international paintings, works on paper
and sculpture for corporate and private
collectors.
Tues–Sat 11–6

Ricky Howell, **Thanks for
the memories, 2007**, gouache
on canvas paper, 16.5 x 13 cm,
courtesy Brightspace, Melbourne.

Christine Abrahams Gallery
27 Gipps Street, Richmond 3121
Tel 03 9428 6099
Fax 03 9428 0809
art@christineabrahamsgallery.com.au
www.christineabrahamsgallery.com.au
Director: Guy Abrahams, ACGA member
Associate Director: Kelli Hulyer
Contemporary Australian paintings and
works on paper, prints, sculpture, ceramics,
photography and glass.
Tues–Fri 10.30–5, Sat 11–5

Christopher Rimmer Gallery
Level 1, 407 Hampton Street, Hampton 3188
Tel 03 9533 4090
Fax 03 9521 9270
chris@roccointeriors.com.au
www.christopherrimmergallery.com
Director: Christopher Rimmer
Blackman, Boyd, French, Whiteley, Hart,
Olsen, Coburn and Nolan in the stockroom
plus regular exhibitions by emerging
artists. Proposals always welcome.
Mon–Sat 10–5

**Contemporary Art Australia
& Associates**
Joan Gough Studio Gallery
328 Punt Road, South Yarra 3141
Tel 03 9866 1956 / 03 9867 2939 /
03 9866 8283
www.panetix.com/caa
Founded in 1989 by Joan Gough, five past
presidents and twenty members of the
Contemporary Art Society, CAA is now in
its seventeenth year. Represented by
Jennifer Tegel in the USA, Anthony
Syndicas in France, Ronald Greenaway, art
consultant in Victoria. CAA is a non-profit
association of artists who wish to explore
the modern and commercial aspects of
contemporary expression and present day
practices in art. Group activities from 8 pm,
the first Monday of every month.
Discussions on evolving works, solo and
group exhibitions on application. Quarterly
newsletter, prize exhibition, workshops,
study groups and interstate tours arranged.
Subscription $60.

**C.A.S. Contemporary
Art Society of Victoria Inc.**
P.O. Box 283, Richmond 3121
Tel 03 9428 0568
Mobile 0407 059 194
mail@contemporaryartsociety.org.au
www.contemporaryartsociety.org.au
Founded 1938 (Bell & Reed), C.A.S. is an
incorporated non-profit art organisation
run by an elected committee of artists, for
artists, with membership across Australia.
10–22 September: C.A.S. Inc. Annual
Exhibition 2007, Eckersley's Open Space
Gallery, 97 Franklin St, Melbourne, Mon–
Fri 9–6, Sat 10–4, Sun 12–3.
C.A.S. holds two major exhibitions
annually, free solo exhibitions of members'
works at Richmond and Fitzroy library
spaces, and changing group exhibitions at
MoorWood contemporary furniture
showrooms, also guided gallery walks and
other social events.
Visit our website: view works and images
from our recent exhibitions, 'Contemporary
by Nature' at The Gallery on Herring Island,
and 'The Collectors' Exhibition 2007' at
Steps Gallery, plus over 150 artworks from
over 100 artists.
Bi-monthly newsletter. Members receive
discounts at several major art suppliers.
Membership $50.

Counihan Gallery in Brunswick
233 Sydney Road, Brunswick 3056
(next to Brunswick Town Hall)
Tel 03 9389 8622
Fax 03 9387 4048
counihangallery@moreland.vic.gov.au
www.moreland.vic.gov.au
Curator: Edwina Bartlem
To view the Counihan Gallery in
Brunswick's 2007 exhibition program,
please visit:
www.moreland.vic.gov.au/services/arts-fr.htm
Wed–Sat 11–5, Sun 1–5,
closed public holidays

Deutscher~Menzies Pty Ltd
Fine Art Auctioneers and Valuers
1140 Malvern Road, Malvern 3144
Tel 03 9822 1911
Fax 03 9822 1322
artauctions@deutschermenzies.com
www.deutschermenzies.com
Senior Executive: John Keats
Chairman: Rodney Menzies
The leading Australian owned art
auctioneers and valuers.
13 June: Major Fine Art Auction, Sydney.
Mon–Fri 9–5.30

Dickerson Gallery
2A Waltham Street, Richmond 3121
Tel 03 9429 1569
Fax 03 9429 9415
melbourne@dickersongallery.com.au
www.dickersongallery.com.au
Director: Stephan Nall
Specialising in original works by Australia's
most collectable young, mid-career and
senior artists. Monthly exhibition
programme and diverse stockroom.
Tues–Sat 11–6, Sun 12–5

Faculty Gallery
Art and Design Building
Monash Art and Design
900 Dandenong Road, Caulfield East 3145
Tel 03 9903 2882
Fax 03 9903 2845
gallery@artdes.monash.edu.au
www.artdes.monash.edu.au/gallery
Director: Lisa Byrne
The Faculty Gallery showcases a diverse
range of exhibitions, addressing the local,
national and international visual arts and
design scenes.
Mon–Fri 10–5, Sat 1–4, closed Sundays
and public holidays
Free admission

Flinders Lane Gallery
137 Flinders Lane, Melbourne 3000
Tel 03 9654 3332
Fax 03 9650 8508
info@flg.com.au
www.flg.com.au
Director: Claire Harris
Fine Australian contemporary art. Also
featuring important Aboriginal paintings.
Extensive stockroom. Exhibitions every
three weeks. Art consultants. Established
since 1990.
Tues–Fri 11–6, Sat 11–4

Gallery Gabrielle Pizzi
Level 3, 75–77 Flinders Lane,
Melbourne 3000
Tel 03 9654 2944
Fax 03 9650 7087
gallery@gabriellepizzi.com.au
www.gabriellepizzi.com.au
Director: Samantha Pizzi
Representing contemporary Australian
Aboriginal artists since 1983: Papunya
Tula Artists, Warlayirti Artists, Utopia,
Aurukun, Ikuntji Fine Art, Maningrida Arts
and Culture, Bula'bula Arts, Tiwi Islands,
as well as artists H. J. Wedge, Michael
Riley, Brook Andrew, Julie Gough,
Christian Thompson, Leah King-Smith and
Lorraine Connelly-Northey. ACGA Member
To 23 June: Christian Thompson, new work
26 June – 21 July: 'Balgo 2007', group
exhibition in association with Warlayirti
Artists
24 July – 25 August: 'New Directions',
sculpture by the artists from Aurukun;
Leah King-Smith, new work
From 28 August: 'Rising Stars 2007'
in association with Papunya Tula Artists.
Tues–Fri 10–5.30, Sat 11–4

Geelong Gallery
Little Malop Street, Geelong 3220
Tel 03 5229 3645
Fax 03 5221 64411
geelart@geelonggallery.org.au
www.geelonggallery.org.au
Geelong Gallery's outstanding collection
of paintings, sculpture and decorative
arts spans the art of Australia, from
the colonial period to the present day,
including the Frederick McCubbin
masterpiece, *A bush burial*.
Mon–Fri 10–5, Sat–Sun and
public holidays 1–5
Free admission

Greythorn Galleries
462 Toorak Road, Toorak 3142
Tel 03 9826 8637
Fax 03 9826 8657
art@greythorngalleries.com.au
www.greythorngalleries.com.au
Specialising and promoting Australian
artists for investment and enjoyment,
advice to young collectors, with over
thirty years experience in the Australian
art market.
Mon–Fri 10–5.30, Sat 10–5, Sun 2–5
during exhibitions

Hamilton Art Gallery
107 Brown Street, Hamilton 3300
Tel 03 5573 0460
Fax 03 5571 1017
hamiltongallery@sthgrampians.vic.gov.au
www.hamiltongallery.org
Outstanding historic and contemporary
collections of silver, porcelain, glass,
oriental ceramics, paintings and prints,
including Australian art, and a collection
of eighteenth century landscapes by
Paul Sandby, 'The Father of English
watercolour'.
Mon–Fri 10–5, Sat 10–12, 2–5, Sun 2–5

Helen Gory Galerie
25 St Edmonds Road, Prahran 3181
Tel 03 9525 2808
Fax 03 9525 2633
gallery@helengory.com
www.helengory.com
Director: Helen Gory
Helen Gory Galerie, established in
1995, is a contemporary fine art gallery
dedicated to the promotion of artists,
providing quality art to established and
emerging collectors. The gallery
continues to be renowned for sourcing
and promoting new Australian artists.
Tues–Sat 11–6

Ian Banksmith Online
Tel 03 9572 2411
Fax 03 9572 2037
mail@ianbanksmith.com
www.ianbanksmith.com
Representing one of Australia's
foremost contemporary artists.
Featuring paintings in oil and acrylic.
ebsite updated regularly.
Melbourne studio viewing by appointment

ICON Museum of Art
Deakin University
221 Burwood Highway, Burwood 3125
Tel 03 9244 5344
Fax 03 9244 5254
oningtonstables@deakin.edu.au
www.deakin.edu.au/artmuseum
Acting Manager: Victor Griss
The ICON Museum of Art at Deakin
University's Melbourne Campus at
Burwood has been designed and situated
to provide great accessibility for students,
staff and the general public. As the hub of
a contemporary arts precinct, Icon
provides substantial space and facilities for
professionally curated exhibitions drawn
from the university's art collection, group
and solo exhibitions by significant
contemporary artists, travelling exhibitions
and selected student work.
Tues–Fri 12–5, Sat 1–5

Indigenart
The Mossenson Galleries
67 Grattan Street, Carlton 3053
Tel 03 9663 4825
Fax 03 9663 4826
Mobile 0412 422 378
indigenartcarlton@iinet.net.au
www.indigenart.com.au
Director: Diane Mossenson
Exhibiting works on canvas, paper
and bark, sculptures, ceramics and
craft produced by leading and emerging
Aboriginal artists from communities
across Australia.
ACGA member.
Thurs–Fri 12–6, Sat–Sun 12–5 and by
appointment

James Makin Gallery
916 High Street, Armadale 3143
Tel 03 9509 5032
Fax 03 9509 5043
info@jamesmakingallery.com
www.jamesmakingallery.com
Tues–Fri 10–5.30, Sat 11–5

John Buckley Gallery
8 Albert Street,
Richmond 3121
Tel 03 9428 8554
Fax 03 9428 8939
gallery@johnbuckley.com.au
www.johnbuckley.com.au
Exhibiting and dealing in modern and
contemporary Australian art for the last
twenty-five years, John Buckley also
consults and advises private and corporate
clients and curates exhibitions in his new
premises in Richmond.
Wed–Sat 12–6

Joshua McClelland Print Room
2nd Floor, 15 Collins Street,
Melbourne 3000
Tel/Fax 03 9654 5835
joshmcclelland@bigpond.com.au
Director: Joan McClelland
Contemporary printmakers.
Early Australian topographical
prints, etchings, linocuts etc.
Natural history prints. Asian art.
Mon–Fri 10–5

Lauraine Diggins Fine Art
5 Malakoff Street, North Caulfield 3161
Tel 03 9509 9855
Fax 03 9509 4549
ausart@diggins.com.au
www.diggins.com.au
Director: Lauraine Diggins
Specialising in Australian colonial,
impressionist, modern, contemporary
and Indigenous painting, sculpture
and decorative arts. Established 1975,
a selection of works is available for
viewing in Melbourne with a number of
exhibitions annually.
Mon–Fri 10–6, Sat 1–5, or by appointment

Libby Edwards Galleries
1046 High Street, Armadale 3143
Tel 03 9509 8292
Fax 03 9509 4696
melb@libbyedwardsgalleries.com
www.libbyedwardsgalleries.com
Monthly exhibitions of paintings, works
on paper and sculpture by contemporary
Australian artists.
Mon–Fri 10–5, Sat–Sun 11–5

Manningham Gallery
699 Doncaster Road, Doncaster 3108
Tel 03 9840 9142
Fax 03 9840 9366
gallery@manningham.vic.gov.au
www.manningham.vic.gov.au
Director: Greg Cleave
The City of Manningham's major
contemporary arts venue, Manningham
Gallery presents a diverse program of
commercial, community-based and
curated monthly exhibitions.
Tues–Fri 11–5, Saturdays 2–5

McClelland Gallery + Sculpture Park
390 McClelland Drive, Langwarrin 3910
Tel 03 9789 1671
Fax 03 9789 1610
info@mcclellandgallery.com
www.mcclellandgallery.com
Director: Robert Lindsay
Set in 16 hectares of wonderful Australian
native gardens, only a one hour drive from
Melbourne, the McClelland Gallery +
Sculpture Park houses an excellent collection
of paintings, works on paper and an
extensive collection of works by leading
Australian sculptors. The home of the 2007
McClelland Contemporary Sculpture Survey
and Award, the gallery presents a vibrant
program of exhibitions, lectures, holiday
programs and guided tours. The McClelland
Gallery Café is available for special
functions, weddings and corporate events.
Tues–Sun 10–5
Café now open Tues–Sun 10–5,
bookings essential
Entry by donation

Melaleuca Gallery
121 Great Ocean Road, Anglesea 3230
Tel 03 5263 1230
Fax 03 5263 2077
slsmith@melaleuca.com.au
www.melaleuca.com.au
Contemporary Australian paintings and
sculpture by leading and emerging artists.
Sat–Sun 11–5.30, or by appointment

**Melbourne Society of
Women Painters and Sculptors Inc**
Ola Cohn Centre, 41–43 Gipps Street
East Melbourne 3002
mswps@yahoo.com.au
http://home.vicnet.net.au/~mswps
Committee: Joan Richard, President;
Helen Carter, Hon Secretary;
Carmel Mahony, Hon Treasurer
Founded 1902. Portrait sessions, life
drawing, general meetings, lectures and
activities. Annual Prize Exhibition.
Membership by application.
Meets Thursdays 10–3

Metro 5 Gallery
1214 High Street, Armadale 3143
Tel 03 9500 8511 Fax 03 9500 8599
info@metro5gallery.com.au
www.metro5gallery.com.au
Manager: Andrea Candiani
Art Consultant: Eliza Roberts
Representing established and emerging
artists: John Olsen, Tim Storrier, Jason
Benjamin, Zhong Chen, Wendy Stavrianos,
Yvette Swan, Yvonne Audette, David Laity,
Tanya Hoddinott, Sharon Green, Mina
Young, Locu Locu, Anthony Lister, Jasper
Knight, Michael Peck, Mari Hirata, Emma
Langridge, Chris Booth, Kate Stevens,
Hazel Dooney, Samuel Leach and Daniel
Truscott.
6 June – 1 July: Jason Benjamin and
Stephen Danzig
4–29 July: Emma Langridge
1–26 August: Sharon Green.
Tues–Fri 10–5.30, Sat–Sun 11–5

Monash Gallery of Art
860 Ferntree Gully Road,
Wheelers Hill 3150
Tel 03 9562 1569
mga@monash.vic.gov.au
www.mga.org.au
Director: Jane Scott
Gallery, gift shop, licensed café and
sculpture park. One of Australia's leading
public galleries, MGA presents diverse
and constantly changing exhibitions
in a wide range of media.
Tues–Fri 10–5, Sat–Sun 12–5

**Monash University
Museum of Art (MUMA)**
Building 55, Clayton Campus
Monash University 3800
Tel 03 9905 4217 Fax 03 9905 4345
muma@adm.monash.edu.au
www.monash.edu.au/muma
Monash University Museum of Art offers a
unique perspective on the recent history of
contemporary art and culture, and is
adventurous, with a forward outlook into
the production, research and exposure of
new art and ideas. Exhibitions range from
newly commissioned projects to surveys
of significant contemporary artists, from
Australia and elsewhere. The Monash
University Collection represents a leading
overview of Australian art since 1961.
Tues–Fri 10–5, Sat 2–5, closed between
exhibitions
Free admission, parking available

Mossgreen Gallery
102–108 Toorak Road, South Yarra 3141
Tel 03 9820 8958
Fax 03 9820 9253
mail@mossgreen.com.au
www.mossgreen.com.au
Directors: Paul Sumner
and Amanda Swanson
Mossgreen Gallery represents emerging
artists and also specialises in the sale and
re-sale of Australian Art: modern,
contemporary and early Aboriginal.
Tues–Fri 10–5.30, Sat 11–5, Sun 11–5
during exhibitions only

**National Gallery of Victoria
The Ian Potter Centre: NGV Australia**
Federation Square
cnr Russell and Flinders streets,
Melbourne 3000
Tel 03 8620 2222
www.ngv.vic.gov.au
The home of Australian art.
To 3 June: 'Top Arts: VCE 2006'
To 8 July: Australian Impressionism
To 19 August: Kitty Kantilla
To 13 January 2008: 'Katie Pye: Clothes for
Modern Lovers'
From 21 July: Geoffrey Bartlett.
Tues–Sun 10–5

National Gallery of Victoria International
180 St Kilda Road, Melbourne 3000
Tel 03 8620 2222
www.ngv.vic.gov.au
A whole world of art.
To 8 July: 'Sneakers: Classics to Customs'
To 9 September: 'Golden Screens'
To 30 September: 'Imaginary Prisons:
G.B. Piranesi and Vik Muniz'
To 29 July: 'Video Resurrection', works
by Vito Acconci, Peter Campus and
Joan Jonas
To 22 December: 'Great Exhibitions!
The World Fairs 1851–1937'
To 30 September: 'Small Worlds', travel
photography of the nineteenth century
From 30 June: 'Melbourne Winter
Masterpieces 2007', 'Guggenheim
Collection: 1940s to Now', New York-
Venice-Bilbao-Berlin
From 22 August: 'Super-Bodies'.
Wed–Mon 10–5

Nellie Castan Gallery
Level 1, 12 River Street, South Yarra 3141
Tel 03 9804 7366
Fax 03 9804 7367
mail@nelliecastangallery.com
www.nelliecastangallery.com
Representing emerging and prominent
contemporary Australian artists working
in the mediums of painting, photography
and sculpture.
Tues–Sun 12–5, or by appointment

Niagara Galleries
245 Punt Road, Richmond 3121
Tel 03 9429 3666
Fax 03 9428 3571
mail@niagara-galleries.com.au
www.niagara-galleries.com.au
Directors: William Nuttall and
Annette Reeves
Niagara Galleries is committed to the
exhibition and sale of the finest modern
and contemporary Australian art. Offering
one of the most extensive stockrooms in
Melbourne, William Nuttall and his staff
can advise on all aspects of creating a
rewarding art collection. William Nuttall
is an approved valuer under the Cultural
Gifts Program.
To 30 June: Helen Maudsley,
Noel McKenna
3–28 July: Gunter Christmann,
Samuel Namunjdja
From 31 July: David Keeling, Helen Wright.
Tues 11–8, Wed–Sat 11–6

Pollock Gallery
270 Church Street, Richmond 3121
Tel 03 9427 0003
Mobile 0401 256 992
carolepollock@bigpond.com
www.pollockgallery.com.au
Director: Carole and Barry Pollock
Representing fine contemporary Australian
artists whose unique and exciting works
reflect outstanding skills, professional
status and serious commitment to their art.
Tue–Sat 11–6, Sun 12–5, or by appointment

Port Art Gallery
384 Bay Street, Port Melbourne 3207
Tel 0409 432 643
info@portart.com.au
www.portart.com.au
Director: Jennifer Anne Webb
A unique, artist-run organisation. Featuring
a stockroom and changing exhibitions
every two to four weeks. Buy direct from
emerging and established artists in the
extensive Port Art network.
Wed–Sun 11–5

Port Jackson Press Print Room
59–61 Smith Street, Fitzroy 3065
Tel 03 9419 8988
Fax 03 9419 0017
info@portjacksonpress.com.au
www.portjacksonpress.com.au
To 17 June: Sophia Szilagyi, 'Somewhere
in the night', recent prints.
2–26 August: Jeffrey Makin, recent prints.
Tues–Fri 10–5.30, Sat 11–5, Sun 12–5

RMIT Gallery
RMIT Storey Hall, 344 Swanston Street,
Melbourne 3000
Tel 03 9925 1717
Fax 03 9925 1738
rmit.gallery@rmit.edu.au
www.rmit.edu.au/rmitgallery
Director: Suzanne Davies
Melbourne's most vibrant public art and
design gallery, presenting Australian and
international fashion, architecture, fine art,
craft, new media and technology.
Mon–Fri 11–5, Sat 2–5
Free admission

Savill Galleries
262 Toorak Road, South Yarra 3141
Tel 03 9827 8366
Fax 03 9827 7454
melbourne@savill.com.au
www.savill.com.au
Director: Denis Savill
Exhibiting works for sale by leading
Australian artists including Boyd,
Blackman, Crooke, Nolan, Dickerson,
Olsen, Shead, Smart and Olley.
Extensive stockroom.
Mon–Fri 10–6, Sat 11–5,
Sun 2–5 during exhibitions

Skepsi on Swanston
670 Swanston Street, Carlton 3053
Tel 03 9348 2002
Fax 03 9348 1877
skepsi@iprimus.com.au
www.skepsisonswanston.com.au
Director: Anna Maas
Skepsi Gallery exhibits works by Australian
artists with an emphasis on Australian
ceramics, also showcasing paintings,
drawings, glass, sculpture and jewellery.
Tues–Fri 10.30–6, Sat 12–6 or by
appointment

Span Gallery
45 Flinders Lane, Melbourne 3000
Tel 03 9650 0589
Fax 03 9650 0591
span@vicnet.net.au
www.spangalleries.com.au
Two large galleries with constantly
changing exhibitions of Span artists and
contemporary art, design and architecture.
Tues–Fri 11–5, Sat 11–4

Sophie Gannon Gallery
2 Albert Street, Richmond 3121
Tel 02 9421 0857
Fax 02 9421 0859
info@sophiegannongallery.com.au
www.sophiegannongallery.com.au
Director: Sophie Gannon
Representing Michael Zavros, Judith
Wright, Selina Ou, John Nicholson and
Nicholas Harding. Extensive stockroom
including Ian Fairweather, Grace
Cossington-Smith and others.
Tues–Sat 11–5 and by appointment

Stonington S tables Museum of Art
Deakin University
336 Glenferrie Road, Malvern 3144
Tel 03 9244 5344
Fax 03 9244 5254
stoningtonstables@deakin.edu.au
www.deakin.edu.au/artmuseum
Acting Manager: Victor Griss
The Stonington Stables Museum of
Art is an innovative and flexible gallery
established by Deakin University in
the refurbished Stonington Mansion
stables complex. It features exhibitions
of significant artworks by established,
professional artists, for the pleasure and
education of the University and the broader
community. The museum provides a focus
for current scholarship, research and
professional practice.
Tues–Fri 12–5, Sat 1–5

Sutton Gallery
254 Brunswick Street, Fitzroy 3065
Tel 03 9416 0727
Fax 03 9416 0731
art@suttongallery.com.au
www.suttongallery.com.au
Directors: Irene Sutton
and Phoebe Dougall
Australian contemporary art.
To 9 June: Eugene Carchesio
14 June – 7 July: Jane Trengove (large
gallery); Brett Colquhoun (small gallery)
12 July – 11August: Helga Groves
From 16 August: Helen Johnson.
Tue–Sat 11–5

Swan Hill Regional Art Gallery
Horseshoe Bend, Swan Hill 3585
Tel 03 5036 2430
Fax 03 5036 2465
artgal@swanhill.vic.gov.au
www.swanhill.vic.gov.au/gallery
Director: Ian Tully
A thriving public gallery with a dynamic,
varied program of exhibitions and events.
Recognised as a leading centre for
naive art.
Tues–Fri 10–5, Sat–Sun 11–5

TarraWarra Museum of Art
311 Healesville–Yarra Glen Road,
Healesville 3777
Tel 03 5957 3100
Fax 03 5957 3120
museum@twma.com.au
www.twma.com.au
Set in the scenic Yarra Valley, TarraWarra
Museum of Art (TWMA) exhibits works
from the TWMA collection of Australian
art from the 1950s to present, alongside
contemporary art exhibitions. The building
designed by Allan Powell, complements
both the exhibited artworks and the
stunning landscape in which the museum
is set. Contact the museum for current
exhibition programme.
Admission $5 (pensioners, students and
unemployed free)
Tues–Sun 11–5

Thierry B Gallery
531A High Street, Prahran East 3181
Tel 03 9525 0071
Mobile 0413 675 466
thierryb8@hotmail.com
www.thierrybgallery.com
Thierry B represents: Diane Dwyer, Lauren
Filippini, Raphael Zimmerman, Thierry B,
James Robertson, Marc Savoia, Tanya
Kingston, Patricia Heaslip, Margaret Marks
Steve Rosendale, Raymond Kelsey,
Mahmoud Zein Elabdin, Peter Daverington
Sarah Leslie, Bernd Kerkin, Jacquelyn
Stephens, Matthew Hooper, Barbara
Carmichael, Suzanna Lang and Liz Cuming
Tues–Sat 11–5, or by appointment

Über Gallery
52 Fitzroy Street, St Kilda 3182
Tel 03 8598 9915
Fax 03 8598 9914
info@ubergallery.com
www.ubergallery.com
Director: Anna Pappas
Über represents a diverse selection of
established and emerging international and
local artists in all contemporary mediums.
To 1 July: New works, Danie Mellor
(Australia), drawing and sculpture
4 July – 14 August: New works, Johnnie
Dady (Australia), painting and sculpture
From 15 August: New works, Jennyfer
Stratman (Australia/ USA), sculpture
Tues–Fri 10–6, Sat–Sun 12–6

Victorian Tapestry Workshop
262–266 Park Street,
South Melbourne 3205
Tel 03 9699 7885
Fax 03 9696 3151
contact@victapestry.com.au
www.victapestry.com.au
Director: Susie Shears
Changing exhibitions of contemporary
tapestries by Australian and international
artists, displayed in a studio setting with
public viewings of works in progress.
Bookings for tours essential.
Mon–Fri 9–5

Wangaratta Exhibitions Gallery
56–60 Ovens Street, Wangaratta 3676
Tel 03 5722 0865
Fax 03 5722 2969
l.mangan@wangaratta.vic.gov.au
www.wangaratta.vic.gov.au
Director: Dianne Mangan
The Wangaratta Exhibitions Gallery
presents a relevant, diverse and changing
visual arts program consisting of national,
state and regional exhibitions, including
local artists, urban artists and touring
exhibitions.
Mon–Tues 12–5, Wed–Fri 10–5, Sat–Sun 1–4

William Mora Galleries
60 Tanner Street, Richmond 3121
Tel 03 9429 1199
Fax 03 9429 6833
mora@moragalleries.com.au
www.moragalleries.com.au
Contemporary Australian and Aboriginal
art. William Mora is an accredited valuer
under the Australian Cultural Gifts Program.
Tues–Fri 10–5.30, Sat 12–5

Without Pier Gallery
A/320 Bay Road, Cheltenham 3192
enquiries@withoutpier.com.au
www.withoutpier.com.au
Director: Terry Earle
Contemporary Aboriginal and Australian
paintings, sculpture and glass. Monthly
exhibitions.
Mon–Sat 11–5, Sun 2–5

South Australia

Adelaide Central Gallery
45 Osmond Terrace, Norwood 5067
Tel 08 8364 2809
Fax 08 8364 4865
acsa@acsa.sa.edu.au
www.acsa.sa.edu.au
Specialising in new works from emerging
and mid-career artists, monthly exhibitions
and stockroom. Exclusive dealer for Pro
Hart in South Australia.
Mon–Fri 9–5, Sat 11–4
Mon–Thurs 9–7 during school term

Art Gallery of South Australia
North Terrace, Adelaide 5000
Tel 08 8207 7000
Fax 08 8207 7070
www.artgallery.sa.gov.au
To 1 July: 'Egyptian Antiquities
from the Louvre'
From 17 July: 'Freestyle: New
Australian Design for Living'
From 27 July: 'Grace Crowley:
Being Modern'.
Daily 10–5, bookshop and art
gallery restaurant daily 10–4.45
Free guided tours daily 11 am and 2 pm
Free admission, charges may apply to
special exhibitions

BMGArt
31–33 North Street, Adelaide 5000
Tel 08 8231 4440
Fax 08 8231 4494
bmgart@bigpond.net.au
www.bmgart.com.au
Monthly exhibitions by leading
contemporary Australian artists. Sculpture,
paintings, graphics and photography.
Tues–Sat 11–5, or by appointment

DACOU Aboriginal Gallery
63 Grand Junction Road, Rosewater 5013
Tel 08 8447 8244
Fax 08 8447 8566
Mobile 0403 324 684
Director: Fred Torres
Gallery Manager: Tate Burford
dacou@dacou.com.au
www.dacou.com.au
Continuous exhibition of fine Utopia art
including work by Barbara Weir, Gloria
Petyarre, Minnie, Emily, Molly and Galya
Pwerle, Emily Kngwarreye and many more.
After-hours appointments are welcome
and can be organised by phoning
0403 324 684.
Tues–Fri 10–6, Sat 11–4

Flinders University City Gallery
State Library of South Australia
North Terrace, Adelaide 5000
Tel 08 8207 7055
Fax 08 8207 7056
city.gallery@flinders.edu.au
www.flinders.edu.au/artmuseum
Director: Gail Greenwood
Flinders University City Gallery conducts
a program of changing exhibitions with an
emphasis on contemporary Indigenous art.
Mon–Fri 11–4, Sat–Sun 1–4

Gallerie Australis
Lower Forecourt Plaza
Hyatt Regency
North Terrace, Adelaide 5000
Tel 08 8231 4111
Fax 08 8231 6616
mail@gallerieaustralis
www.gallerieaustralis.com
Director: David Cossey
Discover the art and culture of Aboriginal
Australia, representing Kathleen Petyarre,
www.kathleenpetyarre.com and Abie Loy,
www.abieloy.com
Mon–Fri 10–6 or by appointment

Greenaway Art Gallery
39 Rundle Street, Kent Town 5067
Tel 08 8362 6354
Fax 08 8362 0890
gag@greenaway.com.au
www.greenaway.com.au
Director: Paul Greenaway
Monthly exhibitions. Artists represented
include Andrew, Bennett, Bezor, Cullen,
Hennessey, Hood, McKenna, Nikou,
Paauwe, Shead, Siwes, Smart, Tillers,
Valamanesh and Watson.
Tues–Sun 11–6

Greenhill Galleries Adelaide
140 Barton Terrace West,
North Adelaide 5006
Tel 08 8267 2933
Fax 08 8239 0148
greenhill@internode.on.net
www.greenhillgalleriesadelaide.com.au
Monthly exhibitions featuring the work
of leading Australian artists, including
paintings, prints, sculpture, ceramics
and jewellery.
Tues–Fri 10–5, Sat–Sun 2–5

Hill Smith Gallery
113 Pirie Street, Adelaide 5000
Tel 08 8223 6558
Fax 08 8227 0678
gallery@hillsmithfineart.com.au
www.hillsmithfineart.com.au
Director: Sam Hill-Smith
Hill Smith Gallery features solo and group
exhibitions by established and emerging
artists from South Australia and interstate.
Mon–Fri 10–5.30, Sun 2–5

Kensington Gallery
39 Kensington Road, Norwood 5067
Tel 08 8332 5752 Fax 08 8332 5066
e.kengall@kern.com.au
www.kensingtongallery.com.au
Interesting exhibitions each month by
leading Australian artists. Agents for
Barbara Hanrahan, John Dowie, Jim Kinch
and Jörg Schmeisser. Specialising in South
Australian women.
Tues–Fri 11–5, Sat–Sun 2–5

Peter Walker Fine Art
101 Walkerville Terrace, Walkerville 5081
Tel 08 8344 4607
info@peterwalker.com.au
www.peterwalker.com.au
Specialising in rare Australian and
international art.
Thurs–Sat 11–5, or by appointment

Port Pirie Regional Art Gallery
3 Mary Elie Street, Port Pirie 5540
Tel 08 8633 0681
Fax 08 8633 8799
portpirieregionalgallery@westnet.com.au
www.pprag.org
Enjoy a changing exhibition program of
Australian visual art and craft with an
emphasis on contemporary regional South
Australian artists. Visit our website for
further information.
Mon–Fri 9–5, Sat 9–4,
Sundays and public holidays 10–4

Western Australia

Artitja Fine Art
P.O. Box 406
South Fremantle 6162
Tel 08 9336 7787
Fax 08 93366901
info@artitja.com.au
www.artitja.com.au
Directors: Anna Kanaris and Arthur Clarke
Artitja Fine Art specialises in high quality
Indigenous fine art from the Central and
Western deserts. Exclusive representation
Western Australia: Julie Nangala Robinson.
By appointment

Bunbury Regional Art Galleries
64 Wittenoom Street, Bunbury 6230
Tel 08 9721 8616
Fax 08 9721 7423
mail@brag.org.au
www.brag.org.au
Situated in the heart of the city in a
distinctive pink former convent, Bunbury
Regional Art Galleries hosts the City of
Bunbury art collection and runs an
extensive program of regional and touring
exhibitions, professional development
workshops and cultural events.
Daily 10–4
Free admission

Galerie Düsseldorf
9 Glyde Street, Mosman Park 6012
Tel/Fax 08 9384 0890
gd@galeriedusseldorf.com.au
www.galeriedusseldorf.com.au
Directors: Magda and Douglas Sheerer
Contemporary Australian Art. Established
1976. New gallery built 1995. Representing
the Estates of Howard H. Taylor and David
Watt.
Wed–Fri 11–5, Sun 2–5, and by
appointment

Goddard de Fiddes Gallery
31 Malcolm St, West Perth 6005
Tel 08 9324 2460 Fax 08 9226 1353
gdef@goddarddefiddes.com.au
www.goddarddefiddes.com.au
Directors: Julian Goddard
and Glenda de Fiddes
Exhibiting contemporary international art,
education programmes, short courses on
understanding contemporary art, investing
in art and advice on collecting art.
Wed–Fri 12–6, Sat 2–5, or by appointment

Greenhill Galleries
37 King Street, Perth 6000
Tel 08 9321 2369 Fax 08 9321 2360
info@greenhillgalleries.com
www.greenhillgalleries.com
Greenhill Galleries represents a diverse
range of leading Australian artists,
including Jason Benjamin, Peter Boggs,
Richard Dunlop, Juli Haas, David Larwill,
Matthew Johnson, Ray Crooke, Euan Heng,
Charles Blackman, Zhong Chen, Shaun
Atkinson, Crispin Akerman, Mac Betts,
Wim Boissevain, Dean Bowen, Madeleine
Clear, Wayne Eager, Dieter Engler, Ian
Greig, Belynda Henry, Nigel Hewitt, Paul
Lacey, Alan Marshall, Leon Pericles, Keren
Seelander, Katarina Vesterberg and Jim
Thalassoudis. Government Approved
Valuers for the Australian Cultural Gifts
Program.
Mon–Fri 10–5, Sat 11–4

Gunyulgup Galleries
Gunyulgup Valley Drive, Yallingup 6282
Tel 08 9755 2177
Fax 08 9755 2258
enquiries@gunyulgupgalleries.com.au
www.gunyulgupgalleries.com.au
Directors: Nina and Ashley Jones
Located in the Margaret River wine region
since 1987. Exhibits fine art and craft by
emerging and established Western
Australian artists.
Daily 10–5

The Holmes à Court Gallery
1/11 Brown Street, East Perth 6004
Tel 08 9218 4540
Fax 08 9218 4545
HaCGallery@heytesbury.com.au
www.holmesacourtgallery.com.au
The gallery's focus is to examine the
diversity and strengths of the Holmes à
Court Collection, a significant collection of
Australian art.
Thurs–Sun 12–5, or by appointment,
closed public holidays

Indigenart
The Mossenson Galleries
115 Hay Street, Subiaco 6008
Tel 08 9388 2899
Fax 08 9381 1708
gallery@indigenart.com.au
www.indigenart.com.au
Director: Diane Mossenson
Exhibiting works on canvas, paper and
bark, sculptures, ceramics and craft
produced by leading and emerging
Aboriginal artists from communities across
Australia. ACGA member.
Mon–Sat 10–5

Indigenart
The Mossenson Galleries
82 High Street, Fremantle 6160
Tel 08 9335 2911
Fax 08 9335 2966
Mon–Sun 12–5

Japingka Gallery
47 High Street, Fremantle 6160
Tel 08 9335 8265
Fax 08 9335 8275
japingka@iinet.net.au
www.japingka.com.au
Directors: Ian Plunkett and David Wroth
Two floors, 400 square metres, extensive
stock room and a full exhibition
programme of established and emerging
Indigenous fine art.
Mon–Fri 9.30–5.30, Sat 10.30–5.30,
Sun 12–5

John Curtin Gallery
Curtin University of Technology
Building 200
Kent Street, Bentley 6102
Tel 08 9266 4155
Fax 08 9266 3878
gallery@curtin.edu.au
www.johncurtingallery.curtin.edu.au
22 June – 10 August: 'Pippin Drysdale:
Lines of Site', Drysdale seeks out places
that have a special character or resonance,
such as the Tanami Desert in the mid-north
of Western Australia. The delicate web of
glazes, etched into the surfaces of her
porcelain vessels, are rich in colour and
generous in their sweeping lines.
Monumental in their presence, they are
evocative of both the wide spaces and the
minute details of this particular part of
Australia.
Mon–Fri 12–5
Sundays 1–4 (24 June and 29 July only)

Johnston Gallery
20 Glyde Street, Mosman Park 6012
Tel 08 9385 0855
Fax 08 9385 0655
info@johnstongallery.com.au
www.johnstongallery.com.au
Director: Felicity Johnston
Representing established and emerging
contemporary Australian artists.
Tues–Sat 11–5, Sun 2–5

Lawrence Wilson Art Gallery
The University of Western Australia
35 Stirling Highway, Crawley 6009
Tel 08 6488 3707 Fax 08 6488 1017
info@LWgallery.uwa.edu.au
www.LWgallery.uwa.edu.au
Changing exhibitions of Western Australian
and Australian art, including works
from the UWA Art Collection, lectures
and floor talks.
Tues–Fri 11–5, Sun 12–5
Free admission

Linton & Kay Fine Art Gallery
299 Railway Road (cnr Nicholson Road),
Subiaco 6008
Tel 08 9388 3300 Fax 08 9388 2116
info@lintonandkay.com.au
www.lintonandkay.com.au
Directors: Linton Partington and Gary Kay
Exhibiting and representing a wide range
of leading regional and national artists.
Daily 10–5

Lister Gallery
316 Rokeby Road, Subiaco 6008
Tel 08 9382 8188 Fax 08 9382 8199
gallery@listercalder.com
www.listercalder.com
Director: Roshana Lewis
Exhibiting and dealing in leading modern
and contemporary Australian art.
Government Approved Valuer for the
Cultural Gifts Program.
Mon–Fri 10–5, Sun 2–5 during exhibitions

LK Galleries
123 Hay Street, Subiaco 6008
Tel 08 9388 0067
Fax 08 9388 0032
info@lkgalleries.com.au
www.lkgalleries.com.au
Gallery Manager: Joie Stevenson
Exhibiting and representing a wide range
of leading contemporary Australian artists.
Mon–Sat 9.30–5.30

**Perth Institute of Contemporary Arts
(PICA)**
Perth Cultural Centre, James Street,
Northbridge 6000
Tel 08 9228 6300 Fax 08 9227 6539
info@pica.org.au
www.pica.org.au
Director: Amy Barrett-Lennard
Through a program of exhibitions,
performances, screenings, studios and
interdisciplinary projects, PICA promotes
contemporary art while stimulating critical
discussion about the arts and broader
cultural issues.
Tues–Sun 11–6

Purist Gallery
Blue Orchid Court, Yallingup 6282
Tel 08 9755 2582
Fax 08 9755 2582
art@puristgallery.com
www.puristgallery.com
Directors: Penny Hudson and Max Ball
Contemporary fine art gallery representing
West Australian artist Penny Hudson and
jeweller Max Ball. Paintings, jewellery,
sculpture in a purpose-built 'retro' gallery,
situated on a bush block in the Margaret
River Wine Region of Western Australia.
Fri–Mon 10–5, daily 10–5 during school
holidays

Stafford Studios of Fine Art
102 Forrest Street, Cottesloe 6011
Tel 08 9385 1399 Fax 08 9384 0966
artstaff@iinet.net.au
www.staffordstudios.com.au
Regular exhibitions of contemporary
artists. Representing Andrew Baines,
Barbara Bennett, Robert Birch, William
Boissevain, John Borrack, Judy Cassab,
Michael Challen, Brendon Darby, Robert
Dickerson, Judith Dinham, Ken Done, Paul
Evans, Tania Ferrier, Tom Gleghorn, Victor
Greenaway, Pro Hart, George Haynes,
Diana Johnston, Heather Jones, Douglas
Kirsop, John Lacey, Gary Leathendale,
Mary Jane Malet, Jane Martin, Dan
Mazzotti, Larry Mitchell, Milton Moon,
Jann Rowley, Jean Sher, Christopher
Spaven, Henryk Szydlowski, Garry Zeck
and Len Zuks.
Tues–Fri 10–5, Sun 2–5

Tjulyuru Regional Arts Gallery
Tjulyuru Cultural and Civic Centre
Great Central Road, Warburton
PMB 71, via Kalgoorlie 6430
Tel 08 8954 0011 Fax 08 8954 0101
tjulyuru.gallery@bigpond.com
www.tjulyuru.com
Artistic Direction: Warburton Arts Project
Presenting an exhibition programme based
on the lifestyles, histories and vibrant
stories of the Ngaanyatjarra.
Mon–Fri 8.30–4.30, weekends and public
holidays by appointment

Turner Galleries
470 William Street, Northbridge 6003
Tel 08 9227 1077
Fax 08 9227 1011
info@turnergalleries.com.au
www.turnergalleries.com.au
Director: Helen Morgan
Gallery Manager: Allison Archer
1–30 June: Matthew Hunt
6 July – 4 August: Jillian Green;
Graham Miller
From 10 August: Julie Gough (artist
in residence exhibition);
Lorraine Biggs.
Tues–Sat 11–5

Tasmania

Art Mob – Aboriginal Fine Art
The Henry Jones Art Hotel
29 Hunter Street, Hobart 7000
Tel 03 6236 9200
Fax 03 6236 9300
euan@artmob.com.au
www.artmob.com.au
Director: Euan Hills
Tasmania's only dedicated Aboriginal fine
art gallery exhibiting works from many
Australian communities including local
Tasmanian artists. Located in Hobart's
historic Wharf precinct. Monthly exhibition
schedule provides a vivid spectrum of
works.
Daily from 10 am

Masterpiece@IXL
Shop 2, 19a Hunter Street, Hobart 7000
Tel 03 6231 3144 Fax 03 6231 3143
info@masterpiece.com.au
www.masterpiece.com.au
Masterpiece exhibits leading Australian
colonial, impressionist, post-impressionist
and contemporary works. Furniture and
ancient Chinese artefacts (Tang and Han)
available.
Mon–Sat 10–5.30

The Salamanca Collection
01a Salamanca Place, Hobart 7004
Tel 03 6224 1341
Fax 03 6223 6800
salcoll@tassie.net.au
www.salamancacollection.com.au
Directors: Jeffrey Thomas and
Diana Harrison
Tasmania's quality gallery in the historic
Salamanca Place. Specialising in twentieth
century Australian art, including work by
Charles Blackman, Sidney Nolan, Russell
Drysdale, Robert Dickerson and leading
Tasmanian contemporary artists.
Mon–Fri 10–5, Sat–Sun 10–4

Sidewalk Tribal Gallery
19–21 Castray Esplanade,
Battery Point 7004
Tel 03 6224 0331
Fax 03 6224 0331
ann@sidewalkgallery.com.au
www.sidewalkgallery.com.au
Director: Ann Porteus
Antique and traditional African sculpture
representing more than eighty-five cultures
collected from twenty-six countries across
Africa. Ethnic jewellery and other items of
adornment, both antique and
contemporary, from every continent.
Daily 10–5

Northern Territory

Gallery Gondwana Australia
43 Todd Mall, Alice Springs 0870
Tel 08 8953 1577
Fax 08 8953 2441
alice@gallerygondwana.com.au
www.gallerygondwana.com.au
Director: Roslyn Premont Lali
Representing the best in Aboriginal fine art,
Australian design and arts from the Pacific
region. Established in 1990, the gallery
works exclusively with internationally
acclaimed artists and sources works from
Indigenous artists and communities.
Mon–Sun 9.30–6, or by appointment

Museum and Art Gallery of the
Northern Territory
Conacher Street, Bullocky Point,
Fannie Bay 0820
Tel 08 8999 8264
Fax 08 8999 8148
www.magnt.nt.gov.au
Overlooking the Arafura Sea, the gallery
covers aspects of the region's art, natural
history and culture with a diverse selection
of permanent and changing exhibitions.
'Transformations' transports the visitor into
a unique and ancient world. Also of interest
is 'Cyclone Tracy' and 'Sweetheart the
famous crocodile'.
Mon–Fri 9–5, Sat–Sun 10–5

Palya Art and Didgeri Air Art Tours
P.O. Box 108, Darwin 0804
Tel/Fax 08 8948 5055
ops@didgeri.com.au
www.didgeri.com.au
www.palya-art.com.au
Recent artworks from artist-owned
Indigenous art centres in the north-west of
Australia. Showing in Melbourne in
November, Sydney in March and by
appointment in Darwin. Didgeri Air Art
Tours enable you to visit artists, and to see
and experience rich, diverse land over the
Kimberley, Arnhem Land and Central
Desert. Information available on request.
All visits are by prior arrangement and in
accordance with Indigenous cultural
protocols.

RAFT Artspace
2/8 Parap Place, (upstairs,
Gregory Street entrance)
Parap 0820
RAFT 11
1 Vickers Street, Parap 0810
Tel 08 8941 0810
Fax 08 8941 0810
art@raftartspace.com.au
www.raftartspace.com.au
A gallery celebrating difference; regular
exhibitions presenting local and visiting
artists as well as art from the regions of the
Kimberley, northern and central Australia
in a contemporary art context.
Wed–Sat 10–5 or by appointment

New Zealand

Gow Langsford Gallery
cnr Kitchener and Wellesley streets
Auckland
Tel 64 9 303 4290
Fax 64 9 303 4302
info@gowlangsfordgallery.co.nz
www.gowlangsfordgallery.com
Directors: Gary Langsford and John Gow
Gow Langsford Gallery represents leading
artists and artist estates from New Zealand,
Australia and further afield internationally,
including Shane Cotton, Tony Cragg, Dale
Frank, John Pule, Judy Millar and Bernar
Venet. Curated exhibitions and projects are
also an important part of the gallery's
activities, working with selected artists
including Thomas Ruff and Michal Rovner.
In addition, secondary market works are
available as part of the gallery's stock, by
artists such as Colin McCahon and Ralph
Hotere, and internationally Cy Twombly,
Andy Warhol and George Rickey.
26 June – 21 July: Katharina Grosse
From 21 August: Gow Langsford Gallery
Twentieth Anniversary.
Mon–Fri 10–6, Saturdays 11–3

International Art Centre
272 Parnell Road,
P.O. Box 37344, Parnell, Auckland
Tel 64 9 379 4010
Fax 64 9 307 3421
richard@artcntr.co.nz
www.fineartauction.co.nz
Directors: Richard Thomson
and Frances Davies
New Zealand's only auction house
specialising solely in fine art. The gallery
represents over fifty New Zealand,
Australian and European artists.
Mon–Fri 10–5.30, Sat 10–5, Sun 11–4

Jonathan Grant Galleries Ltd
280 Parnell Road,
P.O. Box 37673, Parnell, Auckland
Tel 64 9 308 9125
Fax 64 9 303 1071
jg@jgg.co.nz
www.jonathangrantgalleries.com
Three Parnell Galleries.
Jonathan Grant Gallery: 19th and
20th Century British, European and
Antipodean paintings
Artis Gallery: Contemporary New
Zealand paintings and photography
Artis Sculpture Gallery: Contemporary
New Zealand Sculpture.
Mon–Fri 9–6, Sat 10–4

Whitespace – Deborah White
12 Crummer Road, Ponsonby
Auckland 1002
Tel 64 9 361 6331
dwhite@whitespace.co.nz
www.whitespace.co.nz
Director: Deborah White
A contemporary gallery representing
established and emerging artists from New
Zealand, Australia and the Pacific with a
full exhibition program and expansive
stockroom. Deborah White is the president
and founding member of CFADA,
Contemporary Fine Art Dealers
Association of New Zealand.
Tues–Fri 11–6, Sat 11–4

Art & Australia's Art Directory
is a comprehensive guide to museums
and galleries in Australia. To be part of
this guide contact Karen Brown:
Tel 61 2 9331 4455 Fax 61 2 9331 4577
karen.brown@artandaustralia.com.au

RIPE: ANZ Private Bank and Art & Australia Contemporary Art Award

Giles Ryder

Jesse Stein

right
Giles Ryder, installation at John Buckley Gallery, Melbourne, 2006, left to right: **Mirrorchromes R.H.G., 2005**, crystal clear Perspex, mirror, aluminium, 122 x 110 cm; **Space conveyancer, 2006**, neon, transformers, epoxy enamel, timber panels, 350 x 204 x 25 cm; **Mirrorchromes, 2006**, crystal clear Perspex, mirror, aluminium, 124 x 202 cm, collection Monash University Museum of Art, Melbourne; **Spectral magenta, 2006**, metallic and pearlescent lacquer on hand-rolled aluminium, 86 x 120 x 19 cm, courtesy the artist and John Buckley Gallery, Melbourne.

The secret to experiencing the art of Giles Ryder is that the *installation* of his work – carefully arranged in a gallery space – is crucial to understanding his methods and his message. As Ryder explains, his practice involves examining the psychological and phenomenological aspects of colour and light, in addition to a consideration of 'reduction' – of form, colour, line, medium – and a 'compaction' of modern art history.

Ryder works in three modes: hand-rolled aluminium wall-works coated with pearlescent auto-lacquers, neon-light constructions hovering above ultra-shiny panels, and reflective 'mirrorchromes' created from mirrored and coloured Perspex. Ryder has commented that 'the appearance of the painting changes with the fall of light and the position of the viewer'. When installed together, the neon works placed on the floor bounce luminescent colour in complex nuances throughout the architecture of the gallery space.

The artist is a co-founder and Director of Peloton Gallery in Sydney, and describes his curatorial and gallery management activities as an extension of his practice. In 2006 his work was shown at its best: in a large installation at the Australian Centre for Contemporary Art's annual 'rising star' artist showcase 'NEW06' in Melbourne. The space enabled him to show his largest work yet, *Spectragraph [galaxy 5000]*, 2006, a rolled-aluminium work at over 6 metres wide.

Ryder's choice of materials is by no means arbitrary. The artist spent six years working as an industrial painter on the Story Bridge in Brisbane, and describes his technical skills as self-taught, having developed out of his previous employment, as well as study in Brisbane, Edinburgh and Sydney (he completed his Master of Fine Art at Sydney College of the Arts in 2005). Ryder's selection of materials produces a collision between the mass-produced factory product and the custom-made object. He combines 'readymade' industrial materials, such as aluminium and auto-lacquer, with recycled commercial items like old neon signage. There is an element of the production-line when he hand-rolls the aluminium works, but to complete the process each work is meticulously rendered and coated. The resultant works achieve a level of material complexity and resist easy classification.

Nonetheless, some obvious connections can be made. The artist's use of auto-lacquer and stylised stripes evoke car culture and the aesthetics of the automotive industry. Ryder's choice of neon colours and his layering of auto-lacquers and enamel brings to mind the art of Jasper Johns and Kenneth Noland

(1963), where colour, layered coats of paint and an impressive 'in-your-face' materiality is of paramount concern, and that obsessive strand of 1960s car culture is unequivocally described as an art in itself. That said, although Ryder's earlier works, such as his 2002 series 'A Night at the Drags', explicitly reference the optical sensation of headlights and taillights speeding along a highway, he is cagey about the relevance of the car to his more recent – notably vertically striped – pieces.

Describing his work as a 'hybrid between minimalism, abstraction, op and pop art', Ryder suggests that his work is actually 'more abstract' than a direct reference to automobile culture and aesthetics. 'It comes back to art and art history. It's pop but it's not. It's not pure ... it has more to do with Australian culture.' With this comment, a whole new set of references emerge – from striped awnings to RSL Club decor. And unlike earlier modernist forms of abstraction, Ryder's abstraction does not preclude references to popular culture and society.

Academic Carolyn Barnes has commented that Ryder's abstract work has 'moved far beyond its modernist origins' and has opened up to include 'simultaneous allusions to commodity culture and vanguard art practice'. Nowhere is this more apparent than in Ryder's *Fluorochrome/mirrorchrome [transparent radiation] M.I.R.H. 06 portrait*, 2006. Constructed from coloured and mirrored Perspex and aluminium, this large, pink, luminous 'mirrorchrome' is the perfect antithesis to a classic modernist monochrome. The 'traditional' monochrome denied subjectivity, rejecting all references to the outside world. Ryder manipulates this art history, and uses the reflective yet painterly surface of his mirrorchromes to literally *pull in* the contents of the exhibition space, dragging the viewer, and the other artworks in the room, into the surface of his mirrors in a distorted, radiant blur.

In his work *Daze of disco (silver strutter)*, 2006 (as shown on the back of this issue), recycled neon lettering from an old Chinese sign is combined with custom-designed neon lines and a high-gloss door panel. This rests at a slight tilt on the floor, flowing colour out into the exhibition space. Ryder named this work after the band Yo Lo Tengo's song 'Daze of Disco', and it recalls the peculiarity of the disco era, the instability of subculture identification and the intangibility of memory. *Daze of disco* also clearly celebrates – with impurity – the pure concepts of colour, light and form.